LOCAL ENVIRONMENTAL REGULATION IN POST-SOCIALISM: A HUNGARIAN CASE STUDY

Local Environmental Regulation in Post-Socialism: A Hungarian Case Study

CHRIS PICKVANCE
University of Kent

LONDON AND NEW YORK

First published 2003 by Ashgate Publishing

Reissued 2018 by Routledge
2 Park Square, Milton Park, Abingdon, Oxon OX14 4RN
711 Third Avenue, New York, NY 10017, USA

Routledge is an imprint of the Taylor & Francis Group, an informa business

Copyright © Chris Pickvance 2003

The author has asserted his moral right under the Copyright, Designs and Patents Act, 1988, to be identified as the author of this work.

All rights reserved. No part of this book may be reprinted or reproduced or utilised in any form or by any electronic, mechanical, or other means, now known or hereafter invented, including photocopying and recording, or in any information storage or retrieval system, without permission in writing from the publishers.

Notice:
Product or corporate names may be trademarks or registered trademarks, and are used only for identification and explanation without intent to infringe.

Publisher's Note
The publisher has gone to great lengths to ensure the quality of this reprint but points out that some imperfections in the original copies may be apparent.

Disclaimer
The publisher has made every effort to trace copyright holders and welcomes correspondence from those they have been unable to contact.

A Library of Congress record exists under LC control number: 2003056038

ISBN 13: 978-1-138-71596-7 (hbk)
ISBN 13: 978-1-138-71593-6 (pbk)
ISBN 13: 978-1-315-19727-2 (ebk)

Contents

List of Figures		vi
List of Tables		vii
Acknowledgements		ix

1	Introduction: the Hungarian Context	1
2	Hypotheses on Local Environmental Regulation	17
3	Székesfehérvár: Magnet for Multinational Capital and Green Utopia?	43
4	Győr: a Traditional Industrial and County Town	59
5	Nagytétény: Past Pollution and Limited Prospects?	79
6	Dunaújváros: the Legacy Effects of Being a Steel Town	95
7	A Comparative Analysis of Environmental Regulation in the Four Localities	111
8	Settlement Type and Local Government Environmental Policy in Hungary: the Role of Local Economic Structure and Local Government Resources	129
9	Local Economic Situation, Local Environmental Mobilization and Local Government Environmental Policy in Hungary	145
10	Conclusion	163

Bibliography	177
Index	183

List of Figures

2.1	Map showing the four localities	39
9.1	Hypothesized model relating economic situation, environmental mobilization and environmental policy for any settlement type	148
9.2	Counties and 'macro-regions'	150

List of Tables

2.1	Typology of positions taken by local government in environmental regulation based on nature of business and public pressure and whether local government pays attention to these or develops its own position independently	22
2.2	Determinants of strong and weak local environmental policy	32
2.3	Proportion of land in the two worst categories of environmental quality in Poland, Hungary and Czechoslovakia in 1990	38
2.4	The four localities and their main features	40
2.5	Measures of air pollution, 1997, micrograms per cu.m.	40
7.1	Positions of the four localities on the dependent variables and explanatory variables hypothesized to be of relevance	117
8.1	Distribution (%) of first choices of planned measure by local governments to change the local economic structure, by settlement type	133
8.2	Distribution (%) of second choices of planned measure by local governments to change the local economic structure, by settlement type	134
8.3	Distribution (%) of local government responses to the question 'In what period can these changes [in the economic structure] be achieved?', by settlement type	134
8.4	Distribution (%) of first choice environmental problems as seen by local government officials, by settlement type	136
8.5	Distribution (%) of second choice environmental problems as seen by local government officials, by settlement type	137
8.6	First choice responses (%) to the question 'How does the local government plan to solve these environmental problems?', by settlement type	138

8.7	Second choice responses (%) to the question 'How does the local government plan to solve these environmental problems?', by settlement type	139
8.8	Local government officials' perceptions of the likely effectiveness of the environmental policy measures mentioned in Tables 8.6 and 8.7 (%)	141
8.9	Local government officials' perceptions of the effectiveness of local government environmental activities (%)	141
9.1	Characteristics of the Hungarian NUTS2 regions, and how they were grouped into three 'macro-regions'	150
9.2	Percentages of local governments in a given settlement type and region with a written environmental programme	153
9.3	Percentages of local governments in a given settlement type and region with a specific official with environmental responsibilities	153
9.4	Percentages of local government officials in a given settlement type and region reporting the presence of environmental groups in the area	155
9.5	Percentages of local government officials in a given settlement type and region who said that environmental groups had the most influence on environmental decision-making in the area	156
9.6	A measure of the 'conversion ratio' between the presence of environmental groups and the perception that they have 'most influence' on environmental policy, for local governments of a given settlement type and region	159

Acknowledgements

The research on which this book is based was financed by the Economic and Social Research Council (ESRC) under grant R000236579 'Environmental policy implementation by local government in Hungary'. The co-grantholders and project directors were Dr Katy Pickvance and myself. We are very grateful to the ESRC for the confidence they placed in us.

A project of this type incurs numerous debts. Most of all I would like to thank Katy Pickvance for her contributions at all stages of the research, and particularly in the planning, in converting our original ideas into practical research procedures, in choosing and liasing with our Hungarian collaborators, in ensuring that the fieldwork was carried out satisfactorily, and in translating some of the interview transcripts. Without her the research would have been neither possible nor enjoyable.

A second major debt is to the Hungarian academics who conducted the interviews on which Chapters 3 to 6 are based: Dr Kati Hasko (ELTE University, Budapest) in Nagyteteny and Székesfehérvár, Dr Eva Kantor (of Dunaújváros Polytechnic) in Dunaújváros, and Dr Iren Kukorelli (of the Centre for Regional Studies, Hungarian Academy of Sciences, Győr) in Győr. I also thank the numerous interviewees who gave their time to this project. Luca Gabor contributed to our understanding of the legal framework of Hungarian environmental regulation, and Dr Judit Timar (Centre for Regional Studies, Hungarian Academy of Sciences, Bekescsaba) and Dr Iren Kukorelli conducted interviews in two rural localities (Körösladány and Szany) which are not reported here. Miklós Kalman, of MIMIKRI, Budapest was solely responsible for organising the national interview survey of local governments, on which Chapters 8 and 9 are based. Françoise Simmons ably translated many of the interview transcripts.

Lastly, I would like to thank Tamás Fleischer, Katy Pickvance, and Chris Rootes for their comments on parts of this book, Chris Hann who encouraged us to revise and resubmit our research application after it had initially been rejected, and Nick Brawn who prepared the camera-ready copy. I am grateful to all these collaborators.

The book is dedicated to the memory of Gaby Láng, my mother-in-law, and of my parents, Joseph and Else Pickvance, all of whom passed away very recently.

Chris Pickvance
School of Social Policy, Sociology and Social Research, University of Kent, Canterbury.

1 Introduction: the Hungarian Context

The subject of local environmental regulation in post-socialism brings together two of the most important developments of our time: the emergence of the environment as a political issue, and the 'collapse' of state socialism in Eastern Europe[1] and the former Soviet Union.

The rise of environmentalism is an uneven process across space and its political saliency for governments fluctuates over time. Nevertheless the direction of the general trend is not in question. The meaning of environmentalism can range from a 'deep green' concern to transform the economic, social and political system in order to place respect for the environment at the heart of all decision making, to a 'light green' concern to give greater priority to environmental effects without a basic change in economic systems or lifestyles.

In this book we shall be concerned with environmental regulation as practised by governments. Inevitably, given the balance of public opinion and the interdependence of governments with existing economic structures, the environmental measures we shall discuss are at the light green end of the spectrum. They do not involve major shifts in economic systems or lifestyles. They are in fact part of what is called the 'ecological modernization' problematic. This is 'the discourse that recognizes the structural character of the environmental problematic but nonetheless assumes that existing political, economic, and social institutions can internalize care for the environment' (Hajer, 1995, p. 25). This way of thinking can be seen as a response which side-steps the thrust of radical, deep green demands by claiming that a greener way of running existing structures is possible. It leads governments to make

---

1 The term 'Eastern Europe' is used here and, following the practice of the European Bank for Reconstruction and Development (EBRD), excludes the former Soviet Union. Although the term refers back to an ideological divide which no longer exists, its meaning is clear and rival terms are not without their problems. For example 'central Europe' or 'east central Europe' separate the more 'developed' from the poorer countries of Eastern Europe in an exclusionary way as well as making the 'residual' part of Eastern Europe hard to name.

assessments of the environmental impact of new projects, and to use education, administrative controls and economic sticks and carrots, to bring social costs and benefits into firms' and households' decision-making.² In this way negative environmental impacts can be kept within acceptable limits. According to the ecological modernization problematic these restraints are not necessarily at the expense of economic growth, and indeed the pursuit of environmental protection creates new markets for environmentally-friendly products and technologies.

Turning to Eastern Europe, the end of state socialism has had the most drastic repercussions for the people of the region. There has been a fundamental economic restructuring and by 2000 in only a few countries in Eastern Europe had GNP per capita returned to its 1989 level. The result is that the coming of multi-party elections has not ushered in better living conditions on average. Moreover social inequalities have widened. In the political sphere the end of state socialism has transformed superpower politics and has had an impact on domestic Western European politics where it has combined with neo-liberalism to delegitimize socialist policies. Most important for us however is the process of European Union enlargement, in which Hungary is among the group of Eastern European countries which hopes for membership around 2004. This will mean that issues which were inter-national become intra-EU matters too. Industrial location has long transcended national boundaries, and trans-boundary pollution does likewise. However, preparation for accession to the EU means that Eastern European countries have to bring their environmental legislation into line with that of the EU to avoid any possibility that they might obtain an 'unfair' competitive advantage in the market for mobile industrial investment by offering lower environmental standards to firms operating there.

However to tackle broad subjects such as 'How far has the end of state socialism led to privatization and democracy and transformed local economies and political systems in Eastern Europe?' and 'How far has expected EU membership had an impact on local environmental regulation?' would require a different type of research from that on which the book is based. Hence such questions are not of primary concern here.

The aims of the book are both descriptive and explanatory. They are:

a) to provide a picture of some aspects of local-level environmental regulation in one post-socialist country, Hungary;
b) to explain why these differences take the form they do; and
c) to contribute to a cross-national comparative understanding of local environmental regulation.

---

2 An interesting issue is why different measures are seen to be appropriate to different social groups. This was brought out when in 2002, in the wake of UK government hints that households would be penalised if they produced too much waste, it was announced that farmers would receive subsidies to help them reduce nitrate pollution of water courses.

The latter aim involves exploring whether the Hungarian evidence is compatible with the general understanding of environmental regulation developed in the advanced capitalist world and of the 'transition' from state socialism. If a convergence is found with 'Western' patterns we need to ask whether this is because similar causal processes are operating, or, whether different sets of causes can produce similar results. Thus although the book concerns a single country the underlying intellectual framework is a cross-national comparative one.

Environmental regulation refers to the social processes by which regulatory authorities seek to shape human actions with impacts on the land, air, and water and on the human and non-human animal and plant populations dependent upon them. It thus refers to a variety of spheres of action, to a range of objects of regulation (from households to corporations) and to regulatory authorities from the international to the local. We use the term regulation to refer to attempts to secure influence. There is no assumption of success. Regulation thus refers to a process rather than an outcome.

Within the broad field of environmental regulation the present book is concerned with pollution by industrial firms (and especially air and water pollution) and with physical planning, and with the local level of the regulatory process. The local focus is deliberate. While national studies of environmental policy formation show how governments respond to domestic and international pressures, the crucial question from the point of view of people's living conditions is how far policy goes beyond words and intentions to measures which affect activity at the local level. This is the question of local implementation which requires the translation of aims into procedures and targets, and the employment of a skilled staff with adequate technical and financial resources to apply them. Given the appeal to governments of engaging in 'symbolic politics' (Edelman, 1964) in which legislation is passed in order to pacify a particular interest group (and in which interest groups are content to receive symbols), it cannot be assumed that every piece of legislation is intended to be translated into practice.

Environmental regulation can be studied from a variety of disciplinary perspectives. The old idea that each discipline dealt with its own 'chunk' of reality has long ceased to be credible. The subsequent idea that there is a single 'reality' and that disciplines differ in the questions they pose regarding it and the conceptual apparatuses they use to find answers is much more useful.[3]

The approach taken here is sociological in the sense that it is primarily concerned with the influence, perceptions and interactions of the different groups involved in the local level implementation process. This means that it is not concerned with the precise nature of the regulations, the sanctions involved, and the bodies responsible for them, as would be a legal-administrative study. Likewise the study makes no technical assessment of the impact of local environmental regulation. This would require technical expertise about a diverse range of production processes, and about the effects of numerous forms of pollution. Lastly the study does not enter the debate

---

3 The fact that researchers do not stick to disciplinary boundaries is not a serious challenge to this idea.

about whether the economic benefits of environmental regulation outweigh the costs. Like any disciplinary approach a sociological focus involves a degree of naivety about other fields of expertise (Devons and Gluckman, 1964).

In the rest of this chapter we provide some background information about Hungary and about the concepts used here in understanding state socialist and post-socialist societies. The subsequent sections focus on: a) Hungarian state socialism and the environment, b) the concept of and theories of transition and c) the Hungarian experience of transition and post-socialism.

Hungarian state socialism and the environment

It is important to examine the literature on state socialist societies and Hungarian state socialism in particular not for historical reasons but as a way of helping understand the present. The aim is to identify a set of past structures and practices which may act as 'legacies' affecting post-socialist developments. (The term legacy is discussed later.)

The state socialist model

To understand how state socialist societies functioned and what this implied for the environment it is necessary to consider the major institutional structures and how they interacted. To escape from the specificities of the different countries we start by presenting an idealized model. We then discuss variations and the case of Hungary.

State socialist societies had a family resemblance because of four shared features: the dominant role of the communist party, state ownership of enterprises, central planning of the economy, and the repression of political expression (Kornai, 1992). Whereas in capitalist societies, the industrial structure (mainly privately-owned), the governmental structure, and the party political system are differentiated entities, in state socialist societies the opposite was the case. Industry was state-owned and took the form of state enterprises reporting to central, regional or local government units. The economy and the state systems were thus closely integrated. In addition, the state was subordinate politically to the communist party, following the doctrine of the 'leading role of the communist party', so that the first secretary of the communist party was more important than the prime minister. (The term 'party-state' is used to express this form.) At every level of industry and state there was a party branch which was supposed to perform a 'steering' role to ensure this subordination. It can thus be seen that there was an intertwining of state, party and industrial structures. The aim was to create a centrally planned alternative to capitalism which avoided the combination of 'anarchy' of the market, exploitation based on class divisions and social inequality associated in Marx's view with capitalism. It was hoped that the intertwined structures would lead to a stronger steering of society and demonstrate that socialist industrialization could be achieved without class exploitation and without sacrificing the welfare needs of the majority of the population.

In practice, this intertwining of structures did not lead to integration and smooth functioning. 'Central planning' existed in name only for two major reasons. First central economic planning requires a quantity and centralization of information which is impossible to achieve (Ellman, 1989). Whereas capitalist industry operates with supplies of inputs being assured (with occasional disruptions) by bilateral contracts between firms, socialist planning required this coordination to be ensured centrally and administratively. This proved to be highly inefficient. A further reason for this inefficiency was that the existence of sanctions for failure to meet planned production targets gave the lower units (whether farms or industrial plants) strong incentives to conceal accurate information about their performance (Rév, 1987). In the absence of adequate coordination, the economic 'system' stumbled along with the party branches having to become involved in moving resources to where they were needed (Hough, 1969; Andrle, 1976; Rutland, 1985).

The second main reason for the lack of integration was the power of large industrial enterprises, which to a large extent were 'the economy' and were the key to achieving socialist industrialization. This power was such that they were not passive recipients of central 'plans' as socialist doctrine required but were in a position to exert great influence over their content.

The power of state enterprises was also apparent in relation to the localities in which they were based. This was most evident in socialist new towns whose raison d'être was to meet the needs of a major enterprise. It was also apparent in parts of large cities where particular enterprises or administrations had built a lot of houses and related facilities, which gave rise to differentiation between neighbourhoods depending on the resourcing of the enterprises which had built them. The power of state enterprises also meant that local government was in a structurally weak position. The priority given to material production meant that whereas state enterprises were amply resourced, local governments were poorly funded. Indeed many familiar local government functions were the responsibility of enterprises (for example, they often provided housing, health and recreational facilities, and holiday accommodation as well as utilities like district heating and sewage treatment) (Shomina, 1992). Moreover the intertwined party-state apparatus ensured the subordination of local governments to higher level structures and to the needs of local state enterprises: the local executive which ran local government would normally include managers of local state enterprises. This meant that local governments were not in a position to impose regulations on state enterprises' activities (for example, house-building or location of new plant). The expansion plans of a local state enterprise were taken as a given by local governments, not as a matter for debate.

The last element of the model of state socialism is the population. The main channels for public 'participation' were the institutional structures set up by the party-state in the form of official 'mass participation' organizations, for example, peace, women's, youth, and professional organizations. These were set up to secure party control of public participation and pre-empt any independent (that is, non-party approved) citizen organizations. In fact this aim was only partly achieved. The Solidarity movement in Poland was the most striking counter-example, developing in quite unfavourable conditions. But once the Gorbachev era ushered in more favourable conditions for citizen initiatives in the mid 1980s there was a mushrooming of independent and unofficial groupings of all sorts (Brovkin, 1990; Hosking et al., 1992; Pickvance, C.G., 1996a). Moreover it turned out that official organizations were used as covers for unofficial activities. For example in the Baltic republics heritage organizations were used to conceal nationalist mobilization. Thus these official organizations could not contain public pressure. There was also a tradition of people writing to newspapers and officials to draw their attention to citizen dissatisfactions. This was seen as legitimate by the authorities because they saw letter-writers as drawing attention to their individual experience of the failings of systems rather than as advancing a collective challenge to the system.

In some respects state socialism worked: social policy was more highly developed than in capitalist countries of similar economic level, income inequalities were narrower than in advanced capitalist societies (and almost certainly than in capitalist countries of similar income level) (Atkinson and Micklewright, 1992), full employment was achieved (though this involved what specialists call 'on the job unemployment', for example, over-staffing) (Hanson, 1986; Lane, 1987) and the economic integration of the socialist bloc provided short term protection against world market forces though it proved ultimately ineffective.

These gains were achieved at the cost of a loss of international competitiveness due to the extensive intra-COMECON trade, diminished efficiency in agriculture and manufacturing, recurrent shortages of goods, underdevelopment of services and under-investment in urban infrastructure (Ofer, 1977; Pickvance, C.G., 2002).

Within this ideal typical institutional structure state socialism showed significant variations in terms of:

1. levels of national income per capita: there was a rough North-South gradient from East Germany (high) to Bulgaria (low),
2. attitudes to the private economic sector and private housing: private farming was permitted in Poland and private housing particularly in Bulgaria,
3. the degree to which central planning had been reformed: this was most marked in Hungary, and
4. the toleration of 'civil society': the Catholic church was strong in Poland, and dissent existed in Poland (Solidarity) and Hungary and Czechoslovakia (among intellectuals).

State socialism in Hungary

In relation to this model, Hungary occupied a 'deviant' position. This resulted from the 1956 uprising which, although unsuccessful as a revolution, had profound repercussions. It led to the Hungarian regime's subsequent implicit 'deal' with the population in which it facilitated an increase in the supply of goods and services in exchange for an agreement that people would not threaten the regime politically (hence the phrase 'goulash communism' (Swain, 1992)). This was achieved in two

Introduction: the Hungarian Context

ways. First, in the late 1960s, Hungary adopted a looser sort of economic planning which Kornai (1992) calls 'plan bargaining'. State enterprises remained under the formal control of ministries and kept their leverage over 'their' ministries, but they were given looser targets and more choice about what to produce, and expertise became more important in the appointment of industrial managers than party position. Second, the regime allowed the development of a 'second economy' (that is, a small-scale, non-state, capitalist sector) in agriculture (for example private plots), manufacturing (for example using factory equipment after hours), and services (for example car repair, coaching). The aim was to increase the supply of goods and services, mobilize people's efforts, and allow them to earn higher incomes. This policy was successful and by the mid-1980s, the second economy provided one third of wage-type incomes in Hungary. In agriculture the mix of cooperatives and individual plots also proved very successful. This policy represented a deviation from doctrinal orthodoxy but was tolerated by the Soviet Union as long as the Hungarian regime allowed no broad challenge to develop to its political position. The development of dissent, particularly among intellectuals, was not seen as a serious threat because of its narrow social base.

Hungary in fact saw a burgeoning of citizen action. Starting in the 1970s, there was a growth of local environmental protests over river pollution by lead, oil and hazardous waste, dust pollution, and threats to land by radioactive waste (Waller and Millard, 1992; Vári and Tamas, 1993; Pickvance, C.G., 1996a). These protests were tolerated by the regime because they were localized and did not make explicitly anti-regime demands. In some cases the groups taking part accepted co-option by the authorities in order to achieve partial success (Szirmai, 1993). Opposition to the construction of the Danube dam, which started in 1984, was also initially not anti-regime in its demands, but developed to the point where in 1988 the Danube Circle could bring 30,000 demonstrators onto the streets (Fleischer, 1993; Szirmai, 1997). By this time many regime opponents had joined the movement to express their opposition to the regime rather than for 'pure' environmental reasons. The fact that this movement developed in this way is an expression of the weakening hold on power of the Hungarian regime in the late 1980s.

This picture of the institutional structure of state socialism has a direct bearing on the practice of environmental regulation. The peculiar feature of environmental regulation in state socialist societies was its paradoxical combination of extensive and detailed environmental legislation, which in some cases set standards above those in the West, and high levels of pollution (Persanyi, 1990; Fisher, 1992; Carter and Turnock, 1993; Kerekes, 1993, quoted in O'Toole, 1988, p. 50; Manser, 1993). In practice however this legislation was not enforced. The closure to Western markets discouraged cleaner production methods, and the emphasis of industrial managers was on achieving targets. Since the ministries to which the enterprises 'belonged' were either responsible for pollution control, or could influence the bodies responsible for it, the enforcement of standards was never likely to be taken seriously and any fines were very low.

As for local governments, they were far from being in a position to regulate the environmental impacts of state enterprises. The main reasons are that the executive bodies which ran them included managers from the firms concerned, that state enterprises were often major local employers and that local governments were highly dependent on local state enterprises for local taxes and other resources. Their funding came mainly from central grants but households paid no local taxes and enterprises were the only source of local tax.

To summarize, the typical pattern of relations between institutional actors under Hungarian state socialism in the 1970s and early 1980s was that state enterprises, with the support of the party-state apparatus, were able to adopt production methods with virtually no regard to pollution. Local government was in too weak a position to intervene, and public protest where it existed, was limited and at most partly successful. As will be shown, these features constituted important legacies for the post-socialist period.

Understanding societies in 'transition': concept and theories

We now turn to attempts by social scientists to understand post-socialist changes. These centre around the ubiquitous concept of 'transition,' which I shall suggest has been more of an obstacle than a help.

As a concept, 'transition' seems clear enough: it refers to the passage from a starting point to an end-point. The difficulties start when we apply it to society. The first is that societies have multiple dimensions and transition may only apply to some of them. As Offe (1991) has pointed out, whereas the previous 'waves' of transition in Southern Europe and Latin America were 'democratic transitions' and did not involve a change in economic system, those in Eastern Europe have had both political and economic (as well as in some cases a territorial dimension, where there was a change of national boundaries). A second complexity is that, as pointed out earlier, there were considerable variations among state socialist societies and so their starting points were very different.[4] Third, many usages of the term transition assume that only one end-point is possible, namely advanced capitalism with extensive social protection, a multi-party democracy, and a well-developed 'civic culture'. If this is the case it

---

4 In the Hungarian case it has been argued that the transition started with the toleration of a small-scale capitalist sector in the guise of the second (non-state) economy 20 years before 1989. However this is debatable. On the one hand is the view that the second economy was like a genie which once out of the bottle could not be put back and was bound to expand in scope. On the other hand is the view that the development of the second economy was always subject to close party-state regulation and therefore had no inherent self-expanding capacity. The debate is over whether the party-state really could have put the second economy into reverse, a frustratingly difficult counter-factual question to answer. My (retrospective) view is that the second economy probably facilitated change but that it was not a powerful or even a critical factor (Sik, 1994).

becomes a teleological concept, explaining the present as an effect of the future, when in fact, end-points are intrinsically unknowable. For example, in the former Soviet Asian republics, third-world style capitalism with authoritarian political structures and weak welfare states is a more likely outcome. Fourth, as well as involving movement in different directions, transition may proceed at different speeds in different spheres, and is even reversible. For all these reasons in my view the term transition is not an analytical concept with any precise content but rather a fig leaf concealing our ignorance. The danger in using it is that it implies a spurious degree of knowledge about the paths from different starting points to different destinations and suggests that there is a uniformity among them. These uncertainties and differences are important to keep in mind.[5] Stark (1992) has suggested that the term transition be dropped in favour of 'transformation', but this term implies extensive change and also prejudges the character of change.

We now consider three sociological approaches to understanding 'transition'. All have different points of departure. Nee's (1989) theory of transition arises out of his work on China and focuses on changes in social stratification. He argues that the introduction of the market principle will weaken the power and privileges of bureaucrats, facilitate social mobility and provide increased opportunities for those with least resources. This approach however has to take into account the fact that markets existed under state socialism (though to different extents in different cases), and that transition is not coterminous with the expansion of markets. Those who have monopolised economic opportunities may well try and shield themselves from competition. This draws attention to the diversity of economic transition paths.

An alternative approach is that of Stark (1992; 1997) who stresses the role of 'legacies' in transition. Legacies are features of a previous period which continue to influence the present. The previous period may be either state socialism, the inter-war pre-socialist period, or even a part of the post-socialist period before the present time. Examples include:

1. economic, legal and administrative institutions. As we have shown, typical patterns of relationship between state ministries, enterprises, party organs and territorial authorities emerged under state socialism, and enterprises took certain forms because of COMECON;

---

[5] The term transition has various other connotations which may be unfounded. It is often based on an idealization of capitalism as a competitive economy with little government intervention. It also implies a passage from a stable state through a temporary unstable state to a new stable state, which may be more a matter of hope and intellectual convenience than a reflection of reality. Likewise the language of transition implies an end-point without specifying how one is to know that it has been reached. This leads to serious difficulties in empirical research into the 'effects of transition'. Failure to observe predicted effects may thus be because they will occur later, rather than because the prediction is incorrect, a point suggested to me by John Logan.

2. the distribution of economic, social and cultural capital (for example, money and property wealth, social positions and social networks, and educational and technical skills). This distribution acts as a set of opportunities and constraints which affects the ability of groups to realize their aims subsequently. A key issue is how far 'old' assets can be converted into new forms;
3. ways of behaving. It has been argued that state socialism encouraged risk-averseness, dependence on the state, and collectivism. In some countries it also encouraged small-scale entrepreneurialism as well as what have been called 'unofficial virtues' (Elster et al. 1998, p. 61), for example, the self-reliance and flexibility needed to cope with the inefficiencies of central planning described earlier.

Lastly, Elster et al. (1998) point to the way that interpretations of the past can be used in arguments about institution building.

Stark makes the strong claim that change is always based on a rearrangement of existing forms and that 'the new does not come from the new' (1992, p. 301). This does not amount to determinism since it allows for a variety of combinations of legacies to have effects. However the role Stark gives to legacies is debatable and it is more likely that they play a weaker role. First, the idea of legacy underestimates the way that new situations allow new groups to emerge, and give value to new assets. Second, old assets may lack 'survival value' in the new situation because they only survive if they are used. This may apply for example to party-based social networks. Third, an emphasis on legacies implies a level of continuity which may be simply mistaken. Fourth, there is the question of how long state socialist 'legacies' can remain effective as explanations, and whether the 'mode of extrication' from state socialism or later developments (within post-socialism) cannot also give rise to legacy effects. Lastly, there is a problem when legacies of state socialism are classified as negative (for example, risk-averseness) or positive (for example, entrepreneurialism) according to their effects on change. The reason is that 'positive' and 'negative' are judgements which are relative to a particular end-state, for example, a form of capitalism which requires entrepreneurialism and risk-taking, and to ways of reaching it. Since there are numerous possible destinations, use of these terms is teleological. In brief, one should be aware of legacies but not treat them as more than potential explanations, in combination with the effect of new situations, new processes and emergent social groups.

The most systematic study of a legacy effect is the study by Eyal et al. (1998) of what happened to members of the élite (or *nomenklatura*) in Hungary, Poland and the Czech Republic. They address the 'political capitalism' hypothesis that communist officials kept their positions of authority by converting their assets. (This contradicts Nee's theory which emphasizes the vulnerability of such officials to the emergence of the market principle.) Eyal et al. find that the theory applied to about half of all such officials. Within this category 71% members of the economic élite in 1988 were still in a position of authority in 1993 (compared with 44% of members of the cultural élite and 39% of members of the political élite) (Eyal et al., 1998, pp. 117–20). Others accepted lower positions or retired early.[6]

A third theory is closely related to the last: this is known as 'path-dependent development'. This theory originated in economics as a critique of the idea that whatever form of development existed was in some sense optimal for economic and social welfare. In contrast it was argued that initial conditions of development could have a lasting effect and 'lock in' inefficiencies. For example, the QWERTY keyboard, which separated the most frequently used letters in English to avoid the jamming of mechanical keys, was cited as a once-optimal response to a technological constraint which no longer exists, but where the costs of entry for a replacement are too high. More generally, path-dependence emphasizes how timing matters. For example it challenges the idea that there are universally applicable pre-conditions of economic growth which once met allow sustained development. Rather, the economic and political environment faced by countries is ever changing and has strong effects on their prospects of growth. In the case of state socialist transition this approach emphasizes the weight of the past in constraining future possibilities and the particular conditions surrounding the transition. Where it is less clear is in saying how strong the 'weight of the past' is.[7]

It can be seen that these theories fall into two categories: the legacy and path dependence theories emphasize the past, while Nee's theory emphasizes the new. Since there is no reason to think that either polar stance has a monopoly of truth all three theories can be seen as drawing attention to factors whose effect may be combined.

The Hungarian transition and post-socialist experience

We will leave until the next chapter a discussion of our hypotheses about the role of legacies and post-socialist local determinants of environmental regulation. We first outline some aspects of Hungary's 'transition'.

Since the change of regime, which was formalized by the multiparty elections of 1990, Hungary has developed well-structured political parties and a stable legal and institutional framework. The three successive governments have all had different complexions: 1990 – conservative nationalist (Hungarian Democrat Forum in

---

6 The response rate in the surveys on which these figures are based ranged from 50% upwards. The authors suspect the sample is more representative of the higher levels of the *nomenklatura*.

7 No reference is made here to regulation theory, though this has sometimes been used to explain transition as a 'crisis of regulation'; see for example Smith and Swain (1998). In my view the high level of abstraction of the concepts used in this approach lead to vaguely-formulated propositions which allow their users to claim that they 'make sense' of whatever happens. (I am not aware of any study that has shown the inability of regulation theory to 'account for' some social phenomenon.) Regulation theory does not allow the formulation of middle-range propositions about the conditions under which changes of any particular kind will occur, which I see as indispensable.

coalition with Christian Democrat and Smallholders Parties); 1994 – Hungarian Socialist Party; 1998 – coalition of Free and Young Democrats (economically and politically liberal). This shows that an alternation of parties has been established.

In terms of governmental structure, in reaction to the centralized party-state of state socialism, Hungary like other Eastern European countries introduced a decentralization policy which increased the number of local governments and gave them new powers. The 1990 local government reform doubled the number of local governments to 3149. Given that the national population is just over 10 million the average size is 3290 inhabitants making them some of the smallest in Eastern Europe – though in the Czech and Slovak Republics the averages are even smaller at 1680 and 1846 respectively (Bennett, 1998). Nearly half (47.4%) of all local government units had under 1000 people. Inevitably therefore the powers of these units varied with size. Cities have the most powers and villages fewest.

Local governments also acquired state assets such as housing which they were able to sell to willing buyers thereby gaining political support. This policy also had the advantage of producing a painless increase in local government income (in the short term) compared with introducing new taxes which they were also authorized to do. (In the medium term the reduction of the social housing stock will have major repercussions on the availability of affordable housing.) Whereas previously local governments had no scope for independent action, they now have such opportunities which are limited by their economic situation. They are also now regulatory authorities applying national laws, and elected bodies representing local interests and seeking re-election.

The level of decentralization introduced by the 1990 reforms has given rise to considerable criticism by those concerned with the coherence of policy at city level. For example the Budapest city government had few powers over the planning of the city since the 22 (or later 23) districts had extensive planing powers. Interestingly this type of criticism was being formulated as early as 1991 (see the debate in Ladanyi, 1992). But it took ten years before a reform was introduced to strengthen the hand of the Budapest city council against the districts. Lastly, counties are a non-elected administrative level and carry out important powers outside cities.

There are democratic elections for all local governments, so elected politicians occupy the formal places of power. Since 1994 all mayors have been directly elected. There are four sources of local government current income: central grants (based on population and need indices) which are not tied to spending in particular fields, transfers from the social security fund which must be used on health, shares of national taxes (such as personal income tax and corporation tax) where the share is decided annually and which are not tied, and local governments' own revenues from local taxes and charges of various kinds. In addition central government provides specific investment grants. These five sources contributed the following percentages of income in 1997: 29.2, 16.9, 12.1, 23.4 and 15.5 (Temesi, 2000). The fourth figure reveals the small proportion contributed by locally generated revenues. Although local governments now possess the power to raise new sources of income, they have been reluctant to levy new taxes on the population in case they lose votes. As a result

80% of local tax income comes from the local business tax. The other local taxes are a communal tax and taxes on buildings, land and tourism. The rate of the local business tax is set by local governments as a percentage of value added, within a ceiling set each year nationally.

In terms of economic reform there is a mixed picture. On the one hand Hungary's stable institutional framework has helped it to become the most popular Eastern European country for foreign investment in per capita terms. Up to 1993 it attracted 50% of the foreign direct investment going to Eastern Europe and the Baltic republics. But since then this proportion has fallen as other countries have developed their institutional structures, and for the whole period 1989–1999 Hungary received 24% of all foreign direct investment (EBRD, 2000, p. 74). However its per capita foreign direct investment figure for this period remained highest of all at $1764, ahead of the Czech Republic at $1447.

On the other hand the privatization of Hungarian industry has shown a less clear-cut pattern. Initially it proceeded more slowly than in Poland as the government sought to protect employees from the full rigours of a competitive market. But by 1998, in terms of the private sector share of GDP, it was leading the field at 80% (EBRD, 1998, p. 26).[8] However there is some doubt about what such measures of privatization mean since a) there are complex forms of mixed ownership which are claimed to be unique to post-socialism (Stark, 1997), and b) privatization refers to a change in legal ownership which is compatible with varying degrees of change in economic behaviour at enterprise level. For example, privatization can be a defensive strategy (Carlin et al, 1994; Stark, 1997). In fact the main method of privatizing large and medium-sized enterprises in Hungary has been by outside investment. This is a method which has the greatest potential to bring in new capital, skills and management (unlike, for example, the 'insider privatization' common in Russia). This means that it is likely that the cases of 'defensive restructuring' by state firms (such as 'Heavy Metal' described by Stark, 1997) are untypical and represent a passing phase. The privatization of small-scale state enterprises is said to be almost complete and there has been a rapid increase of new small enterprises, followed by a recent decline. But this is a very heterogeneous category covering firms with employees, self-employed individuals, and what are in fact tax minimization vehicles.

The continued economic significance of the Hungarian state is indicated by the fact that it will hold 'golden shares' in 27 enterprises, and long-term stakes in 116 others, and that the level of explicit budget subsidies to enterprises was twice as high as that in Poland and the Czech Republic in 1996 (EBRD, 1998, p. 170 and 1997, p. 83). Such subsidies can be seen as a form of social policy to keep workers in jobs and represent a sort of caution by the government, possibly a long-term legacy of the 1956 uprising.

---

8 This measure includes the informal as well as the formal sector and is very rough. One estimate of the Hungarian informal economy places it at 29% of GDP in 1995, compared with 27% in 1989 (EBRD, 1997, p. 74).

In terms of overall economic performance, even by 1999 the Hungarian GDP in real terms was only 99% of its size in 1989. (This compares with 122% for Poland, 97% for Eastern Europe and the Baltics as a whole and 55% for the CIS (EBRD, 2000, p. 65)). However the Hungarian economy is now growing at 5% per annum. The unemployment rate rose from 1.8% in 1990 to 11.9% in 1993 since when it has declined slowly to 7.0% in 1999 (EBRD, 2000, p. 101). The 1999 figure was the lowest rate in Eastern Europe. This is a claimant rate rather than a population based count and is therefore likely to be an underestimate. Hungary also shows a very rapid decline in the labour force participation rate (the proportion of the population in the labour force) from 68% to 62% between 1990 and 1995 (EBRD, 2000, p. 100).[9] This could be because people are simply withdrawing from the labour force and not presenting themselves as claimants, as well as for other reasons. The 7% unemployment figure is thus rather misleading. Lastly, income inequality in Hungary started from a low point (as in the Czech and Slovak Republics) and has increased a little, but these three countries remain less unequal than other post-socialist countries.

Finally, as mentioned earlier, Hungary has an association agreement with the European Union and is one of the group of countries which hopes to join in 2004. The formal implication of this is that that Hungary has to conform to the *acquis comunautaire* (existing regulations) in the fields of competence of the EU, one of which is the environmental field. There are two logics behind this: that member states are expected to play by the same rules and new members should not attract firms to operate within their boundaries by requiring lower environmental standards, and that citizens in EU countries are entited to similar environmental standards. In pursuit of this objective Hungary is entitled to funding under the PHARE pre-accession scheme for institution building and investment support. This has included funding for work on environmental law and regulatory systems and for investment in water and sewage.

In practice the idea of conforming to EU standards is less clear than it seems for two reasons: the lack of present uniformity in standards and the political character of the accession process. There is a continuous debate about the extent of uniformity of regulations desirable among EU member states. Existing members do not apply common regulations in every case for various reasons. The principle of subsidiarity means that in certain spheres national and subnational governments set the rules, for example, national governments may have discretion about what pollution standards to set. In other cases standards higher than the minimum may be required by EU rules. In addition various derogations and transitional periods have been granted in the past which are a source of diversity (see Soveroski, 2001).

On the other hand the politics of the accession process mean that the EC a) prioritises the demands it places on accession states – environmental demands may be placed below restrictions on the flow of migrant labour, for example – and b) seeks to avoid imposing demands that would alienate the governments or populations of accession states (Kramer, 2001). Conversely, the accession states are likely to emphasize demands which are important to them and may well insist on conditions

---

9 Only in Poland was there a similar decline – from 75% to 67%.

seen as crucial to the economic welfare of the population at the expense of environmental targets.

Thus the image of Hungary moving asymptotically to bring its own regulations and implementation apparatus into line with EU regulations is misleading. It underestimates both the diversity and complexity of regulatory standards within the EU and the importance of political factors in deciding what priority is actually given to bringing environmental regulation into line with EU patterns. While Hungary has strong incentives to adopt an appropriate policy towards the environment, in practice such concerns are in partial conflict with more basic economic objectives such as restoring industrial output and GDP levels (Kerekes and Kiss, 1998).

In sum, Hungary is a post-socialist society where the stable institutional structure, degree of privatization, significance of foreign investment, evidence of environmentalism, and European orientation are all likely to have an influence on local environmental regulation.

The next chapter outlines previous work on environmental regulation and sets out some hypotheses which will be used as the framework for the study. It then sketches in the Hungarian framework for environmental regulation and describes the research method used. Chapters 3 to 6 present the conclusions of the studies done in four cities and Chapter 7 analyses these conclusions. Chapters 8 and 9 summarize the results of a survey of local governments throughout Hungary. Chapter 10 is an overall conclusion.

2 Hypotheses on Local Environmental Regulation

In this chapter we summarize the findings of research on environmental regulation in developed capitalist societies and present some preliminary evidence from post-socialist Eastern Europe. We then set out our hypotheses regarding local environmental regulation in Hungary. In the last two sections of the chapter we describe the institutional framework within which environmental regulation takes place in Hungary and explain the method used in the research on which the book is based.

Local level influences on environmental regulation: the North American and Western European experience

In this section we will explain what we mean by environmental regulation and review past research on what influences its form and strength. It will be shown that research on advanced capitalist societies reveals that there is no single pattern of influences on local environmental regulation, but a range of patterns, each of which tends to occur under certain contextual conditions. Our purpose in setting out these patterns is not to claim that Hungary is fated to choose from this set. New patterns may emerge, in particular because of state socialist legacy effects. But there is no reason to exclude the possibility that Hungary will show patterns found in advanced capitalist societies, and in any case the rationales underlying these patterns are important to understand.

The literature on local environmental regulation concerns four main types of actor:

a) central government as the formulator of national legislation, as an actor involved in enforcing some environmental regulations (for example, via its own regulatory agencies), and as an influence on local governments,
b) local governments as initiators of local environmental policy and implementers of some national environmental legislation,
c) enterprises as the source of much environmental detriment and the object of legislation, and

d) the public as an influence on both local and central government, and on firms.

It is the interaction between these four types of actor which is of particular interest here.

We discuss in turn research on the form taken by environmental regulation, and on the forces which shape its outcome.

A first point about the form of environmental regulation in advanced capitalist societies concerns the balance between educational and punitive action. There are a number of studies of the implementation of pollution legislation which give some insight into the regulatory process by observing how staff working in regulatory agencies go about their task (Richardson et al., 1982; Hawkins, 1984; Lowe et al., 1997, Fineman, 2000). These studies uniformly emphasise that agency staff regard education, advice and persuasion as the preferred means of securing compliance with environmental standards. In other words the primary task of staff is to create a climate in which the firms, for example, adopt the practices which the agency desires because they see it as in their interest to do so. These practices range from minor changes in employee practices to redesigning a production process so that it is cleaner. By inculcating a set of attitudes favourable to the reduction of negative environmental impacts the agency can reduce the share of its work which consists in looking for breaches of standard, and penalising the offender, work which is seen as 'punitive' and which is unpopular with agency officials. Negotiation and persuasion are thus the preferred methods of regulation.

The studies mentioned above show that the majority of firms which breach standards are regarded by regulatory agencies as being amenable to persuasion and negotiation. For them prosecution is a last resort. In contrast the same studies show that regulatory agency staff regard a few firms as belonging to a 'rogue minority' which are considered to be deliberately flouting the regulations and to be unresponsive to argument. In their case the threat of prosecution is introduced straight away.

The result of the agencies' preference for education, persuasion and negotiation is that they undertake prosecutions (as opposed to the threat of prosecution) relatively rarely since they represent the failure of the favoured approach. For example, in Hawkins's (1984) study of water pollution, under 1% of pollution incidents led to prosecution.[1] He argues that agency staff prefer to avoid the 'big stick' of prosecution since they prefer working with local firms with minimal supervision from agency managers, let alone appearing in court. He also claims that regulatory agencies themselves are not keen on prosecution since it takes their operations into the public arena and opens them up to unwelcome scrutiny which involves a loss of control for the agency. Likewise, Fineman (2000) refers to prosecution as the 'poisoned chalice' and notes that inspectors could be humiliated, 'taken to task by magistrates for insufficient prosecutory evidence, or simply outplayed by the superior legal resources

---

[1] Pollution incidents themselves represent only a fraction of the actual pollution since incidents only exist when measures are made.

of the company being prosecuted.' (2000, p. 67). He reports that prosecution also left behind 'a "prickly", "antagonistic", legacy, complicating future inspection visits'(2000, p. 67).

A second feature of the regulatory process revealed by these empirical studies is the pressure to be 'realistic'. Regulatory agency staff are loathe to require costly improvements which would oblige a firm to close. If they were to require the achievement of impracticable standards within tight deadlines this would jeopardise the regulatory relationship. The result is that environmental regulation typically involves a negotiation process in which there is room for manoeuvre concerning whether a breach has happened, the nature of the breach, what standards apply, whether there are mitigating circumstances, what improvements must be made (and their cost) and within what period of time. Terms like 'best practicable means' (BPM), 'as low as reasonably achievable' (ALARA) and 'best available technique not entailing excessive cost' (BATNEEC) (Richardson et al., 1982, Gouldson and Murphy, 1998), which are well-established in the UK context, express the tension between regulatory standards and the costs of meeting them and give a sense of the role of negotiation in environmental regulation. The result is that firms which are already in poor shape economically are likely to be able to argue that they cannot bear additional costs, whereas successful firms are likely to be required to achieve higher standards sooner. Fineman (2000) notes that the very flexibility of BATNEEC:

> was helpful to them [inspectors] in striking deals, 'horse trading', but it also exposed them to accusations of unfairness from wider industry, being seen to give good deals to some, but not to others. (Fineman, 2000, p. 69)

He also writes that many regulatory staff were former employees of the industry they are now regulating and continued to take pro-industry views, and that other staff who came from other backgrounds felt the first group were too close to industry.

The pressure for realism has a direct bearing on the third feature of environmental regulation. This concerns the two poles between which styles of regulation vary. At one pole, legislation may embody precise pollution and planning standards,[2] as in the US At the other pole, legislation may make no mention of specific standards, and leave the standards applied to private negotiation between regulatory agencies and firms about what is practicable, a pattern which places greater trust in officials. This is the UK model (Richardson et al., 1982; Vogel, 1986; Yeager, 1991). European countries other than the UK are placed by Vogel and Kun (1987) in between the two polar types. These differences are linked to the degree to which the law is prescriptive or leaves scope for discretion, and the degree of trust in the public officials who exercise any discretion. Such differences are linked to general differences between

---

[2] The implication is that pollution is permitted if it is below the stated level. Thus paradoxically the setting of pollution limits at the same time involves giving approval to a given level of pollution.

legal systems which relate to historical state-building processes and the balance between public and private spheres.

However, Vogel (1986) goes on to make the provocative claim that these differences in style of regulation are not reflected in differences in outcome. For example he shows that the standards set in US legislation are not in fact observed in practice. The reason for this paradox, he suggests, is that in countries with legally embodied environmental standards the application of these standards is an informal negotiation process in which, as described earlier, considerations of 'realism' and 'practicality' loom large. In other words Vogel argues that informal negotiation between regulators and regulated is universal and leads to a similarity in outcomes. This is because regulatory agencies are reluctant to enforce a measure which has a major negative effect on the well-being of the firms being regulated, and this reluctance is a constant across societies. The only difference between countries is whether informal negotiation is explicitly provided for in the legislation or not. One can interpret the polar types of regulation as symbols of the officially approved relation between the state and the private sector, rather than as indicating real differences in the balance of power between regulator and regulated.

The final feature of the process of environmental regulation in advanced capitalist societies is the obvious one that large firms are privately owned rather than state-owned like the state enterprises of state socialism. This might appear to give state regulatory agencies real independence and freedom in applying policy. However while this is true in a formal sense it is not necessarily true in a real sense. The numerous links between regulatory agencies and large firms mean that large firms can exert leverage over state agencies, both nationally and locally. This leverage derives from the facts:

a) that most industries are dominated by a few firms;
b) that industries are usually well-organized at national level and have informal direct access to ministers. They are also likely to be well-represented on or even to dominate government advisory bodies;
c) that knowledge about production processes and pollutants is likely to be considerably concentrated in the industry itself. (It may even be an object of commercial value which is kept secret.)
d) that those with the requisite knowledge to regulate firms are likely i) to have had careers which have included working in the firms concerned or on projects financed by them, and ii) to hope for such jobs in the future, thus compromising their independence; and
e) that in local areas leading firms are very significant as investors, employers, and sources of demand in the housing market and can acquire 'natural' authority in the local political scene.

As a result of this balance of power, environmental policy affecting an industry nationally or locally is unlikely to be formulated in isolation from its views (Marsh and Locksley, 1983). In the extreme case, where the autonomy of the regulator vis à vis the regulated has disappeared completely, the situation is described as 'regulatory capture'. This means that the roles have become reversed and the firms being regulated have gained control over the regulatory agency in practice if not formally.

Turning to the forces which shape local environmental regulation, the first is local government itself and the fact that local governments have a degree of autonomy vis à vis central government, though it is variable between countries and over time. It is because of this degree of autonomy that central government control is partial and local interests, such as business and citizens, can mobilize with a real chance of affecting local policy. If local government were totally under central control (as local governments sometimes claim) there would be less reason for local interests to mobilize and therefore less likelihood of variation in local policy. This autonomy is very clear in the field of local economic development (Harloe et al., 1990) and concepts such as 'urban growth coalition' (Logan and Molotch, 1987) and 'urban regime' (Stoker, 1995) have been developed to theorize the alliances frequently made between local government and other local interests. The existence of a degree of local government autonomy vis à vis central government is particularly relevant to local regulation affecting the built environment.

A second force affecting local environmental regulation is the public, whether in the form of organizations such as environmental groups, or as individual voters. In recent decades public reaction to environmental threats has become increasingly strong and well organised. The main exception is where local residents are poor and ill-educated and/or are employees of the firm concerned. The power of public reaction acts as a counterweight to the combination of business influence, council ideologies and deregulatory pressures which usually favour weak environmental regulation (Blowers, 1984). The higher level of environmentalist sentiment among the more educated has been widely reported in studies of environmental movements (Muller-Rommel, 1990). There is also spatial as well as social variation in public mobilization over environmental issues. Blowers and Leroy (1994) argue that the spatial distribution of 'locally unwanted land uses' (LULUs) across a country reflects the spatial variation in levels of mobilization among the public. These variations have given rise to the 'environmental justice' movement in the US (Cole and Foster, 2001). (A parallel process operates at international level, so that third world countries are likely to become storage places for hazardous and other waste, and recipients of investment using polluting technologies.)

A third force affecting local environmental regulation is business, as will be described later in this chapter.

What is the outcome of these forces? Studies of local-level environmental regulation reveal a variety of stances from the pro-environmentalist to the anti-environmentalist. These can be modelled as responses to different combinations of business pressure, public pressure and autonomous local government action. Table 2.1 shows six combinations of pressure which might lead to the two patterns. Business pressure can either be pro-environmentalist or anti-environmentalist, as can public pressure and local government. The six combinations will now be discussed.

Table 2.1 Typology of positions taken by local government in environmental regulation based on nature of business and public pressure and whether local government pays attention to these or develops its own position independently

	Main forces acting on local government and nature of force		Local government's own position		Resultant local government position
	Business pressure	Public pressure	Independent of business and public	Responsive to business or public	
A	AE			yes	Anti-environmentalist
B		AE		yes	Anti-environmentalist
C			AE	no	Anti-environmentalist
D	PE			yes	Pro-environmentalist
E		PE		yes	Pro-environmentalist
F			PE	no	Pro-environmentalist

AE: anti-environmentalist
PE: pro-environmentalist

A *Anti-environmentalist,[3] responsive to business pressure:* in this example local governments[4] are responsive to pressure from firms to abandon or demote environmental aims relative to other strategic aims, for example, the protection of jobs, or the attraction of development (Richardson et al, 1982; Blowers, 1984; Yeager, 1991).

B *Anti-environmentalist, responsive to public pressure:* this example, where the public is anti-environmentalist but business is neither anti-environmentalist nor pro-environmentalist seems unlikely.

C *Anti-environmentalist, autonomous of business and public pressure:*[5] a third pattern is that local government officials and politicians downplay environmental

---

3 Anti-environmental is intended in the sense of relative to current norms.
4 I refer here to local governments. In the case of other bodies with environmental regulatory responsibilities such as in this study regional environmental inspectorates (REIs) and water authorities the pattern of influence may be somewhat different but this is very much a matter of empirical study. Does the fact that the latter bodies are made up of professionals and are not subject to locally-elected political leaders mean they behave in a totally different way from local governments?
5 How far local government can be autonomous of local interests depends partly on how far environmental legislation allows scope for local level discretion and innovation, and partly on how far local politics reflects national politics (in the sense that local elections are based on the popularity of the parties nationally rather than being based on local policies and issues) or how far it has some autonomy.

aims and ignore business pressure and public pressure. Here the impression is of autonomous local government action. This may be supported by an ideology which identifies the needs of the locality with those of business.

In between patterns A and C is the case illustrated in Crenson's (1971) classic study which shows how the 'reputation for power' of US Steel was sufficient to keep air pollution off the political agenda in Gary, Indiana. These patterns are supported by the deregulatory thrust of recent decades which has weakened the legitimacy of a strict pursuit of environmental goals.

D *Pro-environmentalist, responsive to business pressure:* a fourth pattern is that local governments take a pro-environmentalist line in response to pro-environmentalist business. It should not be assumed that business is intrinsically opposed to higher environmental standards. Firms may take a pro-environmentalist stance for various reasons; for example, to acquire a reputation as good local corporate citizens and/or to gain a competitive advantage vis à vis other firms in the same industry or same locality. Individual business executives may have strong environmentalist views which they promote and become part of the firm's image, for example, Body Shop. Once a locality gains a reputation as environmentally sensitive this becomes a selling point to new firms.

E *Pro-environmentalist, in response to public pressure:* a fifth pattern is where local government is attentive to the expression of environmentalist views among the public, thereby countering any company pressure in the opposite direction. This would imply a delegitimation of local business views, perhaps because existing firms were in severe decline and a 'fresh start' were needed. It could also happen if an alternative local plan had been articulated perhaps drawing on the environmental assets of the locality as a basis for economic development, for example, tourism.

F *Pro-environmentalist, independent of business or public pressure*: the last pattern is where local government develops an environmentalist policy irrespective of local business or public pressure. This is a difficult option to imagine since the local government has to deny local pressures. One could imagine this happening if a group of politicians were elected on a radical ticket advocating a break with the past.

The alternatives in Table 2.1 could be multiplied if the simple categories were made more complex. For example, business may not have a single voice, the public may also be divided, or policy may not be classifiable as pro- or anti-environmentalist but may be a mixture of the two. Similarly, rather than business and public influence being present or absent, all manner of combinations are possible.

As mentioned earlier, these patterns are not necessarily exhaustive of the possibilities open to local governments in Hungary but they cannot be ignored as possibilities.

Local environmental regulation in post-socialist Poland, the Czech Republic and Hungary: a review of research

New environmental legislation has been passed in all three of the above countries (Jehlicka and Kara, 1994; Slocock, 1996; Slocock and Sowinski, 1996; Bluffstone and Larson, 1997; Emmott, 1997) partly in order to break away from the previous pattern of detailed legislation combined with ineffective implementation, and partly with a view to future EU membership (Matlary, 1994; Caddy, 1997). It is rather early to expect detailed studies of the implementation of environmental legislation, since much of it is very recent, but we can review the research that has been carried out so far.

In his study of environmental policy-making in the Czech Republic, Slocock (1996) argues that what is happening is not a purely symbolic process designed to appease external interests and that the new legislation is being taken seriously. On the one hand he refers to a new clean air act which prescribes penalties which are 'very high' by EU standards and reports that firms have accepted the idea of penalties (to provide an incentive to raise standards) but are asking for a delay in their implementation. He notes that neither lobbyists nor enterprises seem to have considered non-compliance:

> in a political culture so unused to the exercise of economic power for policy-shaping objectives, the legal powers of the environmental authorities to shut down offending processes and plants were assumed to be absolute, and the option of openly obstructing unpopular policies was simply not entertained. (Slocock, 1996, p. 517)

This comment on political culture clearly implies a legacy effect (lack of initiative in policy-making) and is interesting since it hints at a belief that authorities have to be obeyed rather than at any posssibility of negotiation. In my view, following the argument in Chapter 1, this cannot be considered a true legacy effect since environmental rules under state socialism were largely flouted. It is better seen as an example of how images of the past are constructed and used in academic discourse, as Elster et al. (1998) suggest. These images may reflect a 'new legalism', that is the belief that in a post-socialist world legal rules really have to be followed. However there is good reason to question the prevalence of this belief. Slocock notes that there is evidence of significant new environmental investments in large firms, and that the environmental inspectorate expects 75% compliance with the clean air standards. This implies some non-compliance, in contradiction with the earlier quotation. This is confirmed by Stepanek (1997) who points out that different emission standards are applied to existing plant and new plant, but that by 1998 common standards were to be observed. He expects that companies will request delays in meeting them. Another supporting comment, hinting at the diversity of firm policy, is made by Fagin in his study of the Czech Republic who says that 'industries that have not as yet attracted foreign investment have on the whole made little effort at restructuring and abatement' (1994, p. 489).

Turning to Poland, a study by Slocock and Sowinski (1996) concerns the regulation of industrial pollution in Katowice province. Provincial environmental departments issue permits specifying permitted emissions levels, and discuss plans to improve actual emission levels, while provincial inspectorates for environmental protection are responsible for monitoring and compliance. Local governments also have powers but they are more limited. Slocock and Sowinski argue that:

> those firms with a dynamic commercial strategy were concerned with their public image and saw their environmental performance as an important influence on the public standing of the company. In particular, managers whose companies were on the list of major polluters were eager to remove this stigma. (1996, p. 25)

Anderson and Fiedor (1997) describe Polish pollution charges as 'among the highest anywhere in the world' (p. 188) and note that they have increased 20 times from 1990–93 to $400–500m per year. Meanwhile the amounts actually collected fell from 97% to 64% of the amounts levied. They point out that a) the penalty level is non-negotiable but 'the degree of the violation may be subject to negotiation' (p. 194), b) half the facilities lacked facility permits, and c) reliance on self-reporting of pollution combined with the lack of obligation for ongoing measurement, and lack of inspectorate staff make for implementation of limited effectiveness. Another study adds that the execution and collection of fines is 'very poor' (Sleszynski, 1996, p. 131) and that firms refuse to pay charges when they severely affect profits. However it gives no information about how decisions are made to levy charges or fines and collect them or not. A third study describes a 'covenant' between the Katowice provincial inspectorate, Byton city council, and 18 factories which commit themselves to reduce emissions in line with an 'environmental master plan' (Brieskorn et al., 1996). Unfortunately little information is given on the rights and obligations of the different parties to the covenant. However its existence may be evidence of the type of public-private partnership described in the urban politics literature.

Finally a postal survey of Polish privatized manufacturing firms by Angel et al. (2000) with a 36% response rate argues that most firms that need permits have them but that a 'high percentage' (p. 584) fail to meet the standards. However the figures cited contradict this: they show that only 16% of those responding failed to meet waste-water standards and only 29% failed to meet air pollution standards. Since the survey was of privatized firms, and privatized firms could be expected to show better environmental performance than state firms, the authors argue that the survey gives a somewhat optimistic view of the total situation. Angel et al. note that permitting allowed little flexibility but that 'the regulators have responded to widespread noncompliance with considerable flexibility and sensitivity to local and technical and economic circumstances' (p. 585), familiar ideas in all studies of regulation. They also find that environmental fees were on average 0.5% of operating costs which they say means that 'environmental fees and fines are in most cases too low to create significant incentives for pollution prevention' (p. 586). However my impression is that this proportion is higher than in the Hungarian cases to be discussed in this study. So their findings may not be in conflict with the judgement quoted earlier that fine levels in Poland are high internationally speaking.

The Hungarian experience is discussed later in this chapter.

It can be concluded that while new environmental legislation is in force in Eastern Europe the evidence supports the idea that it is not strictly applied, and that it is subject to the same type of negotiation between regulators and regulated that we described earlier.

Before moving to the next section it is worth referring to an interesting study of environmental regulation in China. This country remains officially state socialist but has seen a sustained high rate of economic growth in the 1980s and 1990s based on 'market' forms which include both familiar private companies and unique state-private hybrids (for example when local governments, state firms, or the army are allowed and encouraged to create firms with the promise of retaining the surplus).

Ma and Ortolano (2000) conducted a survey of 76 enterprises in four cities focusing on discharge permits and fees in respect of industrial waste water pollution. They show that regulation in this field is the responsibility of a central Environmental Protection Administration working with local government-controlled Environmental Protection Bureaus (which receive a share of fees that they levy). The authors focus on the informal rules used by the EPBs and reveal the familiar pragmatic negotiation processes described earlier in North America and the UK.

Ma and Ortolano show that the EPBs set low standards for water pollution permits (partly due to a, possibly deliberate, ambiguity in national legislation as to whether standards should concern concentration or mass of pollutants), that they never revoked permits or took court action, and that in setting fines and fees they emphasized the economic status of the firm. This worked to the advantage of state-owned firms which were in a worse economic state than the newer 'township and village enterprises'. They conclude by suggesting that the Chinese system of regulation of waste water is more decentralized and less legalistic than the US one but that it has a similar emphasis on informal rules and 'realism' in regulation.

If, as we saw, Vogel's work suggests that structural differences in environmental regulatory systems do not translate into differences in practice in North America and Western Europe, Ma and Ortolano's study can be said to extend this thesis to China. The impossibility of imposing environmental regulations irrespective of the economic situation of the firms involved thus seems to apply across a wide range of socio-political systems.

Hypotheses on local environmental regulation in post-socialist societies

In this section we present some hypotheses about the local-level determinants of environmental regulation in post-socialist conditions. Features of the enterprise, local government, central government (including regional environmental inspectorates (REIs) as found in Eastern Europe) and the public will be considered in turn. The argument is that the relationship between regulators and regulated, as reflected in the negotiating process, will depend on these features. (Regulators consist of local government and REIs.)

a. The enterprise

We showed earlier that under state socialism the powerful position of state enterprises in the institutional structure meant that environmental regulation was little more than a paper reality. We can thus deduce that one possible legacy effect of state socialism is that private firms (many of which are privatized state firms) will treat environmental legislation with disdain. But we also saw that studies of advanced capitalist societies suggest that under certain conditions private enterprises can also exert great leverage over local environmental regulation. This suggests that in this respect any legacy effects from state socialism could operate in the same direction as forces generated within capitalism. This is an intriguing convergence and one to which we shall return.

To try and identify the conditions under which this pattern will occur we need to refine our argument.

It can be hypothesized that *the influence of private enterprises on local environmental regulation will be greater when one or more of the following five conditions are present.*

The first three conditions are:

- *When firms are sole or dominant employers in an area.*
- *When firms are a major source of local taxes or other income for the local government.*
- *When the demand from investors to establish themselves in the area is low.*

All these conditions refer to the economic power of existing enterprises vis à vis regulators. The first two concern sources of leverage of enterprises over local governments. The third suggests that this leverage is stronger in localities where there are few or no alternative sources of investment, and hence jobs and local taxes, to existing firms. In localities where there is a strong demand for land from industrial investors, the local government will be in a stronger position in its dealings with existing enterprises if it chooses to encourage new investors. Faced with this possibility, one strategy for existing enterprises is clearly to try and 'capture' the local government and encourage it to develop policies which favour existing firms over new ones. New investors can become threats to existing firms in various ways, for example by offering higher wages or 'poaching' workers. Coalitions between firms and local governments can thus either be defensive and inward-looking or proactive and intended to attract new investment. (To point out that linkages between local governments and firms exist is one thing: to identify how these links influence policy is another.) One important point about foreign investment in Hungary is that no less than 85% of greenfield investment in the '6–8 years' up to 1996 was located in western Hungary (Ellingstadt, 1997, p. 18). This suggests that there will be substantial inter-regional differences in the economically-based power of enterprises vis à vis local governments.

The fourth and fifth conditions are:

- *When private firms have a reputation for power even if this does not correspond to their actual power.*

This hypothesis is based on Crenson (1971) and recognizes that there can be a divergence between perceptions of power and 'real' power. The perception that a firm has power will influence actions towards it in the same way as if it actually had the power attributed to it.

- *When private firms have social networks which enable them to put pressure on regulators either directly or via linkages to central government.*

This hypothesis refers to firms' capacity to exercise their economically-based power. Social networks facilitate the exercise of power and therefore where such links exist and help firms reach the target of their influence their effective power is increased. One legacy issue here is whether social networks created under state socialism retain any vitality. This depends on how far the members of networks still occupy significant positions and provide access to useful resources.

However none of these hypotheses refers to the direction in which firms will exercise influence.

A further hypothesis is therefore necessary:

- *That firms may use their influence in either i) an anti-environmentalist direction as part of a cost-minimising strategy or ii) a pro-environmentalist direction when their business strategy depends on improving their image or attracting foreign investment.*

This last hypothesis acknowledges that firms will use their influence in different policy directions, according to the economic, social and political conditions they face.

b. Local government

Local governments in post-socialist societies have more powers than before, though they vary between local government units of different sizes. Whereas previously they were unable to develop independent policies, they are now elected bodies representing local interests and seeking re-election within a national legal framework. Most of the funding for local governments comes from central government, but local enterprises are the predominant source of locally-raised income.

In principle therefore, local governments have greater autonomy in their spending than before but this is constrained by the squeeze caused by meagre central grants and the economic weakness of many local enterprises. Today the constraints are less institutionalized, but privatized former state enterprises and new private enterprises can be powerful local economic actors. It remains to be established how much more room for manoeuvre they leave for local governments than they had before (Pickvance, C.G., 1997).

These constraints together with social network links may favour the cooperative pattern of relationships often observed in capitalist societies between local government and private sector actors, for example in 'public–private partnerships'. Since private firms can be small and unstable as well as large and stable, local governments may be drawn into rescue packages with the former but medium term development strategies with the latter.

This leads to the dilemma for local governments in post-socialist conditions: to adopt pro-environmental policies which harm enterprises which are major local employers and on which they are financially dependent, or to adopt anti-environmental policies and alienate public opinion on which they are dependent for re-election. (In practice this dilemma may not be so real since the public may be more concerned with employment than the environment.)

We would expect the outcome of this tension in terms of environmental regulation to depend on:

- *whether a firm is in a strong position because of its economic importance, for example, as a dominant employer in the local labour market or a major source of income to local government,*
- *how strong local environmentalist opinion is,*
- *how far the firm is motivated to be well-behaved environmentally speaking,* and
- *how far local government is 'captured' by existing economic interests or how far it can distance itself from them, for example, by developing a strategy of economic diversification which reduces the dependence of the local economy on existing firms by exploiting other assets in the area.* This will depend partly on expressions of interest by new investors, but also on the entrepreneurialism of local officials and politicians.

The possibility of divisions among entrepreneurs should not be ruled out. Again everything depends on asset distribution and conversion, social networks, the short or long term orientation of managers, and the scope for local government involvement with new enterprises.

c. Central government

Central government is a significant influence on local environmental regulation for three reasons. It is a source of legislation which allocates responsibilities to local government, it implements legislation through its own structures, for example regional environmental inspectorates, and it continues to provide a large part of local government income (Lengyel, 1993; Bennett, 1998).

The key issue for local environmental regulation is how much priority central government gives to environmental issues, since this determines resourcing levels and the legislative priority given to environmental reforms. The old 'socialist' pattern of economic ministries outweighing environmental ministries is of course equally to be found in advanced capitalist societies and seems likely to continue because of the priority being given by post-socialist governments to economic growth and economic restructuring, and the perception that environmental policies are a source of additional costs on business. Hungary's status as an accession state means that it has to bring its system of environmental regulation into conformity with those of the EU (Kerekes and Kiss, 1998). This involves setting up appropriate structures, ensuring adequate resourcing, and training staff but most of all adopting the EU's approaches to environmental regulation. However as explained in Chapter 1 the accession process does not guarantee that environmental reforms become top government priorities.

The following hypotheses can be suggested.
Central government influence will lead to a weak local environmental policy:

- *when national environmental policy is weak or has a low priority*
- *when regional inspectorates are weak* (for example because of weak national policy and/or under-resourcing), or
- *when local governments are subject to a central resource squeeze which forces them to rely more on local taxes paid by enterprises, and thus be less willing to act against them.* Such a resource squeeze could also lead to greater enthusiasm for levying pollution fines. However the potential scale of such fines is minute compared with the local taxes paid by companies.

On the other hand *central government influence could lead to a tougher policy when these conditions are reversed.*

It should be noted that the strong/weak dimension applies better to the implementation of nationally-set policy than to policy elaborated by the local government itself. Pro-business v. anti-business would be a more useful contrast, but does not distinguish existing firms from newly arrived firms.

No hypotheses will be put forward about causes of differences in regional inspectorate behaviour other than central government policy and funding. We shall advance some hypotheses to fill this gap in Chapter 7 in order to make sense of some of the differences in regional inspectorate behaviour we found.[6]

---

6 We are resisting the temptation to insert some hypotheses to make sense of some findings that were unexpected. This would have perhaps improved the neatness of the presentation but at the expense of misrepresenting the process of research.

d. The public

The main issue here is how far local public opinion is pro-environmentalist. This may be reflected in the extent of organization into environmental groups or in the prevalence of environmentalist attitudes which are not translated into organized action.

It is generally agreed that environmental issues are less prominent in public opinion in post-socialist societies than during the final years of state socialism. This is partly because of the privileged position of environmental activism as a tolerated form of public activity under state socialism and partly because households have had to cope with severe economic dislocation following the end of state socialism (Pickvance, C.G., 1996a, 1999; Tickle and Welsh, 1998). Nevertheless, as mentioned, there are currently several hundred local environmental groups in Hungary.

The *influence of public opinion on local environmental policy depends on*:

a) *the proportion of highly educated groups (which tend to be more environmentalist in opinion) in a locality*,
b) *how far employees in the locality are local residents (in which case we would expect local public opinion to be divided) and how far employees commute in from outside (in which case residents are likely to take more opposed positions to local enterprises)*, and
c) *the extent to which local governments encourage or discourage public participation*. The former can vary from providing more information to providing opportunities for involvement, while the latter can involve co-optation, exclusion or repression of local environmental groups.

The question is under what conditions public mobilization is high and able to influence local government policy, and under what conditions it is low. In general the political opportunity structure strand of social movement theory emphasizes the importance of the context in which political action takes place for the likelihood that grievances will be expressed in collective action, and that this action will be successful.

The above arguments about the conditions under which local environmental regulation will be strong or weak are summarized in Table 2.2.

To explore these hypotheses adequately a large comparative research design would be necessary so as to include localities representing all the different combinations of values of the variables identified as shaping local environmental policy. In practice such designs are too costly to be practicable, and are in any case limited by the actually existing combinations. As described later in this chapter, the four localities studied in the research project on which this book is based covered an array of different possibilities, but fell far short of the ideal design. Inevitably the present study can be regarded as only exploratory since it is not possible to separate out the influence of the different independent variables identified given the small number of cases (Lieberson, 1992).

Table 2.2 Determinants of strong and weak local environmental policy

Actors	Features	Features of actors making for a weak local environmental policy	Features of actors making for a strong local environmental policy
Enterprise	Single/dominant employer	Yes	No
	Reputation for power	Yes	No
	Major contributor of local taxes	Yes	No
	Interest from outside investors	Low	High
	Strong networks to local government	Yes	No
	Environmentalist management	No	Yes
Government	Priority to environment	Low	High
	National policies	Weak	Strong
	Regional environmental structures	Weak	Strong
	Resource squeeze on local government	Yes	No
Local government	Fiscal position (needs taxes from companies)	Weak	Strong
	Local economic policy	No change to economic base (assumed to be polluting)	Diversify (assumed to mean less pollution)
	Policy-making	In line with passive public, or ignores active public	Responds positively to environmentalist pressure
Public	Attitudes	Passive (high unemployment, fatalistic)	Proactive (environmentalist)
	Local residents	Also employees (so divided loyalties)	Not employees (employees commute in)

The framework of Hungarian environmental regulation

Before describing the research method used here it will be useful to explain the role of the different agencies in implementing environmental policy in Hungary. Four levels can be distinguished.

The first is the *national level* which although not the focus of this study shapes what happens at sub-national level. The key to the strength of environmental policy is the political priority it receives vis à vis other policies, the strength of environmental legislation and the degree to which the Ministries responsible are adequately funded. As explained in Chapter 1, the top political priority for post-1990 Hungarian governments has been restructuring the economy and producing the economic growth needed to restore people's living standards. This means that environmental policy has taken a back seat – despite the environmental mobilization in the 1980s.

Three ministries are involved in environmental policy: the Ministries of Environmental Protection and Regional Policy (MEPRP),[7] Transport, Telecommunications and Water Management (MTTWM), and Welfare (which includes public health). The MEPRP was created in 1990. Previously, between 1987 and 1990, Environment was associated with Water Management in the same ministry. According to O'Toole, in this period, 'most analysts believed ... that the water supply interests dominated decisions having to do with water, at the expense of water quality', and the aim of the 1990 reorganization was 'to create a unit that would focus exclusively on protecting the environment and not developing or exploiting it' (1998, p. 52). Kramer agrees that the MTTWM gives low priority to the quality of river water, writing that it 'traditionally places far higher priority on promoting commerce along the Danube River than in protecting the waterway from environmental threats to it' (2001, p. 10).

A regional environmental inspectorate official interviewed in our research, drew a contrast between the water management and environmental functions. The former had a long history, and a professional approach; the latter was a newcomer:

> At the time of the separation [in 1990], the Water (Authority) was particularly strong. It managed to keep an awful lot of its power, both financial and administrative duties, at the expense of the Environment ... The Water (Authority) used to be an extremely stable, well-run authority with great traditions. The same thing could not be said about the environmental authorities. In the 1970s Environment had no ministry. It had only an institution with national authority...This had regional branches, but they did not have any authority. They were just there. People didn't take them seriously. And we must admit that this was legitimate because they had no weight behind them. (H 32)[8]

---

7   This was true at the time of the study. Since then MEPRP has been replaced by the Ministry of Environment and Water Management, the 1987–90 combination. The regional policy function has been joined with agriculture as a separate ministry
8   Interviewee code number.

Observers of the MEPRP since 1990 are sceptical about its performance. O'Toole (1998) sees the weakness of the MEPRP and the under-funding of the regional environmental inspectorates as part of a wider problem of insufficient institutional capacity: 'all these sectors and levels are short on expertise, lacking in budgetary resources, and often handicapped by a lack of pressure group support from the broader society' (p. 75). In the case of the MEPRP the lack of capacity:

> is manifest not only in the relatively limited resources, influence and vertical linkages within government, but also in the very limited ties with ...NGOs and others who remain seriously concerned with environmental questions and might be able to catalyze support for environmental action. The Ministry provides no regular contact with the public, no dissemination of results of environmentally relevant research, and no regular public information on the spending of environmental funds or related matters. (O'Toole, 1998, p. 74)[9]

Likewise, Kramer's view is that:

> the Hungarian Ministry of Environment shares a trait common to its peer institutions in the region: it is relatively weak politically compared to many other sectoral agencies and often lacks the requisite political muscle to overcome this sectoral bias in policy formulation and execution. Such sectoral bias becomes especially pernicious in the accession process given the imperative to integrate environmental considerations into other policy sectors. (Kramer, 2001, pp. 10–11)

He notes that according to the European Commission the legal department of the MEPRP was 'particularly weak; in 1999 only three lawyers worked on this daunting task [the transposition of EU environmental legislation]' (quoted in Kramer, 2001, p. 10).

The same comments about structural weakness of the environmental ministry could of course be applied to environmental ministries and agencies in most capitalist societies.

Turning to environmental legislation, Hungary was slower than Poland and the Czech Republic to pass new measures: the Hungarian environmental framework law was passed in 1995. This was a big step forward. The 1995 law, however, only leads to effective regulation when accompanied by measures specifying objects of pollution and permitted levels. A study by Morris et al. (1997) states that at that time emission limits, a prerequisite of levying fines, had been set for only half of all air pollutants.

Another environmental measure was the creation in 1992 of a Central Environmental Protection Fund which draws primarily on a share of VAT levied on fuel, but also on environmental fines levied by the REIs. In 1997 its total income from fines was 737 million forint (ft) (£2.9 million).[10] Its resources are used to carry out environmental protection measures in association with sub-national governments. To

---

9 Since this was written the MEPRP has created a website with considerable data on the environmental situation: www.gridbp.meh.hu. It includes an English language section.

10 The conversion rate used was that current at the time of the research, £1 = 250 forint.

start with, shares of fines returned to local government could be spent on any legitimate activity of local government. Tighter rules were later introduced so that fine refunds were only sent to local governments which set up a local environmental fund whose use was restricted to environmental purposes.

At the *regional* level are the 12 regional environmental inspectorates of the MEPRP[11] which have existed continuously despite ministerial reorganizations. The REIs have responsibility for:

a) approving new investment which could cause pollution. This must be given before the local government issues a building permit,
b) setting pollution levels in fields where it has this power (pollution from factory and agricultural sources),
c) permitting, that is issuing permits for specified levels of pollution,[12]
d) setting fines for breaches of standard,
e) monitoring the environmental situation generally (based on self-reporting by firms or by the REI conducting unannounced visits),
f) preparing plans, and
g) generally being responsible for the environmental state of the region. This includes responding to public complaints.

The REIs are under-resourced in terms of money, staff and expertise. O'Toole describes their ability to carry out their duties as 'untenable' (1998, p. 64). We found that the REI for the mid-Danube valley (which includes Budapest) is responsible for an area with 450,000 registered companies of which it should have dealings with 30%, but has a staff of 150. In one sense the underfunding of REIs is deliberate: they are expected to find one twelfth of their income by carrying out consultancy work. This can lead to conflicts of interest, as when REIs enter contracts with local factories to check their effluent while at the same time being the monitoring authority (O'Toole, 1998, p. 54). In our interviews with REI officials there were several references to the need for consultancy work to raise income. But even if the REIs had not had to find one twelfth of their income they would still have been under-

---

11 There is also a parallel structure of regional Water Authority offices, which also have regulatory powers and in some cases still share buildings with REIs.
12 An integrated permitting system was put into operation in 1993 under which enterprises are required to obtain licenses from one of the twelve REIs (Emmott, 1997). The concept of 'integrated permitting and pollution control' is based on a critique of the way pollution is traditionally controlled in which a multiplicity of agencies at different levels of government have responsibility for pollution in different media (Weale, 1992, Chapter 4). This fragmentation minimises the likelihood of consistent standards and has no way of dealing with cross-media transfer of pollutants. For example if regulations are weaker or penalties are lower for air pollution than for land pollution there will be incentives to pollute the air. Integrated pollution control is best seen as an aspiration given the practical obstacles it involves but the Hungarian system of pollution permitting and control has taken steps towards it.

resourced. But the underfunding and shortage of staff with sufficient expertise is part of the more general lack of governmental capacity in Eastern Europe already referred to. We can extend this comment to Western Europe too where for example the inspection capacity of the Environmental Agency in the UK has been criticised as inadequate. The general point is that it is easier to pass laws which give added tasks and responsibilities to regulatory agencies than to match this with the extra resources needed to carry them out.

There have been few previous studies of the implementation of Hungarian environmental legislation. However, in an earlier study Morris et al. (1997) argue that Hungarian fine levels are very low[13] and report that by appeals firms 'have been able to delay, reduce or eliminate payment of fines' (p. 169) and that 'compromises, waivers and extensions are frequently granted' (p. 170) when high fines accumulate or firms are in difficulty. They also suggest that the regulatory system relies mainly on self-reporting and that REIs carry out infrequent inspections. Caddy (1997) includes Hungary among the countries with an 'implementation gap'. We shall focus on these matters among others in the next four chapters.

Counties are primarily administrative levels of government which act as intermediaries between Ministries and the 3200 local governments. Since 1994 they have been given extra weight by the introduction of indirect elections. They have a regional development role, and relate to various central Ministries including the MTTWM. There is a parallel system of Drainage Authorities which are responsible for drains, sewers and public sewage treatment plants. They can fine sources of pollution entering their infrastructure. Conversely they can themselves be fined by REIs for polluted water they allow out into rivers.

The 1990 decentralization reform gave new responsibilities to *local governments*, including environmental responsibilities, depending on whether they are cities with county status, other cities and towns, or villages. In the last two cases they have fewer functions and it is county authorities which have the main environmental responsibilities. This poses problems of coordination between cities with county status and counties.

Local government:

a) is responsible for noise pollution, though the standards are set by the REI,
b) is responsible for pollution by the service industry,
c) is a channel for complaints by residents about environmental nuisances caused by factories which it forwards to the REI,
d) levies fines in the case of breaches of standard decided by REI,
e) receives 30% of fines sent to the national level Environmental Protection Fund (provided it has a written environmental programme), and

---

13 As a matter of interest the average fines levied on businesses for pollution incidents by the UK Environment Agency were £8090 in 2000 and £6410 in 2001. The median figures were lower.

Hypotheses on Local Environmental Regulation   37

f) is responsible for town planning including the preparation of plans, issuing of building permits, and classification of land into different categories of protection.

There are a number of additional reasons why firms have an interest in local government and its policies:

a) local government provides infrastructure. It may provide this to attract new investment generally (for example, an industrial park), or it may tailor its provision to the needs of a particular company. It may ask firms to contribute to infrastructure costs,
b) local governments levy local taxes on firms; and
c) local governments also provide services on which firms depend.

Also at the local level is the *municipal public health service* which is responsible for public health: this covers community health, food hygiene, work safety and occupational health. Each local municipal public health service reports to a central office (ANTSZ). Each must keep a register of businesses and can make unannounced visits to firms. In our interviews we recorded cases where they were refused access. They have the power to levy fines up to 30,000 ft (£120) but fine income goes to the ANTSZ. They give advice to the local government on the issuing of permits to build and operate factories. While the local service has a veto power on the issuing of permits, firms can appeal against a veto to the central office.

Overall, therefore, there is what can either be called a developed division of labour or alternatively a fragmentation of responsibility for environmental policy at local and regional level between local government, REIs, county authorities, water and drainage authorities and the municipal public health service. To give an example of this, air pollution by factories is the responsibility of the REI, air pollution by service industries is the local government's responsibility, pollution due to traffic comes under the Ministry of Transport, Telecommunications and Water Management, and the municipal public health service is responsible for air quality.

Lastly it is useful to provide some data on environmental quality. This is only a partial measure of the effectiveness of legislation. Energy efficiency is lower in Eastern Europe as a whole than in Western Europe but air pollution has decreased due to a mixture of decreasing economic activity and improved pollution-reducing equipment in preparation for EU accession. But there has been an increase in car use.

An 'expert' subjective assessment of the proportion of land in the two worst categories of environmental quality in Poland, Hungary and Czechoslovakia in 1990 is shown in Table 2.3. Hungary is shown to be in a less bad situation than the other two countries, and to be below the average for the region.

As far as Hungary is concerned, data on air pollution shows the following trends from 1990–97 (national data, kilotons per year):

SO_2:   decline from 1000 to 670
NO_x: decline from 235 to 200
CO: decline from 1000 to 730
Particulates: decline from 200 to 140
Lead: decline from 700 to 100

(*Source:* www.gridbp.ktm.hu)[14]

These trends are favourable, but the absolute level gives cause for concern. According to the same official website, of the total land area, 3.9% has air which is described as 'polluted' and 9.3% has 'moderately polluted' air. But almost half of the population lives in areas classified in one of these ways.

Lastly, air quality in Budapest, compared with Paris, New York and Tokyo, is worse in terms of sulphur dioxide (39 micrograms/m^3 v. 14/26/18), better in terms of nitrogen dioxide (46 v. 57/79/68) and worse than New York and Tokyo in terms of particulates (55 v. 14/62/49) (EBRD, 2000, p. 48). The better NO_2 figures may reflect lower car use, and the other two figures reflect the greater prevalence of industrial activity in the city. In terms of municipal waste volume the Hungarian per capita figure has increased by about 20% between 1990 and 1998 (EBRD, 2000, p. 46).

Table 2.3 Proportion of land in the two worst categories of environmental quality in Poland, Hungary and Czechoslovakia in 1990

| | Air | | Water | |
	Very poor	Very poor and poor	Very poor	Very poor and poor
Czechoslovakia	20	46	26	53
Hungary	0	5	5	19
Poland	2	14	17	37
Central and Eastern Europe	6	19	10	24

Source: Alcamo (1992), quoted in Pavlinek and Pickles (2000, p. 45). Thanks to John Pickles, who kindly supplied a corrected figure.

Research method

We conclude this chapter by describing our research method. The research was made up of complementary parts: case studies of four localities[15] and a survey.

---

14 These figures are approximate as in some cases they are based on bar charts.
15 The present book reports on the four urban locality studies. Two further studies were done of rural localities.

The aim of the case studies was to explore relations between the major groups with a bearing on local environmental regulation in order to try to gain a deeper understanding of the processes involved than is possible through survey research. We were looking for four localities in which the social and economic conditions were contrasting in ways identified as significant in the hypotheses outlined earlier. We were not looking for typical localities, if such exist, but rather for a purposive sample of settlements which would allow us to test our hypotheses over a fair range of conditions. Thus we wanted a contrast between a dominant employer city and a mixed industry city, a locality which was attractive to foreign investment and one which was unattractive, a council which was dynamic and one which was inactive in terms of local economic development policy, and localities where there were contrasts in the environmental situation and environmental regulation.

In practice (as can be seen from Table 2.4) the localities chosen, Székesfehérvár, Győr, Nagytétény and Dunaújváros, while offering the contrasts we were looking for as a group, were far from the ideal in terms of the distribution of features among them. For example they presented syndromes of characteristics which are understandably linked but which in an ideal world we would have liked to be able to separate. Thus for example the dominant employer city was in the least attractive location for foreign investment, while the city with the most dynamic council was also most successful in attracting foreign investment. These associations are the bane of social science since non-experimental research can only study variation as it actually exists. However the associations between features are of course targets for enquiry, so they are not entirely to be seen as weaknesses in the research design.

Figure 2.1 Map showing the four localities

Table 2.4 The four localities and their main features

	Székesfehérvár	Győr	Nagytétény	Dunaújváros
Location	West-central Hungary	North-west Hungary	Budapest	West-central Hungary
Settlement type	Town	Town	Suburb	Town
Industrial type	Mixed	Mixed	Mixed	Steel town
Foreign capital	Most	Some	A little	None
Council	Most dynamic	Active	Inactive	Low activity

In terms of air pollution, Table 2.5 presents some 1997 data for the four locations. Obviously there are numerous possible measures of pollution. The table does not refer to water pollution or solid waste, and only covers three types of air pollution. However the data are worth keeping in mind in the light of the claims made by actors in the four towns, and especially in Székesfehérvár about the good environmental situation there.

Table 2.5 Measures of air pollution, 1997, micrograms per cu.m.

	Székesfehérvár	Győr	Nagytétény*	Dunaújváros
SO_2	17.9	8.4	20.7	16.4
NO_x	34.8	38.0	27.5	20.5
Residual dust	9.3	8.6	5.2	15.7

Source: www.gridbp.ktm.hu
* Figures are for Budapest.

In each locality we chose one or two companies and set out to carry out 30–40 interviews distributed among their employees (from top managers downwards), local government officials, regional environmental inspectorate officials, and environmental group activists (or, where absent, members of the public). In total 140 interviews were carried out by our collaborators, who were all Hungarian academics. The interviews followed topic guides rather than standardized questions and were adapted according to the interviewee. The interviews were then transcribed and translated.

The interviews were carried out between 1996 and 1998, so when interviewees refer to 'now' and 'the future' 1996–98 is the point of reference. The same is true for our interpretation. We have not tried to update the picture obtained through the interviews but in a few places have noted significant later developments, usually in footnotes. In order to ensure the anonymity of interviewees we have a) given each interview a code number, b) not referred to the interviewees' specific roles but used general terms like official, manager or office-holder and c) in some cases changed the gender of the interviewee in referring to them.

We were aware from the outset that a study based on four localities was open to the objection of atypicality. Although, as explained, we were not seeking typical locations but a purposive sample, we wanted to complement it by a wide-ranging survey. We thus carried out an interview survey of 600 local governments. Details of the sample are provided in Chapter 8.

In choosing in which order to present the locality studies I have started with Székesfehérvár (Chapter 3) because it had the most progressive image in environmental terms and greatest success in attracting new investment. Győr (Chapter 4) is considered next because it has most similarity to Székesfehérvár. Nagytétény is dealt with in Chapter 5 because it has a worse environmental image than Győr but has more assets for attracting investment. Dunaújváros, which also has a bad environmental image and has the least success in attracting investment, is dealt with last, in Chapter 6.

3 Székesfehérvár: Magnet for Multinational Capital and Green Utopia?

In this and the next three chapters we will present our material on the four case study localities in the following format: location, history and economic situation; the local council and its economic and environmental policy; the environmental practices of the firms studied; and the regional environmental inspectorate and its relations with local firms. In Chapter 7 we will assess the four locality chapters and examine whether the evidence fits the model set out in Chapter 2.

Location, history and economic situation

Székesfehérvár is a historic town of 108,000 people located 65km west of Budapest. It was the seat of the Hungarian crown until the sixteenth century and today has county town status. (Its name means 'white castle, royal seat'.) Its location gives it good access in all directions but especially through its position on the main east-west motorway. It was industrialized by the inter-war period, but initially under state socialism its monarchical and religious past was held against it by the authorities. But following visits by the then party leader János Kádár in 1963 and 1965 the town was chosen as a point for industrial growth.

From then on Székesfehérvár grew rapidly in population and employment and gained a reputation as a showcase for high-tech industrial growth which was encouraged around the Videoton radio, television and computer factory, which was based on a former shotgun cartridge factory. By 1988 this firm employed 20,000 people and is said to have contributed 5% of Hungarian industrial production (Radosevic and Yoruk, 2001). In addition the town had many other factories such as the Light Metal factory producing aluminium from Hungarian bauxite, the Ikarus bus plant, a tool factory and a railway repair works. It had a skilled labour force which either lived in the town or commuted in from nearby towns and villages. In the 1980s, Székesfehérvár was one of the first towns to build industrial estates which were located in a ring around existing residential areas.

The change of regime was accompanied by massive unemployment as the existing industrial plants laid off workers. The 1990–94 period nationally saw the breakdown of economic links within COMECON and extensive privatization via the conversion of state enterprises to public companies and the subsequent sale of shares in them to private owners. Videoton and Ikarus, which supplied TVs and buses throughout COMECON,[1] were particularly badly hit.

Throughout the 1990s the town council conducted an active economic development policy which we describe in the next section. Combined with the national economic revival this brought about a recovery of the town's fortunes and a sharp fall in unemployment in Székesfehérvár to 7% (mainly older people) in 1997 and the bussing in workers from up to 70km away.

Companies currently operating in the town include IBM, Stollwerke and Nokia as well as Alcoa, Philips, and Ford (on Ford, see Swain, 1998). The Videoton company subsequently re-invented itself as a successful sub-contracting consumer electronics firm and holding company (Radosevic and Yoruk, 2001). By 1998 it was the eighth largest exporting company in the country, and Alcoa was ninth. The majority of industry is made up of privatized former state enterprises.

Today[2] according to a council office holder (1994–98) the city's income makes it the richest town in Hungary. He claims that 10% of the national GDP is produced in the town. In 1997 a council office holder expected local government income in 1998 to be 14 billion ft (£56 million) of which 1.8–1.9 billion ft (£7 million) would be from local tax receipts.

Turning to the political pre-conditions of this recovery, in the 1990 local election the Young Democrat party gained power and the last mayor of the state socialist period (Istvan Balsay) became the Young Democrat mayor for the 1990–94 period. The Young Democrats' success was partly a response to the brutal effects of economic restructuring which were blamed on the parties in power nationally (HDF, Smallholders, and Christian Democrats) and partly because of the people's confidence in the abilities of Mr Balsay. The fact that Mr Balsay kept his position across the regime change is striking. Evidently he was considered to have shown credentials in the development of Székesfehérvár in the 1980s which people thought would help the town in the new political and economic environment.

At the 1994 local election, a different party coalition won control of the town, made up of Young Democrats, Hungarian Democratic Forum, Smallholders and Christian Democrats. Interestingly the mayor remained a Free Democrat, and one supported by Mr Balsay. For his part, in 1994, Mr Balsay was elected as the local MP (and re-elected in 1998). Several interviewees considered him to be continuing to 'run' the town through the current mayor. We now consider some of the council's policies.

---

1 Economic integration under COMECON involved specialization between countries. Hungary supplied buses to the whole area but was not allowed to manufacture cars and had to import them.
2 At the time of the research.

The local council and its economic and environmental policies

Local economic policy

Against the background of drastic industrial restructuring starting in 1989/1990 the reform-minded and market-oriented town council took an active role in trying to gain investment and jobs. The council sent officials to Western Europe to gather ideas, and distributed information packs about the city to foreign firms and embassies. It placed the emphasis on the location of the town in relation to Budapest and Austria, the industrial infrastructure, the supply of skilled labour, and the council's favourable stance towards investors.

In particular the council offered a five year period (1990–95) totally free of local business tax together with a 50% remission for a further five years to new investors who purchased shares in an existing plant or who set up a new one, as long as the plant was worth 500 million ft (£2 million) or more.[3] This local measure was additional to the national provision that large firms which contributed to approved city causes would pay a lower rate of national corporation tax[4] (6% instead of 18%).

The town also saw the growth of new business parks to add to its existing industrial estates. According to Radosevic and Yoruk:

> The idea of industrial park business in Székesfehérvár emerged when Mr Georg Loranger, an American entrepreneur, made an investment in 1991. Loranger needed a 6000 sq.m. building. The only building of that size in a suitable place was a former Soviet military base of 250ha with 125 buildings. While others had been negotiating with the town to buy that building, Loranger wanted to buy the entire former military base. As a result a joint venture was set up which was the first western business that made a joint venture with the government. This was in line with the strategy of the local government which had decided to do all they could to attract foreign investors, to help provide land and utilities and to promote retraining for the people. A decisive role in that process belongs to Székesfehérvár's visionary mayor, Istvan Balsay. As a director of Ford Hungaria describes 'He created a vision of what this city can become'. Balsay twisted the arms of 40 authorities, including gas and electricity officials, to push through the approvals for the new facilities within 30 days instead of the usual months. In addition, the town offered favourable tax conditions. The three industrial parks have become the drivers of development of the whole town. (Radosevic and Yoruk, 2001, pp. 20–21)

This quotation should be treated with a little caution as it belongs to the 'hero

---

3 One interviewee said that it was the alleged success of this policy in Székesfehérvár which later led the government to pass a measure to ban such policies by local governments. We are unable to say whether this is part of the mythology surrounding the town's growth or whether it has some truth in it.

4 This was one of the taxes mentioned in Chapter 1 of which a share was returned to local government.

overcomes adversity' genre of stories rather than making a balanced assessment of events. For example it ignores the assets the council could build on. Nevertheless it is illustrative of writing about the town.

One other aspect of the financial relations between firms and council is worth mentioning. As we showed earlier, up until 1995 the town offered an exemption from local business tax which was part of its armory in attracting firms to locate there. However this exemption left a growing hole in the town's accounts which officials estimated at between 1.2 billion ft (£5 million) or more. In 1997 a new type of local tax on business based on the value added by the company (that is, income, less outgoings) was introduced nationally. The government would set a ceiling level for this tax each year and each council would be allowed to decide what level they would apply as long as it did not exceed the national ceiling. When in 1997 Székesfehérvár council announced that it would impose the tax at its maximum for that year (1.2%), in place of the 50% remission on the former local business tax which firms were expecting to pay, Philips protested that it would have to pay more than ten times the amount that it had paid in the previous year. It was joined in its protest by other multinational firms. The council responded to this tax revolt by offering firms a 90% relief on this local tax. This indicated both the decision-making autonomy of local government generally and the much rarer situation of a council having a sufficiently favorable financial situation to make use of this autonomy. However this trial of strength made both sides aware that threats to leave the town were bluffs (no firm left or closed because of the tax change according to an office-holder) and in 1998 the council levied a 1.3% rate (the national ceiling had been raised) while reducing the rate of relief to 70%. One consequence of the new tax was that firms ceased to be willing to provide 'generous' voluntary donations to the council as they had done previously, donations which had been a condition of receiving favourable tax treatment.

The state of relations between the council and multinational firms is expressed in this quotation from an interview with a council office-holder:

> I have good personal contacts, official ones, with all the leaders of the multis. They are sometimes fairly generous, give us some 10 million ft (£40,000) as a gift, though it is not such a huge gift considering how generous we are with them by not demanding the 1.2 billion ft tax they would pay in any other city. But now we are increasing the local tax as a result of which they keep decreasing their 'generous' gifts. I asked one of them to contribute to some road construction work, but they refused arguing that I raised the local tax, so they do not feel obliged to contribute on top of that. There was a huge fight at the end of which they did contribute, but their attitude is changing by me increasing their taxes.

> We do not want to fight with them, as a principle, and as a practice. Cooperation is better, especially as we can only lose. Like when Philips had a dispute with the city, they could afford to publish and run a propaganda campaign for 4 million ft [£16,000]. I would not have a fraction of that amount for publicity. So I rather avoid disputes and try to

cooperate because we can only lose against the powerful big firms.

If we look at the local government as a body vis à vis the multis we are obviously weaker. No question about it. They have the money, so they have the power. But if we cooperate it can work better. We don't have any other choice. But we fight our corners, we don't let them do whatever they want. We are not that weak. (H 56)

In sum it appears that having undertaken a very successful local economic policy which gave a lot of concessions to multinationals, the local council has achieved a stronger power position in its relations with companies. Although as the last quotation makes clear the companies retain their dominant position, the council's ability to increase local taxes and reduce tax reliefs shows that it has exploited the power it had and called the bluff on the firms' threat to move elsewhere.

Local environmental policy

We now turn to Székesfehérvár's environmental situation and policy. According to two council office holders the town faces both general and specific environmental problems.

There are three general problems.

1. *Traffic* The first problem has several components. The town is on the major arterial east-west road from the western border to Budapest and there is a lot of through traffic. In addition the location of industry in the town creates a lot of town-crossing journeys by heavy goods vehicles. Finally the buses bringing in workers arrive at the central bus station where workers transfer to local buses which take them out to the industrial estates. Construction of a bypass was planned to start in 2000 but this will not affect the congestion produced by internal journeys. A pedestrianised area is planned in the city centre.
2. *Water* 20% of the supply comes from groundwater, which is polluted, as is the 80% which comes from a mine. This is related to the high level of groundwater in many areas and consequent poor drainage. The cost of filtering is too high for the town at present and additional supplies are being obtained at very high cost.
3. *Sewerage* A major sewer laying and treatment plant programme is being undertaken to connect 98–99% of properties and was due to be complete by 2001. It is financed by the World Bank and PHARE (two-thirds) and the town (one-third) and will reduce pollution of ground water and of Sóstó Lake to the south of the town, a former holiday centre.

In addition there are a number of specific environmental issues or conflicts. These concern:

1. The cutting down of 147 trees in the town centre to make way for an Interspar supermarket and a McDonalds. This aroused a lot of opposition involving the Gaia

environmental movement (and others) and led to the developers being forced to replace the trees cut down by a much larger number of trees, including mature trees. The Mayor uses this as proof of his environmentalist credentials. Certainly the developers' claim that the trees were old and without value was rejected and they bore the costs of the replacement trees, but the development went ahead.

2. There are a number of road-related conflicts. The building of a new link road was due to start in 1998 which needed some land owned by big companies. This was obtained by swaps; in addition firms were made to contribute 70–80% of the cost of traffic lights. A second case was a protest about plans for a link road from the swimming pool to the sports ground (opposed by the then mayor as it did not contribute to the overall improvement of traffic flows). The Gaia movement collected signatures against this but it went ahead. According to a Gaia activist it has led to a 'new bottleneck' with 'serious accidents every week'. (H 26) In a third case, Gaia and the residents affected were successful in getting a planned road abandoned.

3. A plan to build a petrol station in the city centre, backed by the MP Istvan Balsay, was quoted as an exception to the rule that the planning committee makes decisions about planning. Permission had been given without the consent of the planning committee, perhaps an indication of the MP's power.

4. The power station, which burns poor quality coal and provides heating for centrally located housing, has in the past given rise to protest, but in 1996 and 1997 this dwindled. Various plans are being considered, for example, moving it and converting it to hay-burning and/or converting individual flats to individual gas heating, and a World Bank loan has been applied for.

5. Land related issues. There are a number of conflicts where speculators have bought land with development possibilities, for example land adjacent to a former waste dump, land next to a cemetery, and a former Soviet army base with potential as a shopping centre. There is some suspicion of collusion between speculators and local politicians. But the Mayor claims he has not had to pay the prices for which they were holding out.

6. There is a waste dump at the entrance to the town.

What is interesting about these conflicts is that with one exception, the power station case, none of them involves large firms.[5] This means that the publicly acknowledged environmental issues are consistent with the official view that big firms do not cause problems. According to a council office-holder,

> the big multis do not cause [environmental] problems in our city, they even try to provide help for us, they always try to do something for the city. Both Alcoa and IBM are

---

5 Although journeys to work and lorry journeys are induced by firms, they are not conventionally regarded as the firms' responsibility.

good examples of this. Only [name of big firm] caused some trouble for us, but this is off the record, I cannot talk about it. (H 56)

This interviewee claims a strong commitment to environmental aims – for example they were included in his manifesto – but he believes these were irrelevant in the 1994 local election and that they are not central in local politics. Certainly there is evidence of environmentalist pressure being partly successful (for example, the protest against trees being cut down mentioned above), or totally successful (the abandoned road plan) and the Mayor has instituted a 'green line' for telephone complaints on environmental matters. However the Gaia movement admits that it is much weaker than it once was. (Nevertheless since winning a competition for funds it has an office which is open every day and a full-time employee.)

The official discourse goes further than this and claims that large scale environmental problems at least are a thing of the past in Székesfehérvár. Firstly it is claimed that the big polluting state enterprises (Videoton, Light Metal, and Ikarus) have collapsed, and that their foreign-owned successor companies have solved their environmental problems by introducing the rules of their own country. Secondly it is claimed that only non-polluting firms are now welcome in the town. There is some evidence for this. There is an example of a firm which wanted to process rubber tyres having its application to set up in the town rejected. The reclassification of the land on Alcoa's site so as to tighten standards of air pollution (see below) is another example of an environmentalist measure.

Against the official view, it has to be pointed out that the majority of industry in Székesfehérvár consists of privatized former state enterprises which did not have to undergo a 'non-polluting' test. This means that one should treat the official view that firms only caused major environmental problems in the town in the past as an aspiration for the future rather than a description of the current situation. Also there is acknowledged to be a continuing pollution problem among small firms. A former Videoton employee drew a contrast between the effective environmental control achieved in that firm and the lack of control among the hundreds of small companies into which it had been fragmented. He described the 'industrial park' attitude where such small firms are not subject to any checks. However while this view of the present may be accepted, the view of the past is debatable since Videoton is one of the three big firms allegedly responsible for much pollution in the past. For example Videoton was forced to build a sewage system and install filters, and was made to stop its galvanizing operations.

In sum the local council presents a selective picture of the environmental situation in Székesfchérvár which draws attention to the improvements associated with the arrival of foreign firms and plays down the continuing problems associated with privatized state firms. Undoubtedly the council has taken stronger proactive environmental measures than councils in any of the other three towns studied here. This has been driven partly by the council's own aspirations for the town, but has also been a response to public pressure including through Gaia.

In order to examine the case of one firm we chose Alcoa.

Alcoa and its environmental practices

Alcoa is a producer of intermediate or semi-finished products and was the ninth largest exporter in Hungary in 1998. The factory includes among others a foundry, a rolling mill, a pressing factory, a gradual processing unit, and a lorry chassis-producing machine. There is considerable continuity between the production structure of the former Hungalu and the Alcoa-owned firm. In 1993 the Light Metal company was bought by Hungalu (51%) and Alcoa (49%), and in 1996 Alcoa bought out the Hungalu interest. At the same time the employment level in the firm fell from 5000 workers in 1989 to 1500. Several Alcoa interviewees thought the firm was less prominent in the local media than it deserved to be and that it suffered in this respect by not being producers of consumer products.

A key issue following the privatization of Hungalu and the involvement of US ownership was the relative environmental standards of the Hungarian firm and of the US owners.

One manager who had been there before privatization said that:

> I'm not saying that environment wasn't important before. But the attitude and practice were different. With regard to the environment, this company wasn't bad in the past either. You can see that from the surveys of Alcoa when they bought up the company. Of course it did not meet the American and Alcoa standards, but we did have standards. (H 10)

He stated that:

> This company operates on all continents and its standards have to be implemented everywhere. Naturally they have to be adjusted to the local practices. Local rules have to be observed everywhere in the world but if the norms of Alcoa are stricter then we have to stick to them. (H 10)[6]

On the face of it this statement could be regarded with suspicion since it is sometimes argued that foreign direct investment is in part motivated by cutting production costs by using environmentally damaging technology in countries where environmental standards are low or not enforced.

In fact there was evidence to support the company's claim about its practice and against the sceptical view. In two cases, Alcoa regulations prohibited practices which were allowed in Hungary: the use of asbestos and the use of uncheckable underground storage. In both cases Alcoa took action to bring the local plant into line with its company policy.

---

6 One manager claimed that 'if the Hungarian regulations happen to be stricter in certain areas than that of Alcoa then Alcoa would choose the stricter one' (H 23) but said that 'of course, there are hardly any examples of this.' However another manager suggested that the Hungarian standard was higher than the US standard in the case of effluent flowing into sewage systems, and higher than German standards regarding buried waste (H 24).

In the case of asbestos, the company had adopted a ten year programme to remove the asbestos in the plant. A company manager noted that this was in line with the company's policy of not using asbestos. It had found 30,000 cubic metres of asbestos in walls and large workshops and 10,000 cu.m. in roofs and pipes. At the time of the interviews about one third of the asbestos had been removed at a cost of 800 million ft (£3.2 million). An interviewee said that 'we're doing this without any obligation to the authorities, since there aren't even any regulations which forbid the use of asbestos.' (H 10) Another Alcoa interviewee said that:

> there are many problems which the country isn't ready for. The asbestos removal was a case in point. The country is not ready for it yet. In many cases there aren't even apposite Hungarian regulations. For example, in this case [the local council] had to consult the Ministry about the position they should take, what guidelines they should follow. Therefore I think we're well ahead of the Hungarian regulations. (H 24)

Likewise the company has replaced underground storage tanks by surface tanks where possible and introduced damage-averting equipment where it left them in place:

> The regulations of Alcoa stipulate that no containers which can't be checked can be left under the ground, because if they perforate it will pollute the soil and the underground water. We had to check all our underground [containers], all sixty of them. This covered underground tanks, pits, everything which is used for storing dangerous materials like emulsions, acid or alkali which can cause pollution if it gets into the ground. These had to be made safe. The initial aim was that everything which was no longer needed had to be finished with. Those which were still needed had to be brought up from underground and were equipped with a 110% secure piece of damage-averting equipment. These included some of our fuel tanks and other tanks. Two of these of 200 cu. m. capacity were put back underground and one 200 cu. m. one was left above the ground all equipped with a 110% secure piece of damage-averting equipment... Therefore I can say that we don't really have this kind of equipment under the ground because we have brought up whatever we could above the ground. (H 24)

A sceptic could point out that these statements are by interested parties and that they fall short of direct observation. This is undeniable. All one can say against this view is that the evidence that does exist supports the company's claim to be introducing its own standards in advance of Hungarian standards. Finally, a single case is insufficient to show that multinationals never adopt lower environmental standards when operating abroad. All it can do is show that the case of Alcoa in Székesfehérvár appears to be a counter-example.

We can now pass to the question of Alcoa's environmental practices as perceived by Alcoa staff and others. Five types of problem were reported:

1. air pollution caused by waste incineration;

2. the presence of asbestos;
3. the pollution of ground water from leaking storage tanks;
4. excessive salt content in waste water; and
5. air pollution due to nitrous oxide emission.[7]

The fact that the company did not report any problems with dangerous waste is surprising since the tightening of regulations on dangerous waste in 1996 was mentioned by many interviewees in firms in the other three localities studied.

In response to the above five problems the company had taken various measures.

1. It had installed a dust separator in the waste incinerator (in 1995, at a cost of several hundred thousand ft, or £1000).
2. It is removing the asbestos over a ten-year period as described above.
3. It is ensuring all chemicals and waste are stored safely.
4. The excess salt problem has come about as the company has saved on its use of water. The company said it is working on it.
5. The nitrous oxide emission problem has not been solved.

The reason for the nitrous oxide problem is as follows. A few years before 1996 the site of the plant was re-classified by the council from protected area category 2 to protected area category 1, which meant emissions had to be cut by half. The company has had to pay fines of symbolic amount. According to a manager, 'the penalties are based on our admissions and levied according to the Hungarian regulations. I don't think this is a bad system.' (H 10) Another interviewee said that:

> we can't afford to consider whether the fines will cost more or [whether to invest] to be below the limits. This is true for air pollution as well [as oil pollution of effluent]. In the past we did have problems with air pollution which was due to letting out too much nitrous oxide because of the gas-fired furnace. And the company said that it's true that we paid fines, symbolic fines, because it wasn't much, about 1000 forints [£4], which is nothing for a company like this one, but we had to take measures to eliminate this minimal pollution as well. (H 24)

Managers had proposed to raise the height of some of their 63 chimneys but the council had rejected this. It was also said by the company to be impracticable. New regulations were awaited which would not refer to the number of chimneys and 'I don't think we'll be among the ones who have to pay fines.' (H 23) (The changes will involve a different method of calculating emissions. It is not clear whether the actual emissions will be changed.)[8]

In sum Alcoa is an example of a company whose environmental practices, at least in respect of asbestos and underground storage, show the role of internal corporate

---

[7] Until the end of the 1980s pollution of waste water by oil occurred 'but we haven't had such problems for some time now'. (H 10)

rules being applied to raise standards above those prevailing in Hungary. (This contrasts with the role of pressure from customers in raising environmental standards revealed in the Rába case in Chapter 4.) However there were a number of other cases (air pollution, polluted waste water) which were admitted to be unresolved although they seemed not to be major or to occasion large fines.

The REI and Alcoa

As we explained in Chapter 2, the role of the regional environmental inspectorates includes advising on new investment in agriculture and manufacturing industry (before the local government issues a building permit) and establishing permissible pollution levels, checking emissions from existing plant (by companies' self-reporting and unannounced visits) and levying fines, as well as general responsibility for the environmental state of the region.

The REI for Székesfehérvár is the Central Trans-Danubian Environmental Inspectorate which was claimed by an official to be the largest in area covered and in environmental problems. It covers three counties (Fehér, Veszprém and Tolna) and Lake Balaton, and interestingly according to an official the environmental problems that give rise to the most complaints are to do with pig farms rather than manufacturing.

Officials said that there were no serious environmental problems in the area covered by the REI but that Székesfehérvár 'was and still is a moderately polluted town'. (H 32) This is an interesting remark to counterpose against the council's own image of the town. It is supported by the figures given in Table 2.5, which showed that Székesfehérvár is the second most polluted town of the four being studied here in respect of SO_2, NO_x and residual dust.

Pollution was described by REI officials as having fallen since 1990 due to the decline or closure of former factories, and their replacement by cleaner new factories. The role of foreign firms was explained thus by an official: 'when there is a discrepancy between the regulations (Hungarian and that of their home country) foreign companies tend to choose the stricter ones'. (H 32) An example given was a resin used by Ford in spark plug production which was not regarded as dangerous by Hungarian legislation but was treated as such by Ford. As we saw this was backed up by the Alcoa example.

The remaining problems identified by the REI officials were: air pollution due to domestic heating and traffic (neither of which are within the REI's remit), water

---

8 The Hungarian system sets fines according to a) the level of protection of the area (strictly protected, protected area category 1, protected area category 2) and b) the measured emission levels which are adjusted to take into account the height of the emission, for example, low or high chimney. According to Morris et al. (1997) the formula gives incentives to firms to build high chimneys. In our example the power of the council to rule out this 'solution' is shown, a factor not taken into account by Morris et al.

pollution by industry, and pollution by smaller companies (especially dangerous waste). Many smaller companies are unregistered and said to be ignorant of their environmental responsibilities. Their activities are only likely to be discovered following a complaint. Again this supports a point made earlier in this chapter. Water pollution was said to be not a serious problem because 'in the case of Székesfehérvár ... 90% of the large companies have some kind of filtering system and then they let their waste water into the public drains'. (H 35) Industrial air pollution was regarded as 'not significant'. (H 35)

Turning to how the Central Trans-Danubian Environmental Inspectorate works, its first responsibility is to give permission for new investment in manufacturing and agriculture. An Alcoa interviewee confirmed that 'most of our technology is such that permission must be obtained from the authorities for its use'. (H 23) Another described the relationship between Alcoa and the REI as follows:

> It would be an exaggeration to say that we have daily contact with the Inspectorate. We don't molest each other. I mean it, because in my opinion the cooporation is exemplary. We discuss all our problems with them. We co-ordinate our new improvement plans with theirs, they are our partners in this. It's very rare they play the Inspectorate role towards us. Of course, if it's necessary, they would do it. But I think that we do have a good relationship. We try to have good relations with all authorities. (H 10)

The REI operates two systems for monitoring pollution levels. The first is the system of self-reporting whereby larger companies are obliged to send in the results of their own monitoring. The second is the system of inspection visits in which the REI carries out regular and, what is more, unannounced inspections.[9] These visits follow a regular schedule and it is claimed that factories are visited once or twice per year:

> We never announce ourselves in advance ... The person in charge tends to organize the inspections by scheduling several inspections for one day, two or even three, but that is unusual. There is a list issued every monday on which it is indicated which company the laboratory should visit each day of the week ... I'm sure that there are people who would like to know the dates of our visits in advance, but it wouldn't make much difference because if they have a waste water treatment (plant), it has to work all the time.(H 35)

The occurrence of these inspection visits was corroborated in our interviews with Alcoa staff. According to one Alcoa interviewee:

> Environmental inspection is based on self-assessment. We have to tell the authorities if we pollute the air, if we have dangerous wastes, etc. ... We make sure our assessment is accurate. These are often checked. Our company cannot afford to submit false figures, because we can easily be found out during inspection. But we don't need to submit false

---

9 Interestingly neither interviewee at the REI here mentioned a problem of under-staffing.

figures anyway, because all our data is within the permitted limits. (H 23)

Likewise, another said that:

> the penalties are based on our admissions and levied according to the Hungarian regulations. I don't think this is a bad system. Because why would it be better if I didn't admit it? If I admit air pollution then, in a way, I'm making a statement. And if the following day the Inspectorate comes out and my statement doesn't correspond to the reality then it's the company's responsibility. (H 10)

The evidence of regular inspection visits by the Central Trans-Danubian Environmental Inspectorate in Székesfehérvár contrasts with the situation reported for the Mid-Danube Environmental Inspectorate in Nagytétény (Chapter 5) which appears to be too under-staffed to conduct any visits. However perhaps more surprisingly it also contrasts with its own operation in Dunaújváros, as we shall see in Chapter 6.

The REI officials listed a number of large firms in Székesfehérvár which had had problems. Videoton had let out waste water with a heavy metal content from galvanising, and Alcoa had once let out sodium nitrate above the permitted level (probably the salt problem referred to earlier).

As far as fines are concerned the officials emphasized the discretion they possessed:

> These chemicals don't have their own limit [that is, a single maximum level]. There is a favourable limit and a strict limit. We use the former for certain components if the company cannot afford to carry out the changes we would require. The most important thing is that the waste water of the company does not affect the quality of the water by being above the allowed limit. This is our first criterion. The second is that we don't force a company to carry out investments which they can't afford. (H 35)

Another official explained that:

> The amount of a fine is decided in a specific way. We measure the amount of pollution and then use a mathematical formula to work out the amount [of the fine]. In addition to this there are other factors which can influence the amount of fines. There is room for judgement by the authorities here. This is also based on a mathematical formula but it goes from 0.5 to 5. We have to take many factors into consideration when we use the mathematical formula for water. When the authorities increase or reduce the fine they will have to give a very good reason for it. (H 32)

In other words, the actual fine imposed can vary on a scale around an indicative figure, thus allowing the official to take into account the economic circumstances of the offending firm and the environmental effects of their pollution. These quotations illustrate precisely the way that scope for negotiation is built into the regulatory process as described in Chapter 2. Standards are subject to adjustments to take into account the ability of the firm to meet them.

The officials did not regard the level of fines as being high enough to have a serious effect. The fine levels had been revised from their 1984 level in 1993 to allow for inflation. But in one official's opinion 'It is still just some pocket money for the companies. It's nothing. It has no particular effect on the companies... 10,000, 60,000 forints won't deter them from polluting.' (H 35) Two firms were quoted as having paid fines: SZIM (61,000 ft, £240), IR3Video (formerly part of Philips) (15,000 ft, £60). Alcoa, it was said, had not been fined. (In fact, as we have seen, it has been fined but rarely and by only symbolic amounts.)

Finally we refer to a comment by a council office holder, according to whom the REI is:

> extremely strict when it comes to following the regulations. They never allow any concessions. Sometimes I even feel they are too rigid but at the end of the day they are absolutely right and we all have to give in to them. (H 56)

However, given what has just been noted about the discretion available to the REI, this statement should be treated as more of a 'political' statement than an accurate description.

In sum the Central Trans-Danubian Environmental Inspectorate seemed better resourced than the others we shall encounter and the fact that it conducted regular unannounced visits was distinctive. Its assessment of the continuing pollution problems in Székesfehérvár was in contrast to the picture presented by the council.

Conclusion

Székesfehérvár is a town which has built on its socialist past (Videoton, infrastructure, skilled labour) and its advantageous location through an entrepreneurial policy of investment attraction, including the unusual five-year period free of local tax. It might seem paradoxical that a town which had so many initial advantages should have introduced such a policy. While this may be so objectively, the logic of local economic policy is based on subjective judgements and local yardsticks. Faced with a rapid rise in unemployment the council introduced powerful incentives to attract firms which added to its locational advantages. It is not part of local economic policy to consider the competitive effects of these measures on other localities. Only a supra-local policy can take these into account. Thus the paradox is that the local council which claims to be the richest in the country (relative to its size) is heavily and successfully engaged in the competition for investment.[10]

---

10 Attempts to restrict local economic development measures to the most needy localities have rarely succeeded. Governments are faced with lobbies of better-off local governments which resist the idea that they should be excluded from the competition for investment and employment (Harding, 1988, Pickvance, C.G., 1996).

The fact that the same person was Mayor pre-1990 and again in 1990–94 (despite a change of party label) and took a leading part in this local economic policy is significant. Together with the fact that Istvan Balsay subsequently became the local MP it is strong evidence of a legacy effect. The nature of this effect is more difficult to pin down. In one sense local economic development in the town was itself a continuity across the 1990 change of regime. But it is likely that Balsay's pre-1990 connections locally and nationally were valuable enough to be redeployed, and that his post-1990 activities in developing a pro-active economic policy themselves gave rise to new (shorter-run) legacy effects. The possibility must be that there was a considerable continuity in local power structure before and after 1990. The result is that Székesfehérvár has been extremely successful in attracting multinationals.

The town has the strongest environmental policy of the four localities considered here. However its claims that only non-polluting firms are welcome and that company-produced environmental pollution is a thing of the past cannot be fully accepted. But the evidence of rejection of plans by polluting firms to set up in the town, and of a tightening of environmental standards as well as of environmentalist influence support the idea of a relatively strong environmental policy. Also the Mayor is willing to engage in conflicts with large firms, though he sees the local government as ultimately being in a weak position towards them. The town has made considerable efforts to tackle collective environmental problems. Indeed it is characteristic that the Mayor claims environmental credentials himself – though it is difficult to separate what is deep-rooted from what is part of the city's image-building efforts.

A recurring theme in our interviews in Székesfehérvár was the debate over whether multinationals investing in the town adopt higher environmental standards than those prevailing or whether the town allowed them to operate with lower environmental standards than were found in more advanced capitalist societies. At Alcoa our interviewees gave evidence of the benign first scenario, but one cannot rule out that there is also evidence to support the second scenario.

Lastly Székesfehérvár is interesting because the pro-environmental policy of the council is matched by a tough REI inspection regime which will be shown to be stronger than in the other three localities. The REI's behaviour is particularly striking since in Dunaújváros, where the REI is also the Central Trans-Danubian Environmental Inspectorate, there is no pattern of regular inspection visits. The differences in REI behaviour among the four localities will be addressed in Chapter 7. Despite these positive aspects, REI officials' insisted on the continuing pollution problems of the town and of the lack of effectiveness of the fines regime at their current level. This is backed up by the figures showing Székesfehérvár to be the second most polluted of our four case study localities.

4 Győr: a Traditional Industrial and County Town

Location, history and economic situation

Győr, a town of 130,000 inhabitants, is one of the six largest provincial centres in Hungary. It is located in north western Hungary close to the border with Slovakia and not far from the border with Austria, and lies 130 km from Budapest on the main road to Vienna. After Székesfehérvár it is the second most important provincial industrial centre. It has a mixed manufacturing base and its industries include food, engineering, transportation and textiles. The town's unemployment rate of 8% is below the national average.

In the early 1990s, as elsewhere, firms in Győr were badly hit. Many firms in traditional industries were privatized and there was some new investment by both domestic and foreign owners. As will be shown the council took an active role. Nevertheless employment growth failed to make good the job losses. Győr was slower to attract new foreign investment than Székesfehérvár, United Biscuits being the largest example at the time of the research.[1]

The rise in unemployment led to serious problems for local residents and to conflict between residents and local council. According to a council officeholder there were demonstrations of unemployed people instigated by a 'skilful organizer' who allegedly had a political agenda, objecting to the way the town was run. Its unemployment rate at the time of the study was more than pre-1990 but not as high as in the worst affected regions of the country.

---

1 Later, however, other major investors arrived, such as Audi and Philips. In 2001, after the research period, the largest employers were the Hungarian owned Rába (see below), Audi and Philips with 6400, 4800 and 4150 employees respectively. (2001 was also notable for a protest/boycott campaign in defence of the 100 year-old Győr Keksz [biscuit] factory. Bought by Danone from United Biscuits, Danone planned to close it, but abandoned its plans after the campaign.)

The local council and its economic and environmental policies

The local government reform of 1990 made Győr a county town of county rank. This means that it is not only the most important town in its county (Győr–Moson–Sopron) but also exercises county-level functions as well as city-level functions. Whereas pre-1990 it was subordinate to the county level of administration, this is no longer so (Hajdú, 1993).

Politically, Győr was run by a Free Democrat–Christian Democrat council led by a Free Democrat mayor from 1990–94. In 1994, the Socialist Party gained control of the council and a Socialist mayor was (directly) elected.

Local economic policy

According to a council officeholder the council's policy towards the local economy is to combine its traditional industries with high-tech industries:

> It's important for our town to preserve traditional industry, such as textile, food, and mechanical engineering industry. We emphasise that we'd like to help these industries to recover. We'd also like precision machining, technical appliance industries to operate in our town on a larger scale. (K 4)

He argued that 'fundamental [economic] changes are not necessary'.

Likewise a council official said that 'our strategic aim is to attract better quality industries, especially micro-electronic industries' but that:

> In the case of industry, those with tradition, their strengthening is definitely among our strategic aims. For example we encourage certain branches of heavy industry to stay. (K 8)

Regarding the types of firm desired, the council is aware of environmental considerations:

> What we don't want is industries which cause environmental damage. We're very careful with those. Our bylaws concerning investments are much stricter than the Hungarian parliamentary laws. This isn't difficult to enforce when western firms come to the industrial park. For them protecting the environment is self-evident, although not in every case. (K 4)

This interviewee cites the example of a German firm which wanted to set up a foundry and 'nobody believed that it wasn't to pollute the environment' but where the authorities gave permission after a visit to the firm's plant in Germany. (It is located in the Industrial Park mentioned below.) This indicates that, despite its aspirations, the council is not yet in a position to pick and choose among firms wanting to locate in Győr.

The council took quite an interventive approach to local economic policy:

1. In 1995 a development plan was drawn up laying out general outlines rather than specific details, and a detailed zoning plan is being drawn up now.
2. The town has built a 125ha Industrial Park 5km from the town. In 1992 the first 36ha were inaugurated. The company which owns and is responsible for it is 60% owned by two Austrian firms and 40% by Győr town council. The industrial park cost 600 million ft (£2.5 million). The companies based there include: Amoco, Phillips, VAW (German – aluminium cylinder heads), Skiny (an affiliate of Austrian Huber Tricot), Qehenberger Forwarders (Austrian), and United Biscuits (Győr Keksz). By 2000 it accounted for 1000 jobs, about 2% of the town's total.
3. By-laws have been passed to give firms two years free of local taxes and big investors can obtain a ten year tax free period. These apply 'especially to those settled in the Industrial Park and those outside it, depending on the value of their investment, their profits or their reinvestment of generated income'. (K 4)
4. The council has also taken some steps in a cultural direction which will have an economic impact. It has created a theatre, set up the Győr Cultural Summer festival, a Győr archive and there are plans to restore Esterhazy Palace as an art gallery.

The council officeholder quoted earlier, who had worked in the town for ten years prior to 1990, expressed some surprise about current policy saying that:

> prioritizing certain parts of the city, in fact putting lots of emphasis on this [the industrial park] ... today in a market economy should not be an obligatory role of a local government at all.

and that:

> the role of the town doesn't lie in creating the local economy per se so much as in providing the right conditions for the players in the local economy. (K 4)

One suspects that his view of the proper role of local government was more a reflection of free market models than of the characteristic interventionism of the real world.

Local environmental policy

Turning to the council's environmental policy, as suggested above the town has environmentalist aspirations. It has an environmental committee which examines the general and detailed town plans before they are passed by the council. Since January 1996 the town has also had an Environmental Fund, but we were told that it was 'rare that the environmental committee is opposed to a policy'. One case where it was, is discussed in the section on Gardenia's expansion plans below.

The officeholder quoted above felt that there was a risk that environmental considerations became too prominent but thought that the town had got the balance right:

We establish various committees, groups of people responsible for the environment but these should be reduced because what we need is that such a view is built into the professions, that's to say that if you make that official decision, financial decision then you should build into it the point of view of environmental protection as well. At the moment we tend to blow these issues up. Here in this town it's kept in perspective but those who regard themselves as environmentalists occasionally blow the matter out of proportion. (K 4)

An example of the difficulties of making decisions on environmental matters was quoted. A firm that had moved to the Industrial Park to produce the backing for woven carpets used a sprinkler system in case of fire instead of the special paint on inside walls the law prescribed. This was cited as an example of a solution not covered by Hungarian law.

The case of Gardenia's expansion plans which were opposed by the Environmental Committee but which were eventually allowed is discussed below.

Lastly the council aims to make the town greener by establishing parks and planting trees, and is piloting a selective rubbish recycling system in the Szentivan district.

The influence of environmental groups

The Council is aware of the local environmental group Reflex. The Chair of Reflex is a member of the environmental committee. The group was credited with initiating various proposals, for example, a parking ban in a central square. According to a council official:

The [parking ban] proposal had already come up in the office of the council in town, but nobody had the courage to carry it through the decision-making of the council. There were various suggestions about the way to carry it out within our own building and therefore there was a passive reaction to it. When someone from outside made the move, we were glad that eventually we could do something. (K 8)

This comment sounds defensive but the interviewee clearly acknowledges the key role of Reflex in instigating council action. Pressure from Reflex had likewise forced the council to build a wall to protect residents from traffic noise in one area. Interviewees agreed that there was a constant information flow and communication between the council and Reflex:

The council does listen to them because they have good opinions. Those few exaggerations which didn't seem to be realistic haven't soured their welcome. The council is still receptive to their advice, even if it doesn't agree with everything. (K 8)

More generally in answer to the question 'How far can local residents influence the environmental policy of the local council?' a council official claimed that 'They have a profound influence on it, which one should be pleased about'. (K 8)

The council had undertaken major investments in sewage and was planning new investments in waste collection.

Overall, Győr does not seem to have had as active a local economic policy as Székesfehérvár, nor has it been as successful in attracting foreign investment. Its ability to impose high environmental standards has also been less than in Székesfehérvár. However in both respects it has been more successful than Nagytétény as we shall see in the next chapter.

The council's view of its relations with firms

In describing the council's relations with firms the council office-holder makes a contrast between the old 'top-down' style of administration and the new style where firms are seen as 'partners'. The town's relation with firms is described by officials as generally cooperative and the Mayor is seen as taking the leading role in keeping good relations between the council and the firms:

> We're in continuous communication with the large companies, or with everybody who contacts us. We aspire to a good relationship with everybody. It's in the interests of the town that they feel comfortable here and the relationship between us is continuous and not limited merely to the beginning. [It extends into] cultural relationships, sport and other areas as well. (K 4)

The town's image in the eyes of outsiders is seen as something important.

> When they [outsiders] visit firms already in Győr they report back about the helpful attitude of the town. It is us who has to help.. of course we keep to the regulations but at the same time we consider the interests of the firms. (K 4)

Regarding the general influence of local companies on environmental policies:

> they [companies] do influence them more or less. This means that we have to accommodate them in our town development plan. I say this as a self-criticism. Our present plan is quite rigid. It'll be more flexible in the future. Our present plan is rigid in the sense that when they come to us we should agree with them. For example, there is a factory in the industrial park which wants to build a chimney, necessary for its operations. According to our present town development plan the maximum permissible height in the industrial park is 8 metres. This is ridiculous when technology requires something higher. (K 4)

Overall therefore the town seems to take a business-friendly approach. We will follow this up in discussing the particular firms we studied. There is a belief in the council that close relations are in the general interest of the town. The exception is in the case of 'traditional' firms which cannot afford to change their technology, where we were told conflict is likely.

We now turn to an examination of the environmental practices of our two case study firms in Győr, Rába and Gardenia. Both are long established firms located outside the industrial park.

Rába and its environmental practices

Rába Rolling Stock Factory is a 100-year old firm specializing in the production of axles, engines, automotive components, and agricultural and military vehicles. Axles are its main source of income. It is Europe's second largest axle producer and the world's fifth largest. Its exports to the US (for example, for International Harvester) comprise 25% of all Hungarian exports to the US.

At the time of our interviews it was still publicly owned (80% by the state privatization agency, which had taken over the share previously owned by the Hungarian Development Bank, and 20% by local governments, including Győr council), and we were told that investment plans had been put on hold pending privatization. It was one of the last Hungarian state firms to be privatized but privatization took place in late 1997.[2]

In the 1980s, Rába was the town's largest employer and at its peak in employment terms it employed 20–22,000 people. At that time its scale meant that it carried out a vast training function for the local labour market. After a loss-making period following 1989 and large-scale redundancies, its work force has aged and it has lost skilled workers to Audi which has been successful in attracting younger workers. Rába returned to profit in the mid-1990s. By early 1997 it had 'only' 6200 employees but was still the largest employer in Győr.

Rába's post-war activities were said to be the product of COMECON industrial policy. It was a self-contained factory, being made up of a smelting works and foundry as well as its production activities. We were told that this ensured quality control over materials. Its technology dates mainly from the late 1970s and 1980s.

Rába is mainly located on a former airport on the edge of Győr, but also has three 'village factories'. Rába previously had a foundry located in the centre of Győr but following public protest about the noise it made, supported by the REI which required Rába to close it, the foundry was moved out, helped by EU PHARE funding. This cost 200 million ft (£800,000) (by comparison the firm's annual investment budget is 1.8 billion ft (£7.2 million)).

Pollution: paying fines

The firm produces four types of pollution, which we examine in turn.

Solid waste Galvanic waste was previously stored at Sas hill but this was declared

---

[2] In late 1999 Győr council still owned 11% and other owners included EBRD 10% and Graboplast (a local floor-covering firm) 8%.

dangerous and the firm was forced to find a solution and given a 1994 deadline. Various options were considered whose costs ranged from 10 to 200 million ft (£40,000–800,000). There were two issues: removal of the waste itself and dealing with the soil which it had polluted. The dearest solution for the removal of the waste was to take it to the sole national specialized dangerous waste site at Aszód (50km north-east of Budapest) where a per ton charge was payable. A second solution (estimated to cost 130 million ft) was to enclose it in its present site with a concrete wall, and rely on the clay acting as a seal underneath. The former was chosen. For the polluted soil one solution (36 million ft) was the 'poker' method where an excavator picks up the polluted soil and neutralises it by adding a mix of chemicals which bind the heavy metals together, and then leaves it on its clay base and covers it with soil. The cheapest solution (10 million ft) was to spread a chemical on the soil which filters down and binds the heavy metals together. The poker solution was chosen. The project was completed by late 1996, two years after the deadline. New waste will be dried and granulated to reduce its weight by two-thirds and sent to Aszod.

Other types of waste (foundry sand, asbestos dust, paint waste, metal turnings) which had previously been considered acceptable had been declared dangerous (under the 1996 102nd regulation) and the company was making representations to try to get exemptions from parts of this. The fact that it was doing so indicates the possibilities open to major firms which are well-linked into industry-wide organizations. Before 1981 only poisonous waste required special treatment.

The firm did not pay fines for dangerous waste at the time of the interviews but this situation is threatened by the 102nd regulation.

Air pollution The main sources of air pollution are the (relocated) foundry and granule sprinkler. There are plans to install improved filtering systems (dry instead of wet filtering) in 1998.

Rába does pay fines in respect of air pollution of about 300,000 ft (£1250) per annum. These are based on self-reporting (based either on measurement or on calculation). For example:

> we have a chimney that lets out 1kg of dust per hour. In 1996 I worked with it for 100 hours, so I let 100kg of dust beyond the limit, for which I will pay this amount of fine. We'll have to tell the Environmental Inspectorate of Győr. (I 12)

External checks are carried out twice a year.

Air pollution in Győr is said by a Rába employee to have increased by 50% between 1982 and 1997: 'not because of Rába but because of the traffic' (I 12). In 1993 a decree was issued to reduce air pollution (of all sorts, traffic as well as industrial) 'above the limit' by 2000 in Ajka, Miskolc, Budapest and Győr.[3] Rába was said to be on target to do this.

---

3 Ajka (a town) and Miskolc (a city) are two other highly polluted places.

Waste water Rába was paying fines ('not much') for pollution of both the foul sewers (for example by oil) and of the surface water drainage system which flows into the Danube (for example by coolants).

There are some cleaning processes on the site, for example, a decomposter, but the company acknowledges that it needs to invest in a water treatment system. This would allow all its effluents to go into the public sewers and would end pollution of the Danube. But this would be very costly. As we shall see this shows parallels with Gardenia (discussed later in this chapter), and Chinoin (in Nagytétény, discussed in Chapter 5).

Effluent which cannot be let into the public sewers, such as water which has been used for cleaning, is kept in storage pits and taken away by tanker.

The REI checks the fresh water and the water company checks the surface water drains. Each makes checks two to three times per year. The water company can make unannounced visits:

> What happens is that they come out. It's in the regulations so they don't have to make an appointment and they say that today there'll be a drains check-up from seven in the morning until two in the afternoon at the railway site and then they take samples every hour. These samples are shared between them and us. We examine it in our own laboratory and they examine it too and within a month they send the result if there was an overpollution. In such cases we can explain what caused it, and can ask for a second inspection or if we think the result was correct, we just pay the fine because it's possible that another inspection result would be even worse. (I 12)

The company pays waste water fines of 500,000 ft (£2,000) per year. We were told that 'Neither our pollution nor the fines are significant'. (I 12)

Noise and vibration This is subject to inspection by the municipal public health service (ANTSZ). In this respect Rába does not pay fines.

In total Rába was paying under 1 million ft in fines per year (£4,000).

Environmental practices

Investment decisions at Rába are initiated by the section concerned but are checked centrally to ensure that they meet environmental criteria. 'I don't think that we could make such a mistake that a machine which seriously pollutes the air would be installed.' (I 12) We were told that the possibility of fines 'influenced the company. But not the overall strategy.' 'Always the cleanest technology is chosen'. (I 12) As an example, a recent purchase of air conditioning equipment was cited where:

> we had to make sure that we buy one that doesn't damage the ozone layer – from Italy. First they wanted to supply us with the one that damages it. It might have been cheaper but we chose the one that does not damage the ozone layer. (I 12)

However another interviewee also said that:

> when I plan the environmental investments, I have to calculate that if I don't install something, then I might have to pay, let's say 5–8 million ft fine.[4] The figure will appear in the investment analysis. The most recent calculations were made for the granulator in connection with the shutting down of Sas hill. (I 13)

On the other hand the decision rule in use was a tough one:

> not only us but all the other companies can afford environmental investments only if the investment can be recovered within one or two years. The usual pay-back period is not allowed. (I 12)

The latter point is an interesting one. It suggests that tougher criteria are applied to investments with environmental aims than other investments and implies that such investments have a lower priority in the firm's ranking of investments. The short pay-back period means that any savings on fines consequent on new environmental investment will be less. This will act in the same direction as the low level of fines itself, namely to reduce the incentive to undertake environmental investment.

An interviewee also made the point that Rába 'is amongst those few [companies] which didn't get government support to cut its environmental pollution. And perhaps there aren't any other companies like us.' (I 12)

Decisions on what materials are used by Rába were also said to be made with environmental effects in mind. Two pictures were presented of the initiation of such choices.

On the one hand, these may be customer-led. The typical customers are other manufacturers since Rába produces many intermediate goods. 'It's possible that an American customer stipulates that we can't use materials which have contents that would damage the ozone layer.' (I 13) 'When we need a certain material we ask three or four suppliers to recommend them and we also have to ask for the data about its safety.... We take into consideration the price, quality and environmental points when we choose.' (I 13) Another employee said that:

> Americans and Germans gave environmental demands. The Americans ask us whether the products they buy contain materials that could damage the ozone layer or are they made with such material. The Germans are even stricter. They say they are going to give us their environmental rules which we have to keep to. This finishes with us passing the list to our suppliers, asking them to give us the same information. We have to make declarations to our customers, and our suppliers have to make declarations to us. We try to

---

4   This is a dubiously high figure in view of the fact that the firm pays under 1 million ft per annum for environmental fines of all types. To pay as much as 5–8 million ft for one type of fine would suggest the calculation is over a 5–10 year period. This is in contradiction with the claim that investments have to pay for themselves over two years.

exclude products from the list which are not popular abroad. This isn't difficult to keep to but one thing is sure, the oil which complies with these demands is much more expensive. (I 12)

Another interviewee agreed:

We have western contacts, mainly American, where the rules are much stricter than elsewhere in Europe ... The American market has trained us severely. Chemicals we use are lubricants, cooling oils, washing materials, delubricators. In the area of hydraulics, coolers, oils we use the latest in Europe. Companies with which we are in contact are the Aral, Castrol, OMV, Austrian companies. We buy almost all our lubricants from them. (I 14)

On the other hand, when talking about recycled materials, we were told that Rába itself may seek to initiate changes though here too customers exert influence: 'the new materials we would like to use have to be approved by our customers. We can't change the paint unless our customers agree beforehand.' (I 13)

These examples can be related to the findings of Baylis et al. (1998) whose survey of manufacturing industry in South Wales found that 'customer pressure (supply chain)' was cited by 34% of companies as a stimulus to adopt environmental improvements. In that study it came behind compliance with environmental regulation (75%), potential for increased profit by reducing costs (57%), good neighbourliness (56%), personal environmental concern (54%) and employee concerns (41%). This is quite a strong contrast and suggests that there is less self-direction at Rába than in the Welsh case.

Rába, the REI and Győr council

As a major firm Rába is a leading member of three industry wide associations (Hungarian machine producers, Hungarian foundries and Hungarian manufacturing industry) which come under the auspices of the Association of Hungarian Employers. The Rába director is co-director of the Machine Producers organization. In 1994 the Rába environmental manager was nominated by the Hungarian manufacturing association to be a member of the environmental committee of the Association of Hungarian Employers and in this role she evaluates environmental legislation on behalf of these organizations. Rába is also a member of the national-level Environmental Information Club and attends their meetings where they are relevant.

In general the company feels itself to be always under pressure from new regulations. As mentioned above, wastes such as foundry sand, for which Rába had certificates stating that they were safe, were later declared unacceptable.

Before 1981, everything was dumped on the waste site except poisonous materials. Galvanic waste was stored on a separate site with the approval of all the relevant bodies. In 1981 the first regulations (56th Act) came out saying dangerous waste had to be collected. The galvanic waste site was in accordance with waste regulations of the time but it is no longer acceptable. In 1990, Rába had 3,5000 tons of waste.

Moving this 'took away our money for 2–3 years'. (I 12) It cost several hundred million ft.

In 1995 the 53rd Act came out and its enacting clauses are still coming out. In 1996 the 102nd regulation came out which revises the 53rd Act concerning hazardous waste (200 pages long). It meant that all the dangerous wastes listed had to be collected. In 1992 the first REI decision was made about dangerous wastes, specifying a 30 June 1994 deadline: this involved granulating asbestos brake pad dust as well as transportation.

In general Rába feels that fines at their present levels are manageable but fears that in the long run they will be increased to the level of clean-up costs they lead to.

An interviewee complained that regulations passed in June are supposed to come into force in September. Regulations were seen as becoming stricter but the staff necessary to implement them was becoming less: 'stricter administration should not be imposed since there is no-one who can carry it out.' (I 12)

As mentioned above, the introduction of the 102nd regulation on dangerous waste had led the Rába employee to press for an exemption for the company. This employee was asking the REI to change the way the diary is kept and computerise it. 'I'm sure it will not be allowed, because it [REI] can't change it.' (I 12) This example also shows that either industrial lobbies are not able to secure everything they want through initial influence on the form of legislation, or that Rába's needs deviated from those of producers in its sector generally and that it had been unsuccessful in influencing the original legislation. It also shows that it was considered feasible to influence the REI to implement the regulation in a way more satisfactory to Rába. Presumably this was based on past experience or some indication of a future favourable outcome.

Lastly, concerning relations between firm and council, Rába felt that it had little contact with the town council[5] and that there was an irregular flow of information to the council:

> The local council does not care at all. We make contact with them occasionally. It's possible that without the waste incinerator [a possible joint project] we would not have contacted them either. One of the reasons we keep in touch with them is because our Head of Environment used to be a [co-opted] member of the environmental committee of the local council in the old times [in fact 1990–94]. He used to do a kind of volunteer work. We tend to approach the local council more often than they do us. I can't recall an occasion when they approached us. (I 11)

Gardenia and its environmental practices

The second firm we studied is Gardenia. The Gardenia Lace Curtain Factory was

---

5 There was said to be 'considerable' professional consultation between environmental experts at Rába and at other companies in Győr, for example Tungsram and Graboplast, but no general inter-company collaboration.

founded in 1912 and today is a producer of synthetic curtains, bedspreads and embroidered table cloths. It is the market leader in its field in Hungary. On the European scale however it is small relative to German producers, and occupies an 'upper middle' area of the market. Its aim is to move up market. Its factory and office is on a site in Győr where it employs a mostly female work force of 660. Gardenia also has contracts with ten firms employing 200 or more workers which work exclusively for it. It also produces ready-made curtains which are made up by outworkers. It has franchising agreements with over 60 shops throughout the country.

The firm was privatized in 1991 and is now 95% Austrian owned[6] – Győr council and the OTP savings bank each own 2%. (The origin of the council's share lies in the council's ownership of the land and the prohibition on transferring land to a foreign owner.) The firm's directors are Austrian and Hungarian.

Since 1991 Gardenia has always been in the black and its fortunes have fluctuated from fair to good. It had a turnover of 3–4 billion ft (£12–16 million) in 1995 and 60% of its production was exported.

Gardenia's location in Győr is considered satisfactory by the management. The border is nearby (which is important for exports to the west), skilled workers are available, and its costs are competitive. The average salary of workers is eight times less than that of comparable workers in Austria, but the real saving on wage costs is much less since labour productivity is one quarter of Austrian levels. This is partly because machines are working at lower capacity. A further advantage of the Győr (or a Hungarian) site was that four-shift operation was possible whereas in Germany and Austria it was unpopular with workers.

The company considers itself a 'good citizen' environmentally speaking, and this was no doubt a factor in their agreement to be part of the study. (Graboplast, a synthetic floor covering firm, with a bad reputation for pollution, refused to take part.)

We will examine its environmental impact under two headings: pollution and expansion plans.

Pollution: avoiding fines

The production process at Gardenia involves various stages: washing the polyester, whitening it, dying it, drying and fixing it, and knitting it. These create effluents, air particles and solid waste. New machines reduce air pollution but increase the effluent-borne particles. They also give off heat, which is recycled.

The firm's general approach to pollution is progressive. They take the view that it is always best to introduce equipment which places them ahead of today's environmental regulations since these are changing and always in the direction of tighter control. Hence, they say, equipment which is most economic in the short-term may not be most economic in the medium term. This decision rule would imply a payback period longer than the two years described above for Rába. However,

---

6 In Győr–Moson–Sopron county, Austria is the largest source of foreign investment (60%), followed by Germany (26%) (Győr–Moson–Sopron County, n.d., probably 1995).

without access to detailed costings, it is difficult to know how far this maxim is followed in practice.

Gardenia claims to be adopting EU practice regarding the techniques of measuring pollution, and says that their pollution emissions were below the EU level except in the case of waste water. The company contrasted itself with another local firm, notorious for its 'dirty' image, which it said would have far greater problems in terms of EU standards.

The reason for Gardenia's problem with effluent is the effluent content and the fact that both effluent and rainwater go into the same pipes. But the company is planning to separate them as part of a 40 million ft (£160,000) investment. As at Rába, and at Chinoin in Nagytétény (Chapter 5), the treatment of industrial effluents was a key issue and one that was not resolved in the study period. This seems to be one field in which environmental practices in Hungary have been backward.

The company also conforms to the ISO 9001 quality management standard.

Finally the company's exports to Germany and Austria oblige it to respect certain regulations regarding the safety of the products themselves.

Gardenia's air and water pollution are subject to monitoring by the regional environmental inspectorate and water authority. We were told that there had been only two cases of water pollution exceeding the permitted levels when the water authority had sought to fine them.[7] In the first case, which was associated with starting up after the Christmas closure, the firm successfully appealed to the water authority. In the second case, the water authority took the view that a second violation within a year could not be an accident. The firm appealed to the water authority but its appeal letter did not arrive. The authority made a re-test, 2½ months later, and during this time the firm paid the fine. The company appealed against this fine to the local authority, on the grounds that new equipment had been coming into operation and that their appeal letter to the water authority had failed to arrive. As a result the fine was reduced to a 15 day fine. Managers referred to these fines as though they were real blots on the company's clean and modern image. The company paid fines for water pollution much less frequently than Alcoa in Székesfehérvár.

Expansion plans

The other environmental impact concerns Gardenia's expansion plans. The firm's present site is fully used. Old buildings and machinery have been demolished to make way for new buildings and plant, but these are insufficient to allow the firm to expand. Since its site is hemmed in by a dam, Gardenia proposed that it should pay for the dam to be moved and to acquire the reclaimed land. It threatened to move away unless its plans were approved. Permission for this depends on the town council.

The company started discussions with the town in 1995, putting forward three

---

7 There had also been public outcry at the dark blue smelly particles being emitted through the firm's chimneys but Gardenia staff, while denying the particles were harmful, admitted that such judgements could change over time and quoted the example of carbon tetrachloride.

options which varied in cost to the company in a ratio of 1:10. For the town council the issue was the loss of green space which was involved in all three options. The cheapest option for the firm involved the most loss of trees, and the dearest involved most reinstatement. The explicit threat was that if the council did not agree to the proposal to move the dam the company would itself move.

The town council was described as being divided, with a few officials objecting to the scheme while most supported it. In particular the Architect's and Planning Department, which is responsible for the protection of green spaces, objected to the loss of trees, since a water-side site a few hundred yards away had also been cleared of trees (and remained vacant). The Environmental Committee also objected and the water authorities were also concerned, but public opposition was limited.

In early 1996 the council wrote to the company saying that it had set up an environmental fund and inviting it to make a donation to it. The company replied, shrewdly, saying that it agreed to make a donation but that its size would depend on the town's decision on the dam. In May 1996 the council approved the expansion plan and the company was seen as having 'won'. However it will have to undertake some tree planting as a condition. A council official said that Gardenia had also agreed to pay 10 million ft (£40,000) to the environmental fund.

The council's own description of its relations with Gardenia can be quoted. In the case of Gardenia, an office holder said that:

> we can't say that Gardenia does not influence the policies of the local council. They can exercise influence over certain issues which affect them. But this has happened only once concerning an environmental protection issue. (K 4)

Gardenia was described as:

> partners even when our town has demands towards them. Gardenia has had a good relationship with the Mayor's office during the past four years. It's not formalised and not regular. They contact us when they need to. This has happened frequently. If it wasn't like this then it couldn't be called a good relationship. (K 4)

Overall, our impression is that Gardenia is economically successful and that the management is committed to cultivating an image as a good citizen environmentally. This image is presumably helpful in negotiating with the town and in its relations with the public. Its purchases of environmentally-friendly plant and equipment appear to reflect this image, but without technical knowledge it is difficult to assess how far it is justified. In the case of effluent the company seems to be benefiting from lax standards operating throughout Hungary. There is some evidence that Gardenia's dependence on exports to Germany and Austria is a factor in raising the environmental consciousness of the management.

The REI and its relations with Gardenia and Rába

We now consider the environment as seen from the perspective of the North Trans-Danubian Environmental Inspectorate based in Győr. This office covers two counties, Győr–Moson–Sopron and Komárom–Esztergom, which together form a 200km long strip about 20–50km wide along the north-west border of Hungary (see Figure 9.2). The Győr office is located in the centre of this strip but the remotest places from it such as Sopron to the west and Nagymaros[8] to the east are each about 100km away. The REI employs 110 people and its office is adjacent to that of Győr town council. Our REI interviewee contrasted the post 1990 REI with its predecessor when:

> there used to be party representation at work, and daily politics was much more to the forefront ... Today I have no idea whether there are people among my colleagues who are members of a party. None of them in a management position [are], otherwise we would know about it.' (I 17)

The work of the REI includes dealings with firms and with the public. The REI is also involved when urban planning decisions concern areas exceeding a certain size in which case it has to carry out an environmental impact study.

The REI has to approve the environmental aspects of company investment decisions and deals with some 100 such cases each year. There is a tolerance for expansions of less than 25% of capacity. However this assumes that the current capacity is known. But we were told in answer to the question: 'Has it ever happened that you asked for data from a company but they refused?' that:

> Yes. It often happens, especially in the case of activities where a study of environmental impact is compulsory and when we need, for example, data about current capacity. And then the company says that it's a company secret and therefore they can't tell us. At present we have *exactly* such a case with Firm X. (I 17)

Most visits to firms seem to be in response to invitations by the firm, and our interviewee placed a lot of emphasis on the location of the firms concerned:

> We're called out to companies to see what they're doing, and if there are environmental problems, we discuss how we could solve the problem. On these occasions the managers always ask about the possible changes in the regulations, what kind of requirements they would have to fulfil in the future. If we're called out, mainly around Győr, we are pleased to go, but we can't go further than that because of the cost, cost, cost. (I 17)

> It's due to where we are that throughout the county [Győr–Moson–Sopron] we tend to have contact particularly with companies which are in Győr. I've mentioned before that

---

8 Nagymaros is the location of the proposed dam on the Danube which gave rise to the well-known Danube Circle movement in the 1980s (Fleischer, 1993).

they tend to invite us to show us their technology. We also issue [orders], there are quite a few of those, about what pollution they should reduce. For example, Firm Y has a case about soil pollution which has been going on for many years. *We tend to turn up in these places occasionally and carry out the appropriate examinations.* Of course, whenever it's necessary, we go to the other county [Komárom–Esztergom] as well. We have to do that. It is much more difficult to go to places for an occasional meeting. Therefore those are limited mainly to Győr. For example, I've visited places like the Industrial Park, the oil factory, and so on, which is very useful for a bureaucrat. He can see what kind of activities are going on in reality. (I 17, italics added)

The results of these contacts were described as follows:

We managed to achieve that these companies, who already have a positive attitude to environmental issues because it's them who tend to contact us, tend to pick up the phone much quicker to ask us for help because they know who deals with what. They indicate to us their problem and that they would like to apply for a permission. They'd like to plan things ahead so that it doesn't cause any further problem at the permission [stage]. In many cases we can avoid a lot of letter writing. (I 17)

These informal visits were undoubtedly an opportunity for the REI officials to educate firm managers in the values and methods of the inspectorate so that they would be less likely to infringe environmental standards. To carry out its responsibilities to monitor pollution of different kinds the REI is largely reliant on self-reported data by firms.

Air pollution, the so-called local polluters, are within the [remit of the] authority, we decide the obligatory limits. It is to us that the data should be sent by the companies which operate air polluting sources and if the pollution is over the limit we'll penalise them. (I 17)

We were interested to see whether the REI conducted unannounced visits to check pollution levels. No mention of unannounced visits was made by the interviewee. The only reference that might have involved them was the italicised passage in the quotation cited above. The REI also carried out joint inspection programmes with other authorities, for example, of non-ferrous metal collection sites, but there was no suggestion that these were unannounced.

The REI responds to complaints from the public. 'The most common cases are about neighbours disturbing one another.' These relate to for example to smells from keeping animals, or waste water being let onto someone else's land. But they can also relate to the dumping of dangerous waste. Complaints are also made about companies disturbing the people living nearby. According to the official:

We also received complaints from the sacked drivers of a company serving the locals that there were dangerous wastes mixed with household waste. Which is very important because the waste incinerator of Dorog is in our area. Also there is an environmental organization in Dorog and they constantly show interest, complaints concerning the waste incinerator. (I 17)

Again the spatial constraints were mentioned:

We receive many complaints, personally, by phone or letter and we try to respond to them quickly, although it's not easy because the county of Győr–Moson–Sopron and that of Komárom–Esztergom come under us. If we receive some complaints from a settlement 100 kilometres away, its investigation, the cost and time will be on us. (I 17)

The REI tries to investigate all complaints coming from local people:

There is a provision of law issued in 1997 about complaints concerning public interest. There is a prescribed way we have to proceed. If a [local person] complains to us, we have to investigate the matter and inform him about the final result. If the complaint is anonymous, then, in theory, we don't have to investigate the matter. However, if the matter is such that we think we ought to look into it, we tend to go out to the scene, even if we discover that there is nothing in it. We have to investigate what had happened and have to see what we should do and whether we have the authority to do so. If we have the authority then we often have to investigate who committed the environmental pollution and if the case is outside our responsibility than we always try to find the organization in this complicated bureaucratic system who has the authority to deal with the case. We always inform the person who complained about the final outcome. (I 17)

In response to a question about whether there was any difference in the complaints of local people before and after 1990 we were told that:

Yes. People tend to be much braver when complaining. The negative side of it is that these complaints tend to have less grounding than before. The way things are investigated has not changed since 1977, nothing has changed which determines the procedure of what we have to do. But the fact that people are more sensitive about environmental matters has definitely changed. (I 17)

This is an interesting observation about how professionalized bureaucracies can feel little affected by political change.

We now examine the REI's perception of the world. The biggest problem in dealing with firms about the enforcement of environmental issues in the eyes of the REI lies in the area of dangerous waste. As we have seen a new regulation was published in 1996 extending the list of wastes that were classed as dangerous and as requiring separation and special treatment.

The REI interviewee said that:

it hasn't yet become general knowledge that dangerous wastes can't be mixed with household wastes, that they have to be collected separately and can only be given to organizations which have permission to handle them. This is such a problem that when our waste supervisors go out to inspect these wastes, in 90% of the cases they have to penalize. Which for a small business can be very high and they often feel that it's unfair, because in most cases it isn't a matter of breaking the law deliberately but merely not knowing it. (I 17)

Regarding Rába, we were told that:

They have several workshops. These workshops usually pollute the air, I think here, first of all, of the smelting works. In fact, this is a major air polluter here in Győr. Because of the make-up of Rába, there are dangerous wastes. Some of its waste water, or not the waste water but some of its precipitation goes into the industrial sewage system, and therefore we have to examine this area, but they don't really mean a big problem for us in these two areas, in the field of waste handling and water pollution. They used to have a dangerous waste site in Sas hill. After a great many years we achieved that they cleared the area and now take care of the proper treatment of these wastes. This was a sensitive point between us but now it has disappeared. (I 17)

This confirms that the galvanic waste dump was Rába's worst source of pollution and that the remaining air and water pollution are less serious.

Regarding Gardenia, the interviewee said that:

I don't really remember the environmental problems of Gardenia. I think that they use various chemicals, and at the time when they purchased these poisonous materials, we expressed our opinion, but it doesn't really come up among the environmental problems. (I 17)

As in Nagytétény and Dunaújváros, but unlike Székesfehérvár, our interviews with REI officials in Győr drew attention to the shortage of resources they experienced. The earlier quotations in this chapter have placed considerable emphasis on cost as a constraint on meeting firms and responding to complaints from members of the public. Further evidence on the shortage of resources can be given.

We were told that:

Since we've existed, we've always suffered from a lack of budget [that is, funding], and we even find it difficult to plan the right circumstances to carry out the tasks which we have to according to the regulations. (I 17)

The pressure of urban redevelopment was also mentioned:

I must admit that it is very difficult to cope with the volume of work, because in Hungary in the past few decades settlement replanning was non-existent and now everybody is trying to utilise the situation, so the cases tend to pile up for several years. (I 17)

Lastly, the REI makes little use of outside experts which may also be related to its resource situation.

> We employ outside experts very rarely, only if there isn't the right technical condition in our laboratory to give a professional opinion on something. For example our laboratory can't measure the often talked about air polluting dioxin of the Dorog waste incinerator. In this case we do use outside experts. Otherwise we don't have to because we [can] deal with it. (I 17)

We were told that this happened 'Very rarely, once or twice a year' (I 17)

Overall the REI seems heavily absorbed by giving obligatory opinions on new investment and new urban plans, holding meetings with firms to discuss their future investment plans, dealing with self-reported air pollution data, and investigating public complaints and waste disposal. What is apparent is that it gives priority to cases closer to Győr which given the strip-like shape of the area it covers means that large areas are more lightly controlled. The time spent on meeting firms to discuss their plans has an important educational function. All studies of regulation[9] show that regulators prefer to educate than to penalise and these meetings are an obvious venue for this. However such meetings mean that less time is available for unannounced visits. The fact that fines are levied by the REI and water authority means that their efforts have some 'bite'.

Gardenia's concern not to be fined at all shows that fines can have a symbolic importance which goes beyond any economic impact they may have.

Conclusion

Győr falls into the category of an established industrial (and administrative) centre with a mixed manufacturing base. It thus contrasts with the traditional socialist 'new town' of the Dunaújváros type based on a single large plant, and with towns such as Székesfehérvár whose industrialisation started more recently and where there was a smaller share of older firms.

The town council of Győr is committed both to its existing industries and to the attraction of new firms. It shares the prevailing idea that firms are 'partners' working with local government. Its creation of an industrial park is a useful symbol of its active policy, but its economic measures do not reach the level of those in Székesfehérvár. The neo-liberal opinions expressed by one interviewee perhaps suggest some of the tension within the council about its adoption of an activist economic role.

Its activism in the area of the environmental policy is moderate, and is less than at Székesfehérvár. Moreover its efforts were primarily responsive to public opinion (including the Reflex environmental group). Public pressure had instigated the relocation of Rába's foundry from the centre of the town, had secured a parking ban

---

9 See the studies referred to in Chapter 2.

and a noise-shielding wall, and was a constant source of pressure on the REI.[10]

The two case study firms were in contrasting positions. Although both were long-established, one was a major player within Hungary's national economy and one was medium-sized. Rába, the former, was very active in industry-wide employers' organizations, and was consulted about environmental legislation. The management was environmentally concerned but less so than at Gardenia. Rába regularly paid fines in respect of air pollution and waste water. Its problem was that the cost of investment needed to reduce pollution to a level where no fines were levied was too high. In particular given the low level of fines paid (£4,000 per year in total) the economic incentive to undertake costly investment was simply absent. If the idea that a two year payback period mentioned by an interviewee is accepted the likelihood of such investment is even smaller. The most important driver of environmentally-friendly investment at Rába was pressure from purchasers, especially foreign firms.

At Gardenia the management seemed particularly keen to appear as environmentally conscious as witnessed by their concern about being fined even once. This suggests that fines can have a symbolic importance which exceeds their economic significance. Gardenia claimed to anticipate higher environmental standards in their investment strategy, in contrast to Rába. If so, they were taking a longer term view of investment than suggested for Rába. They did not cite pressure from purchasers. The case of Gardenia's expansion plan shows how detrimental environmental impacts can be overcome by a firm trading on its long established role in the town and good relations with the town council. It got what it wanted at a fairly small cost in terms of its contribution to the council's environmental fund. However public opposition to Gardenia's expansion plan was limited.

Lastly the North Trans-Danubian Environmental Inspectorate, despite experiencing some resource constraints, probably gives considerable attention to the environmental situation in Győr at the expense of the more peripheral locations in its region. Its regular meetings with firms are likely to have an educational role. Although fines are levied by the REI and water authority it seems unlikely that they are large enough to have much economic effect.

---

10 Also, after the study period, as mentioned, there was a successful campaign against the closure of a long established biscuit making firm.

5 Nagytétény: Past Pollution and Limited Prospects?

Location, history and economic situation

Nagytétény is an industrial suburb on the southern edge of Budapest, about 12km from the city centre. It is located in the XXII district. It developed as an industrial area from the early twentieth century onwards. It has a mix of older single houses and new estates which have gradually crept up to the factories. It is well served by roads and rail and its fringe location gives it good accessibility in several directions. In the 1980s its industries included chemicals, army engineering, rubber, pharmaceuticals, paper, a pig farm and sparkling wine production, By the time of the study the main employers were Chinoin (a French owned chemical factory) and Pannonplast (a South Korean owned plastics factory).

In 1990 Nagytétény was listed among the 12 most polluted places in Hungary but it also has a reputation as an area of environmental activism as a result of a widely-reported conflict in the late 1980s period (Pickvance, C.G., 1996a; Szirmai, 1997). The origins of this go back to the 1970s and are relevant to an understanding of relations between institutions and residents in the area today.

The existence of lead pollution caused by the Metallochemia metal-processing plant was discovered in the 1970s. However attempts to get the plant closed were unsuccessful. In 1989 a public meeting was held about environmental conditions and health in the area. This initiative was taken by local intellectuals, doctors, and employees of a local community health centre. It was decided to form a local 'social environmental council'. This group linked up with activists of the M0 group (which was trying to resist a motorway ring which cut the district into two), and with an environmental group linked to the local branch of the HDF (the largest party in the 1990-94 national governing coalition). As a result Green Future was formed and was registered in early 1990. Its President was Peter Mészáros, who was subsequently elected as the area's MP (standing for the HDF) in the May 1990 general elections. Initially, like other environmental groups such as the Danube Circle, Green Future acted as a magnet for opponents of the regime. However after 1990 most of them left and by late 1991 the group had declined in size to 60 members, of whom eight to ten were the main activists. Green Future made use of the resources of the local community health centre. But when it applied to the local council for a grant to enable it to employ two people the council said it would only agree if it gave up its autonomy which Green Future refused to do. As a result Green Future lost the use of the centre, and an employee-activist was sacked, but it succeeded in obtaining other resources. These were partly external (from the George Bush Foundation and Parliamentary Environment Committee) and partly internal (membership payments). By late 1991 Green Future had £30,000 in the bank.

In May 1990 the group held a protest march and handed in a petition to the local council listing 22 complaints about the environmental situation in the area and also wrote to the Prime Minister asking for Nagytétény to be declared a disaster area. Green Future was successful in getting Metallochemia closed (though there may have been economic reasons for this too). But its demands for the removal of polluted soil, compensation for those affected by pollution and the redevelopment of the site were rejected. Instead the government set up an inter-ministerial committee to look into pollution in Nagytétény. This funded a Dutch investigation and held a competition for solutions. This was the high point of Green Future's impact. The fact that this committee was set up was undoubtedly due to the appointment of Peter Mészáros, the local MP, to the Parliamentary Environment Committee. (Cases of pollution elsewhere in the country did not receive parallel treatment.) Subsequently no action was taken to implement any of the proposals and in 1993 Mészáros was removed from the Parliamentary Environment Committee. He did not stand for re-election in the 1994 general election.

Green Future's next step was to change its tactics in favour of cooperation with the local council. Green Future agreed to support the council as plaintiff in a legal case against the plant's owners and the government for compensation. In March 1993 the council launched a £40 million claim. The rationale for Green Future's change of approach was its belief that a local government was more likely to be successful in a legal case. The group may also have judged that its declining strength meant that continued action in isolation from the council was not likely to be fruitful. The present situation is that the lawsuit is stalled. The Ministry did not place the Nagytétény case among its top ten cases requiring action, allegedly because the list was made up of easily resolved issues and the Metallochemia case would be very costly. In 1997 the Ministry had a budget of 1 billion ft (£40 million) for areas requiring the removal of contaminated soil, hazardous waste, etc. for the whole country. This was the figure that the council was hoping would be given to Nagytétény. An offer by the Ministry to make an out of court settlement was rejected by the local government.

Meanwhile the local council is under pressure to develop a plan for the affected area. However there is a stalemate between the council and the REI. The council is unwilling to prepare plans for the area until it is told what level of lead is in the soil and suspects the REI of wanting to set abnormally high levels of permitted lead. The REI for its part is refusing to advise on what levels of lead are present because it says the acceptable level varies according to the planned activity. The permitted lead level is more than a technicality since the higher it is the lower the potential costs of the cleaning or soil replacement it would require, costs which could fall on the government on which the REI depends. Thus while the council has the power and duty to plan, knowledge of the environmental state of the land is held by the REI and used as a bargaining counter to try and persuade the council to plan 'realistically'. For example, non-residential uses such as a logistics centre (in which lorry loads can be broken and re-assembled) and a railway station have been discussed.

As well as leading to an impasse, this conflict has resulted in deep hostility between the REI and the council. The REI feels that the council has behaved in a populist way by allying itself with the protestors and that it is making irresponsible demands regarding the removal of pollution. The council on the other hand feels the REI has given in to government pressure to relax the permitted lead levels and cut clean-up costs at the expense of the health of local residents. The situation is further complicated by the council and REI's hopes to make Metallochemia (or its owner Metalloglobus) contribute to any compensation payments. It is feared that the privatization of Metallochemia will put an end to these hopes.

Nagytétény's industrial history has thus been associated not only with pollution problems and residents' protest, but has led to hostile relations between the REI and local council.

The local council and its economic and environmental policies

We now consider the local council's policies. From 1990–94 the local council was controlled by a Free Democrat–Young Democrat coalition and had a Free Democrat mayor, and from 1994–98 by the Socialist Party with a Socialist mayor. Interviewees reported that there was an awkward transition from the pre-1990 period when officials had not needed to pay attention to elected representatives, and this led to alienation among local people who saw the council as absorbed in conflict rather than taking effective action.

In terms of resources, the local government is in a poor position. The council has three broad sources of income.

1. Central grants. Most of these come with strings attached to finance compulsory functions such as education and health.
2. A share of national taxes such as income tax, and of taxes levied by Budapest City on industry and tourism. A share of the income tax is channeled to Budapest city council. Budapest city council sets the rate of industry and tourism tax. The total income from all these taxes is then shared between itself and the local governments of Budapest based on their population and needs.
3. Locally-levied taxes and incomes. These include taxes on buildings and land, a communal tax, the environmental fund income, and the proceeds of asset sales.

In this way the council's income depends on local firms via the tax on buildings but not on the (nationally collected) business tax.

In total the budget of Nagytétény was 4 billion ft (£16 million) in 1997. The contribution of the three income shares was roughly: 69%, 15%, 16%. The council nominally has freedom over the spending of 30% of its budget. In practice these levels of income are quite inadequate to the council's needs and it attempts to raise income via permitting development in previously green or undeveloped land, increasing densities of development, and offering incentives to attract large developers including multinationals (Hasko, 1998, pp. 12–15).

Local economic policy

The council's general priorities for local economic development are:

1. to renew the Danube bank area;
2. to renew parts of inner Nagytétény (but not the Metallochemia site which is centrally located); and
3. to prepare a 'tourist vision' stressing the cultural heritage of the area, for example, attractive sites and buildings, the old 'wine culture'. According to a senior politician:

> In fact we'd like to base the whole of our programme on the fact that there is a very old and valuable wine culture here. That this is a city of wine-making, to which the welcoming of visitors is attached, that during the centuries a kind of bourgeoisie has developed here and we can enjoy its benefits.[1] (H 5)

The council has other plans such as tree planting, and runs a competition for the best flower garden. But almost all of the above priorities are future intentions and it is clear that the council does not have a developed industrial attraction policy based on industrial estates and economic incentives as in the other three localities in our study.

As far as relations between local government and local companies generally are concerned, the newly elected senior local politicians visited all the local firms in 1995 in order to discuss their problems and to inform them about the council's plans. According to one of them 'unfortunately the relation between companies and local government is not close. But there are companies which we meet regularly' (H 5), for example, wine making companies with which they organize festivals. The council set up a foundation with Pannonplast to 'save' the castle of Nagytétény (and convert it into a museum of applied arts). The council also supports company-owned sports clubs, thereby opening them up to non-employees.[2]

With Chinoin a senior politician said there is 'no close cooperation'.

> There is no official contact. They don't have to provide us with information. The need

---

1 There are 40km of limestone caves in the area which are used for wine storage and mushroom production.

for a meeting comes up only if we have mutual interest in it. Like the building of the water purifier because of the complaints of the locals. (H 5)

In 1996 Chinoin invited a senior politician to a meeting and showed the two alternative proposals for a water purification plant, and the schedule for building it, but the council was not kept informed of progress subsequently. This was confirmed by a senior manager of the plant who said he meets senior politicians two or three times per year. 'This is a mutual need.' The firm had also discussed its plans for a water treatment plant with the council Environmental Protection Committee.

Local environmental policy

The council Environmental Protection Committee, which reports to the Planning Committee, has three councillors and a number of (co-opted) 'external' members. In 1990–94 the committee had a number of Green Future members and was infused by their activism. According to a senior politician, in that period 'the atmosphere was more euphoric, the way of looking at things was more radical'. (H 5) In contrast the 1994–98 committee is described as more 'responsible'. It was less likely to raise issues itself and stuck to the tasks allotted to it by the local council, for example, commenting on the district plan. (One of the external members of the Environmental Protection Committee in 1994–98 was the leader of Green Future and former MP, Peter Meszaros. By this time Green Future had dwindled in size but Meszaros continued to be active on environmental issues in the area.)

There is no specific budget for environmental protection. The council has established an environmental fund, from the 30% share of fines levied locally which are sent to national level and then returned. In 1997 these amounted to 3 million ft (£12,000). Some environmental spending also took place under other categories.

In terms of staffing, one staff member is responsible for environmental protection but has other responsibilities too, and only one quarter of his time is spent on environmental protection. This is allegedly less than before the regime change.

As an illustration of this paucity of resources, we can cite the case of a firm[3] which is 'extremely noisy and according to some people it also polluted the air.' (H 4) Recently the local environmental protection official had imposed a fine and the firm

---

2 This relates to a major problem encountered in the transition period. Under state socialism state enterprises had developed a range of leisure and non-work facilities for employees such as sports facilities to holiday homes. However, privatization meant in most cases that new owners did not want to bear the costs of non-essential activities. One solution was therefore for the local government to step in with financial support but at the same time to open access to local residents as a whole.

3 The firm had been opened (and approved by the council and by the REI) ten years earlier at a time 'when there were no [environmental] regulations in force' and 'despite the opposition of local people' (H 4). The council's only concern was said to be whether it met building regulations.

had reacted by commissioning an expert opinion. In response the official commissioned another expert opinion and subsequently levied a fine of 120,000 ft (£500) plus the expert's fee. But according to an official 'we haven't seen a penny of it so far. This is very risky because sooner or later we have to pay the expert.' (H 4) The fact that the council could not pay the expert until it had received the fine indicates the hand-to-mouth existence of the environmental control function in local government.

As far as environmental policy is concerned, according to a senior politician the main general environmental problems in the area are:

1. *Sewage* A sewer laying programme between 1990 and 1994 paid for by the council had raised the proportion of households connected from 20% to 50%. The major task of building a collector and treatment plant could only be considered for 2008–10.
2. *Roads* The M0 motorway which cuts through the area was built despite protests by residents. But there is a lot of traffic congestion and exhaust pollution within the district.
3. *Lesser problems* Include rubbish dumping by people wanting to avoid the journey to the official tip.

The main problems relating to factories are:

1. the Metallochemia site where, despite the closure, the waste is still lying and when disturbed by the wind blows over the area,
2. the area filled with slag from the gas factory. This was placed on the Ministry's priority list but the local government has not been informed as to what the Ministry proposes to do about it.

In contrast 'the problem of Chinoin [the company selected for study here] is third order. It'll come to the fore only when we really start to put the bank of the Danube in order.' (H 5)

A senior politician said the council has 'occasional contact' (H 5) with the Environmental Inspectorate – partly through an ex-REI employee who attends the Environmental Protection Committee. The local official with environmental responsibilities responsible however (see below) said he was in daily contact with the Inspectorate.

On the other hand, environmental considerations are not totally lacking in the council's thinking:

1. the location of Nagytétény within the urban structure of Budapest gives it undoubted potential advantages – especially compared with locations in the east of Hungary,
2. environmentalist mobilization among the population (as witnessed by the Green Future movement) ensures that environmental concerns are not ignored.

Nevertheless in contrast to Székesfehérvár and Győr we found no sense of a strong economic policy or a strong environmental policy even at the level of words. It seems likely that difficulties of dealing with past pollution problems have affected the council's ability to think ahead. This is a clear example of a significant legacy effect.

We now consider the case of one firm, Chinoin, its environmental practices and its relations with the local government and the REI.

Chinoin and its environmental practices

Our focus is on the plant owned by Chinoin at Nagytétény which produces plant protection products (insecticides, fungicides and herbicides). Chinoin has another plant in the Ujpest district of Budapest.

The Nagytétény plant was founded to produce shotgun cartridges and mining detonators in 1910, and in the 1970s was taken over by the Chinoin pharmaceutical firm which was outgrowing its plant in Ujpest. Subsequently detonator production was run down and the plant was used to produce pharmaceuticals and chemicals, and packaged medicines. The plant had originally been isolated and remote, but the expansion of the city had brought housing close to the plant.

In 1989 Chinoin[4] became a limited company and in 1991 40% of its shares were purchased by a French multinational, Sanofi, for $75m. (A manager of Sanofi had been part of a French delegation to Hungary led by President Mitterand in 1988). Subsequent purchases made Sanofi the 98% owner. Some pharmaceutical production was moved to Ujpest and the Nagytétény plant became more specialised in plant protection products. Employment at this plant fell from 1700 before privatization to 550 today.

As far as environmental effects are concerned, as explained above, the company was not considered to be the main polluter in Nagytétény, though it was partially targeted by the Green Future campaign against Metallochemia. Interviews with Chinoin staff make clear that the plant has become used to paying fines for pollution. This was also part of the perception of the council: a senior politician described Chinoin as 'regularly fined'. (H 5)[5]

We now examine the company's practices in relation to waste water and air polution.

Waste water

Chinoin's main problem was that for decades it had done without a central waste

---

4   From here on Chinoin will be used to refer to the Nagytétény plant.
5   As in Székesfehérvár, we came across the comment made by a large company interviewee – in this case Chinoin – that small companies who were 'almost never inspected' were to blame for a lot of pollution.

water treatment works and its effluents had flowed into the Danube, although it has purification equipment linked to particular processes. (A former senior manager said he even felt that production should have been switched to products which did not require a water treatment works but this did not happen.) 'What happens is that the effluent goes through a pre-purification process... and then it goes straight into the Danube through an outflow pipe (via the communal sewage system)'. (H 8) (By contrast at the Ujpest plant effluent flows into a public waste water treatment plant.) The reason for the lack of a treatment works was cost.

We were told that the effluent is checked daily by the company for ten to 12 elements and that it was easy to trace the source of any excessive pollution found. In addition water treatment systems in each part of the factory are checked at least once a week. According to an interviewee 'we have reduced pollution but if it's still around the limits and economic pressure is strong then we might decide to continue with it and pay a small amount in fines'. (H 8)

Chinoin usually keeps to the standards for effluents, we were told, but 'every year, once, twice, six times or eight times we exceed the limits. Simply because of the limits of our capabilities.' (H 8) These standards concern salt content, where the firm has its 'own limits'. What this means is that the firm is allowed a higher than normal level of salt in its effluent: 3 grams per litre instead of 1.5 grams. The standards also concern ammonia content but:

> at present one isn't fined for chemical oxygen absorption which is a characteristic of organic materials. From the point of view of the environment, however, this means that if our effluent needs oxygen when it flows out into the fresh water, then it will absorb all the oxygen from the fresh water in order to break itself down. This isn't desirable. At the moment, the Danube is able to handle the amount coming from us since we don't let out a vast amount and not in big spurts. The main purpose of the water purifier is to solve this problem. (H 8)

In addition the firm investigates complaints made by local residents to it rather than to the health authorities or regional environmental inspectorate. (This reduces the risk of publicity and of being fined.) For a long time residents had complained about the gas, steam, and smells coming out of the outflow pipe before it entered the sewer and as a result in the 1970s Chinoin spent 49 million ft on a sealed and pressurised pipe which was routed away from the houses.

From the mid 1980s the firm's management pressed for a waste water purification plant 'because of the fines they had to pay for their sewage.' (Hasko, 1998, p. 19), and for air filters in the chimneys, etc. The firm also became more open to complaints from the population 'after the slackening of party hierarchies within the government.' 'It also opened its gates to Green Future activists and promised to [respond to their demands], particularly for the building of the waste water purifier' (p. 20) Because of Chinoin's 'flexible behaviour', Green Future activists showed more tolerance towards it, compared to the 'tough' Metallochemia.

The sale of the firm in 1991 did not lead to the abandonment of the idea of building the water purifier plant but it was not built. In 1996 a decision was made to build a water purification plant by September 1997 in order to reduce by 80% the quantity of organic materials passing into the Danube as well as the ammonia. This deadline was not met. It has been suggested that the REI and council supported the plans even if they were not perfect but that the Medical Officer for Health rejected them as not effective enough. A delay of course meant that Chinoin was saved from undertaking the expenditure. However as explained in the next section it meant the firm could benefit from a provision which allowed leniency or exemption regarding water pollution fines in situations where firms had plans to improve the situation.[6]

Waste

Chinoin also has to deal with its waste products. An interviewee stated that in the late 1980s it paid fines for letting zinc into the water.[7] It now precipitates the zinc and sells the zinc carbonate. According to an interviewee this is 'a positive example of how one can make profit out of fines' (H 8), though the profit is not big. Chinoin also has an accumulation of waste containing zinc which may be extracted by a specialist firm. The firm's dangerous waste is kept in containers which met the old regulations fully and 'almost' meet the new ones. This has to be taken to waste collecting stations or directly to the incinerator at Dorog, the national facility for dangerous waste (which has itself been the target of environmental protest).

Air

Air pollution is stated to be less of a problem than at Ujpest. It is checked by the company and by independent firms. According to an employee at Chinoin:

> The figures for air pollution are based on measurements and on how much the company is willing to admit. We admit everything. We examine any changes and carry out new measurements. The fines will be based on these figures. We check places where there used to be air pollution. If it has improved, then we no longer have to pay the fines. (H 8)

This interviewee said that firms tell the truth because of the fear of paying extra fines if caught and because of their professional consciousness. However he admitted that getting caught was unlikely: 'In practice a sudden inspection is out of the question.

---

6 In 1997 Sanofi, owner of Chinoin, sought to sell the firm. The reason given was in order to refocus the group's activities. In 1998 a sale of the firm to a US company fell through when the Russian market, to which it sold 30% of its output, collapsed. In 2000 the waste water plant had still not been built, but Sanofi sold the company to its management. It seems likely that the cost of the water purification plant was relevant to Sanofi's desire to sell Chinoin.

7 The amount quoted in the interview transcript, 50 million ft (£200,000), is out of line with all other fines referred to by interviewees and we place little confidence in it. A figure of 500,000 ft (£2,000) is more likely.

The [Regional Environmental Inspectorate][8][9] has no capacity for it and is not prepared for inspection.' (H 8) Later he describes how new environmental laws mean administrators are 'overworked' and underpaid:

> the best people leave. Therefore this kind of inspection isn't a solution. There is no point in having a good law if nobody keeps to it, or if it isn't checked whether people keep to it. Most of the inspections are only for appearance, they are randomly selected inspections, since one can't expect conscientious work from them for the above-mentioned reasons and they don't have the resources either. (H 8)

This interviewee rejected the idea that the firm was careless: 'when we go beyond permitted limits in the area of water or air, we do it with regret. It's always due to some kind of constraint, either economic or technological.' (H 8) However the same interviewee later admitted that they don't have the equipment to check air pollution, 'but there is one in Ujpest and people come out from there to take some measurements if we ask them.'

The overall picture provided by the interviewees with Chinoin staff thus support the idea that inspections are relatively rare and ineffective and that the firm has got used to paying modest fines. This corresponds to the image of the firm in the eyes of local government officials and local politicians.

However, this leaves unexplained why, after doing without a waste water treatment plant on site for so long, a decision to build one was taken, even if the plant was not eventually built. Several interpretations can be given of the firm's stated commitment to build the plant. One is that it was a way of buying off growing pressure on the firm. According to a senior politician, it was 'because of the complaints of the locals' (H 5) which suggests that resident protest was greater than admitted by the firm. Another is that investment in a purification plant was seen as worthwhile economically in view of the likelihood of tougher regulations and larger fines in the future. A third is that, as mentioned, having plans to deal with effluent allows a firm to be exempted from the fines for breaching effluent pollution levels. Since, as we have shown, the current level of fines is low the economic incentive to build the plant seems weak unless a huge increase in fines was expected. It seems more likely that there was no intention to build a plant but that the announcement of the intention was useful in defusing complaints and in avoiding the imposition of fines. This is supported by Chinoin's subsequent failure to build the promised plant.[10]

---

8 The transcript refers to the Environmental Committee which has no powers of inspection; only the power to report complaints to the Regional Environmental Inspectorate and to levy fines if a breach is found to have occurred. We assume the interviewee had in mind the REI.

9 Morris et al. (1997) argue that the steep increase in fines if a repeat violation is found creates an incentive for firms to under-report in the first instance. Following the same argument it could be suggested that the rarity of unannounced inspections reduces the incentive to under-report. However, whether firms' behaviour conforms to economic models in this way, or whether other considerations apply too, is a matter of speculation not fact.

The REI and Chinoin

We have already touched on some of the ways that the REI impinges on Chinoin. We now present a general picture of the REI, before discussing its relation with the firm.

We interviewed four staff at the Central Danube Environmental Inspectorate which is responsible for the Nagytétény area. The Central Danube area includes Budapest and contains 450,000 registered companies. A common concern among the interviewees was the understaffing of the REI relative to its functions. The REI deals with 20,000 cases per year, and these include both applications to build new plant, and to dismantle old plant.

The office is divided into sections (water quality, environmental geology, hydrology, air pollution, environmental technology, etc.), each of which has around six professional staff, and deals with 400–500 cases per month. One staff member said he had prepared 664 official opinions in the previous six months and that at any one time he had 150–250 cases pending. He explained his approach to prioritization:

> The truth is that if someone keeps phoning in every day, I have to do theirs first. I sometimes suggest to the clients to do so. If it's very urgent they should phone several times. (H 39)

The shortage of skills is at the technical level. An interviewee said the office would need 150 people to deal with the companies it was responsible for, instead of less than half of that. At the time of the interviews in 1997, a new law was due to come into force (in July) which fines the REI if it fails to respond within six months to requests for opinions on planned investments. The interviewees could not see how they could meet this requirement:

> There would be no point in punishing the inspectors because we work more than eight hours a day anyway. What else could we do ... The higher authorities must know about our situation. (H 36)

Turning to the REI's practices, their policy towards inspections was described as follows:

> We go out together when the inspection is complex. These are bigger inspections. We do this in the case of bigger polluters, so that we don't have to go out separately, we go out together to check the air, waste, noise and water. It makes them (the firm) quite busy. Therefore we usually tell them in advance to get their permission ready, we tell them what we're interested in etc. And then we investigate everything. (H 39)

---

10 After the research period, Chinoin was involved in a major pollution incident. In May 1998 an insecticide spill at the firm led to pollution in the Danube and dead fish at a fish farm. The company promised to build an emergency retention pool and expected a very large fine.

Another activity of the REI is to inspect firms which do not have connections to the sewerage system since the REI is responsible for the leakage of effluents into the soil. Firms are supposed to show receipts to prove that the sewage has been emptied. However firms pay less to have sewage removed if no receipt is given. There is therefore a mutual interest between firms and sewage collection operators in avoiding using receipts. The result is that the REI has no way of checking that firms' sewage has been properly removed. 'It's impossible to check things then. We give out several thousands of such permissions a year which (are) impossible to check'. (H 39)

Another interviewee described how the REI gives permissions: 'We should visit places but we hardly have time for that. Therefore we only look at the plans. But we can't do our work well without looking at the place.' (H 36)

Thus the effect of the understaffing of the REI is apparent in their lack of ability to carry out inspections.

Turning to relations between the REI and Chinoin, it was clear that the REI did not view Chinoin as the major polluter in the area. Metallochemia occupied this status. However there was a contrast between the view of the most senior of the interviewees and the others. According to the former 'We don't have any particular problems with Chinoin. There are small matters, but I know things are all right there.' (H 20) The other three staff members however referred to two issues: effluents, and the storage of fuel oil.

The effluent question has already been referred to. Chinoin allowed its effluent to go through the city drains, which are the responsibility of the Drainage Authority, into the Danube, for which the REI is responsible.

Three issues were identified by REI staff:

1. that the effluent was not treated before leaving the plant;
2. that it did not go into the central part of the Danube but into a lake which only slowly emptied into the Danube and so was not dispersed quickly;[11] and
3. that the firm took advantage of differences in the levels of fines between the REI and the Drainage Authority.

An interviewee noted that:

This is a very convenient situation as far as Chinoin is concerned because the fines for letting its sewage into the drainage system are much lower than for letting [it] direct into the fresh water. They would be charged much more for that. Therefore it was worthwhile for [Chinoin] to build a 20 metre long drain pipe. But through this the sewage gets into

---

11 This lake gave off strong smells which irritated local residents. However, the attempt to get rid of this lake by filling it in with building rubble had given rise to further conflict over who had jurisdiction to authorize this tipping (and receive a payment for it). The Waterworks Directorate who owned the lake gave the permission but the building works authority contested this since it is responsible for issuing (and charging for) permits for constructions above one metre high, which it claimed applied to the building rubble.

the fresh water nevertheless. (H 39)

The reason for this is that according to the division of labour between authorities, the Drainage Authority fines Chinoin for polluting its sewer, and the REI fines the Drainage Authority for allowing the sewer to pollute the fresh water.

The same interviewee noted that Chinoin had been promising to build a sewage treatment plant for 15 years but had benefited from the provision for 'progressive exemption'. This applies if a firm has plans to resolve a problem or is making technical modifications to improve the quality of the effluent. It explains why having good intentions has an economic value.

The other issue associated with Chinoin was its containers for storing chemicals and fuel oil. These were of different ages and conditions 'and are only partly equipped with some kind of technical protection.' (H 36) They required REI permission to ensure they were safe and that there was no leakage into the soil. The REI gave this permission provided the firm set up a monitoring system. (According to an REI official, in fact they had a partial system but 'they didn't use it... as often as we would like them to. We had no knowledge of them taking regular samples from the water and examining it'. (H 36))

Lastly one REI interviewee reported on the REI's practice regarding fines:

> because I work with many other companies as well I can see that they [Chinoin] try to follow these rules [ISO 14000] ... At the same time we also know that they have a problem which they try to solve from inside. Because if the authorities [the REI] learn about it, they'll levy fines. Therefore I think that we should make a distinction between the facts that, on the one hand, they [Chinoin] do try to fulfill the highest standards, but on the other hand they don't want to involve the authorities when they have a smaller problem, especially if they can solve it themselves. But we don't always levy fines. If they can solve the problem immediately or start to do something about it, then we don't levy fines. It's not at all sure that all the cases reach us as an official case. On many occasions we only hear about them and if we see that there is an attempt to remedy the situation then we don't make it into a case.' (H 37)

This again makes clear the discretion which the REI applies in dealing with firms. Also when fines are applied there is scope for variation according to circumstances: from 10% to 150% of the basic fine which is applicable. (Compare Chapter 3, where a ratio of 50% to 500% was quoted, a 1:10 range instead of 1:15.)

Overall then the picture is of the REI as endowed with extensive responsibilities but subject to understaffing and penalties for failing to meet deadlines for decisions. The effect is that it concentrates on processing applications for new plant as opposed to regular inspections of existing plant. It is unable to carry out inspections in more than a minute proportion of applications to install new plant, and where there is an inspection of an existing plant it is likely to be announced in advance. The REI is not aware of all breaches of level. Where it is aware it can vary the levels of permitted pollution according to the circumstances, and in relation to fines it has the option to exempt a firm from a fine or ask for the imposition of a lower fine where the firm is making efforts to improve the situation. All of these practices can be seen in its dealings with Chinoin. These are exactly the types of negotiation between regulator and regulated referred to in Chapter 2. As a result while on the one hand Chinoin is not perceived as a serious polluter on a par with Metallochemia, its failure to build a waste water treatment plant over decades of operation shows the lack of teeth of the previous and current regulatory system.

Conclusion

Nagytétény is the locality among the four chosen where pollution has given rise to the most serious and long-term conflict. The Green Future environmental group seized upon pollution as an issue and succeeded in gaining national attention for it. This led to a government-funded study of the problem and then to a legal case between council and government which remains unresolved. On the face of it in such a situation one might expect the local council to be strongly motivated to develop strong economic and environmental policies to reduce the suburb's dependence on polluting industry and to improve the environment.

In fact the opposite has happened. The council had not built industrial estates or tried to use economic incentives to attract new firms, and its efforts in the environmental direction have not left the paper stage. What seems to have happened is that the council has been overwhelmed by the scale of environmental problems in the area and its failure to achieve a satisfactory outcome in its legal case. It has also found itself in conflict with the REI. The REI is pressing for a compromise but the council and Green Future are opposed to this. The result is that there is a stalemate which has had a debilitating effect on policy making. This is a clear example of a legacy effect.

As a result, in terms of environmental policy Nagytétény occupies an intermediate position between localities with a dynamic local industrial policy, a strong environmental movement, and the power to deny access to polluting firms (as in Székesfehérvár) and localities with a weak labour market situation (for example due to a dominant employer, or lack of attractiveness for industrial location) and no environmental movement such as Dunaújváros (which is discussed in the next chapter).

Our study of Chinoin showed that it was accustomed to paying fines in respect of air pollution and effluent pollution. The emergence of a firm such as Chinoin with a reputation as a regular payer of fines is symptomatic of the weakness of local economic and environmental policy in Nagytétény. It is a district which lacks a dynamic industrial policy and is thus more dependent on existing firms. It cannot afford to antagonise them too much.

There had been a long understood need for a purification plant at Chinoin for the effluent to pass through. The fact that this had been planned for many years had allowed the company to pay lower fines. The REI noted that by emptying effluent into drains rather than the river directly the company had kept its fines down. However the plan for a purification plant had never been realized, thereby perpetuating the level of pollution in the area. There was no evidence of pressure within the Sanofi group to make this investment (of the sort we saw in Alcoa in Székesfehérvár). Nor was there demand-led pressure as we saw at Rába in Győr. The often suggested argument that foreign firms invest in Eastern Europe and third world countries to take advantage of lower environmental standards seems more applicable to Chinoin than to Alcoa.

Lastly, we have seen that the Mid-Danube REI is in a weak position due to its lack of resources and is unable to carry out more than occasional unannounced inspections. The already small fines are often reduced because of the economic situation of the firm concerned and the legal provision that firms with plans to improve their effluent standards are entitled to pay reduced fines.

6 Dunaújváros: the Legacy Effects of Being a Steel Town

Location, history and economic situation

Dunaújváros is located on the Danube 70km south of Budapest. Like the other three towns it is in the western half of Hungary which is more favoured from the point of view of foreign investment. Within the western half however it is somewhat less favoured than the other three localities. This is partly because it is not on the major highway to Austria (and Germany), and partly because it is not on a through road in an east-west direction. It lies on the road south from Budapest to the provincial city of Pecs and then to the Slovenian border. Strangely, however, there is no bridge over the Danube within the town and traffic going in an east-west direction has to go 30km south to cross the Danube, or take a ferry. Thus on a national scale of attractiveness to investment Dunaújváros is in a better position than places in the east of Hungary but within the west of the country it occupies a somewhat worse position than the other localities in the study. However, more important than its geographical situation is its economic structure.

The town was created in 1949 as a 'socialist new town' centred around a new steelworks. Its present name means Danube New Town in contrast to its original name Sztalinvaros which was changed in 1961 reflecting the political reassessment of Stalin.

Dunaújváros was originally planned to grow to 20,000, but by the 1980s had grown to 60,000. There has since been some out-movement to the surrounding area by people able to afford to build houses and also out-migration further afield and today it has a population of 57,000. There are 32,000 employees in the town of whom 22,000 live in the city and 10,000 commute in from outside. The Dunaferr steelworks is by far the largest employer, with 17,000 employees, over half of the total for the town. All other employers have under 1000 employees. They include a paper-mill (600 employees), Ferrobeton (reinforced concrete products), Momert (clocks) (200 employees), Red October (menswear), Junior shoe factory, MAV (railways), Dunaqatherm, a bread factory, and an agricultural cooperative (150 employees).

The local council and its economic and environmental policies

In 1990 the first multiparty local elections were held and from then until 1994 a Free Democrat–Young Democrat coalition ran the town, with a Free Democrat mayor. From 1994–98 a Socialist council was in power with the same mayor (this time directly elected). This shift towards the Socialist party parallels the national trend in the 1994 general elections.

Local economic policy

There are a number of long term plans with the potential to affect the economic situation of Dunaújváros. The first two are part of national plans. There is a national plan for a bridge across the Danube in the town. This bridge would also serve as a link in a new motorway allowing east–west traffic to by-pass Budapest. At the moment the plan is on the drawing board. The intention is that the bridge would be located to the south of the town. The present pattern of industry is that the older and heavier industry is to the south and the newer and higher-tech industry is to the north. By siting the bridge in the south, the north would be sheltered from the traffic generated by the southern industrial area.

A second plan is part of an international project to link the Rhine and Danube by a canal. This plan would involve building a port on the Danube which would be one of five ports in its Hungarian section. Originally the plan was for the port to be built on the site of Dunaferr wharfing facilities to the north of the town. But this would have threatened the adjacent recreational area and would have increased lorry traffic though residential areas. This port would serve the rapidly growing nearby town of Székesfehérvár as well as Dunaújváros itself.

At the town level the council's intention is to attract medium size firms to the town but to accept that the steelworks will always be there. This policy is one of economic diversification which would reduce the dominance of Dunaferr within the city. The council also expects Dunaferr to expand by making more processed products, but acknowledges that it has no influence over this.

To encourage investment, the council offers two main types of incentive to businesses. For large firms, with a turnover of 500 million ft (£2 million), a reduced local company tax rate of 6% is levied if they support causes which the local government approves, for example, in the spheres of sport, culture, or social welfare. In the case of small businesses (of up to 2 million ft turnover – £8,000) the council offers relief from local taxes (for example, 0% instead of 30–40% for three years). The council does not however provide free sites. Also, since 1996, the council has arranged with a major bank that firms it recommends should be eligible for loans at preferential rates of interest, though this does not guarantee that they will in fact obtain loans.[1]

Other council ideas for development include tourism (to attract those interested in socialist new towns) and speed-boating, but the lack of hotels is said to be an obstacle. A proposed huge food market would be impossible 'before we clean up the environment' according to a council office-holder. The council also intends to improve the southern zone and to make sure Dunaferr has the land it needs. According to a council office-holder (who is also a Dunaferr manager) the priority is to move industry from the centre of the city to a new industrial zone in the outskirts, and convert the land thus freed to residential and park use. An obstacle to this is that the city owns little peripheral land. The exception is the site of a former Soviet military base where it is planned to create an 'Inno(vation) Park' through cooperation between the council, the polytechnic and Dunaferr. In practice little is happening beyond the Inno Park.[2]

Thus the town council wants to encourage in-migration and new investment. Despite this there is no clear development plan to provide guidance in responding to enquiries. The pre-1990 plan is out of date and, for example, contains an area for council housing which is no longer being built. And nothing was achieved in the 1990–94 period. A potential legacy effect should be noted here. Before 1990 councils had no control over land. State enterprises used land as they chose and councils rubber-stamped their decisions. This means that councils today lack a pro-active tradition of visualizing a future town then taking the measures needed to achieve it.[3] What this implies for legacy arguments will be discussed later in the book. An opposition councillor described the council as riven by conflicts and unable to set priorities: 'the mayor drifts along with the events.' (E 7)

Some new investment has come to the city but nothing like the amount in Székesfehérvár. There has been a small amount of foreign investment, for example investment in one or two units of Dunaferr. Most companies are privatized and have shrunk their workforces. Dunaferr is exceptional in not having been privatized.

Local environmental policies

Turning to council policies affecting the environment, the main perceived environmental problems are air pollution, traffic congestion and water pollution caused by untreated household and industrial sewage. (Only the paper-mill in the town has its own treatment plant.) An incinerator for dangerous waste has been built but is itself causing some problems. There are also parking problems for residents of apartment buildings.

Nevertheless a number of decisions with impacts on the environment have been taken by the local council. The most significant one is to invest in a biological sewage filtering system – to be financed by the town, the state and EU (under the PHARE scheme for pre-accession countries). Dunaújváros was subsequently one of three

---

1 However, since it is difficult to prove that a preferential rate of interest has been applied (since this assumes that a standard rate existed rather than a risk-dependent rate) this may be little more than a symbolic measure.
2 This has been constructed. It is 25ha in size and is 67% owned by the council and 23% by Dunaferr.
3 Székesfehérvár council, as discussed in Chapter 3, was unusual in its pre-1990 activism.

cities (Budapest and Székesfehérvár being the others) which benefited from a $79m loan coordinated by the World Bank to improve the municipal sewerage system between 2000 and 2006. This loan is financed 28% by the World Bank, 20% by the EU (PHARE), 20% by the government and 32% by water and sewerage companies, and will provide for new sewerage and treatment works, and technical and managerial assistance to help reach new water standards.

A ban on lorries above 10 tons in the central area has been introduced with great success and tree-planting has been undertaken within the town.

There has been no attempt to impose to impose environmental conditions on firms wanting to set up in the town.

The relationship between Dunaferr and the local council

We now explore the relationship between the local government and Dunaferr, and ask how far the council can influence the practices of Dunaferr and how far Dunaferr can influence the policies of the council just described. Power is a notoriously difficult concept to investigate: there are many ways of conceiving it, and a corresponding number of ways of measuring it (Lukes, 1974).

If power is conceived as the ability of a group to secure its interest in an overt conflict then conflicts can be studied to see who (if anyone) wins. This however requires that the interests of the groups are defined at the outset to provide a point of comparison. This in turn raises the question of whether interests can be measured by studying explicit statements of position or whether explicit statements conceal a group's interests more or less. An alternative, which avoids the possibility of interests being implicit is for the analyst to impute them. This is obviously risky and can simply lead to the analyst's preconceptions being introduced without check.

Alternatively power may be seen as more elusive as when it is conceived as the ability to keep an issue out of the public arena, or the power to exert behind the scenes influence. In this case no public debate happens so one cannot look for 'who wins'. The problem is of course that empirical evidence on such behind the scenes processes is intrinsically harder to find. There is therefore a tendency to impute an interest to a group and say that if this interest is secured this demonstrates the power of the group even if no conflict has occurred. Again this is open to the danger that imputed interests are unverifiable.

The alternatives of imputing interests and accepting statements of interests at face value are both unsatisfactory. When a group has reasons for concealing its interests there is every reason to treat its stated interests with caution. So some imputation is unavoidable. If imputations of interest are based on comparable cases we may place more confidence in them, but as can be seen power can never be assessed purely on empirical grounds because different conceptions of power lead to different ideas about what empirical evidence is relevant and what weight should be given to it.

Another way of looking at power is to look at the concepts and language of debate on the grounds that the way we think itself contains and perpetuates relations of power. This is a point well made by feminist writers for example. In this case statements of interest or imputed interests would be less relevant.

A cross-cutting issue concerns whether power should be seen as something which varies by issue so that groups which are powerful in one sphere are not powerful in another, or whether one group, or elite, is powerful in all spheres. This is the famous debate between pluralist and elitist pictures of the distribution of power (Judge et al., 1995). It has obvious implications for the choice about how power is to be studied.

If this study was primarily focused on power we would have developed an elaborate methodology. In practice the evidence regarding the relative power of Dunaújváros council and Dunaferr is varied though it reflects my preference for an interest-based approach to power.

We shall start by examining the structural linkages between the council and Dunaferr through personnel, contacts, employment and finance and then go on to examine the mutual influence between Dunaferr's influence and the council.

Personnel The origin of personnel linkages is as follows. According to one interviewee, before 1990, Dunaferr treated the town as 'nothing but a large housing estate' created for the firm. But with the change of council control in 1990 Dunaferr's attitude changed and it realized that it needed to ensure that its employees were well represented on the council. In the 1990-94 period there was a weaker representation of Dunaferr employees, which worried the company and led it to ensure better 'representation' from 1994. At the time of the research seven of the 28 councillors are Dunaferr employees and some of these are members of the council environmental committee. The two Deputy Mayors are both managers at Dunaferr as is the president of the financial committee. A Dunaferr manager stated that 'we [Dunaferr] represent ourselves in the local government via the seven councillors who work for Dunaferr.' (E 2) These councillors were not the only channel of company influence since councillors who do not themselves work at Dunaferr are likely to have indirect connections with the company through spouses, relatives and friends.

Contact There are regular informal meetings between the Mayor and President of Dunaferr arranged as and when necessary, and between senior staff of the council and Dunaferr. For example the City Notary and the Financial Director of Dunaferr met to discuss local taxes. Other contacts are in connection with cultural, sports, social policy, labour market and economic issues.[4] The council has recently completed a reorganization plan for the steelworks according to a manager (E 7). This involved the chief architect and the Dunaferr director of privatization.

Employment In terms of employment the overwhelming dominance of the company as a local employer gives it huge leverage. In addition a lot of other jobs in the city are

---

4 The importance of Dunaferr sports teams in the town can be seen by entering 'Dunaferr' into a web search engine!

indirectly dependent on the existence of Dunaferr. However this would change were there to be a significant decline in Dunaferr's economic and labour market position.

Finance We consider in turn potential evidence of council influence over Dunaferr and then of Dunaferr influence over the council.

1. On the face of it the fact that the council owns 15% of Dunaferr suggests that it has influence over it. But this was not considered to be the case by a senior office-holder. Another interviewee pointed out that Dunaferr does not pay a dividend. In practice the ownership pattern of the company is complex and local government is a passive shareholder.
2. On the other hand there are several indicators of Dunaferr influence over the council.

Several interviewees claimed that the local government 'lives from' the local taxes Dunaferr pays. About one quarter of the city's income comes from local taxes and of these 90% are paid by Dunaferr. Likewise the company contributes directly to the hospital, cultural events, sport and education, for example by sponsorship, contacts, providing equipment, and voluntary labour. This is not entirely altruistic since as mentioned earlier such support entitles the company to pay a lower rate of local company tax. The company also has leverage over the council because it supplies hot water to the town and if threatened with higher taxes can retaliate by threatening to raise hot water charges (or less plausibly by cutting the hot water supply).

If these structural linkages exist between Dunaújváros council and Dunaferr what evidence is there that the firm influences the council or vice versa?

A first possible domain of influence is council local economic development policy. From the point of view of Dunaferr, the idea of economic diversification is one which could potentially threaten its dominant position in the local labour market and in local society and politics. New employers could introduce competition in terms of wages and alternative employment for skilled labour. From what was said earlier it is clear that compared with Székesfehérvár (see Chapter 3) the council is not very dynamic in terms of its planning for the future of the town. The council has no development plan and the Inno Park is its main effort in this sphere. The fact that its achievements in attracting investment are modest is partly because of the relatively low level of demand from investors to locate in the town but must also be attributed to the council's own lack of enterprise. As far as Dunaferr is concerned this means that its own position in the town is not jeopardised. Moreover Dunaferr is closely involved in the main industrial development policy being implemented at present, the Inno Park. Also the relief from local company taxes for large firms is one from which Dunaferr gains substantially. Thus, so far, there is little to suggest that the council was undertaking policy which worked against the interests of Dunaferr.

It would be reasonable to conclude that this situation is the result of Dunaferr's dominance over the council, but conclusive evidence would require more research. All we can say is that the fact that Dunaferr part owns the Inno Park means that it has a stake in the main form of economic development in which it is not involved directly and which has the potential to create a rival demand for labour. This involvement is consistent with the structural links between the council and Dunaferr outlined above.[5]

A second issue of concern to Dunaferr is the level of local taxes. In 1996 the City Notary proposed to raise the level of the corporate tax, but this was voted down by the council. According to a council office-holder 'Everybody was convinced that this was because there are so many people representing Dunaferr interests directly or indirectly among the councillors'. (E 8)

More generally according to one interviewee the dominance of Dunaferr employees among councillors means that 'the interests of the steelworks prevail.' (E 7) A qualification of this was offered by one interviewee who suggested that in the 1990–94 period when Dunaferr's ownership structure was unresolved this weakened the position of Dunaferr vis à vis the town. He considered that once this was resolved the firm was in a stronger position. Further evidence of Dunaferr's influence is that the town has never initiated any action against the company on environmental issues and is generally regarded as lacking expertise as well as power.

In sum the relation between the local government and Dunaferr is a very unequal one.

The picture that emerges about the relation between company and council in connection with policy is strongly favourable to Dunaferr. The council has no powers to regulate pollution caused by Dunaferr and as we shall see later the REI is rather lax about implementing standards there. On the other hand the council's own policies regarding the development of the town, although favouring diversification, are in practice constrained by the limited interest from investors. This situation could change if the Danube bridge is built and the town becomes a key point on a cross-Hungary motorway. This scenario may be more threatening to Dunaferr than anything the town can do on its own. However there is equal evidence that the council is not very determined to act against Dunaferr. The structural strength of Dunaferr in relation to the council and its involvement in the Inno Park make clear that it possesses considerable resources which could be deployed in the unlikely event of the council adopting policies which worked against its interests.

The influence of the public on local environmental policy

Lastly we consider the question of public influence in getting environmental issues onto the political agenda. We indicated earlier that two-thirds of local employees are resident in Dunaújváros. On this basis one might expect quite a large degree of concern among people about their environment.

Analysts of urban politics in the west argue that the distribution of government functions between levels of government, ministries, and agencies of different kinds

---

[5] It could be argued that the most obvious measure of Dunaferr influence would be for a refusal to allow diversification in the town. But this is so obviously a short-sighted measure that its absence cannot really be used to deny that Dunaferr has influence.

has a shaping effect on the expression of political opposition (Friedland et al., 1977). Put simply, public opposition will only be directed at bodies with the power to take action on an issue. The implication of the distribution of environmental responsibilities in Hungary between ministries and local government is that local government is a less useful target for public opposition than if local government was solely responsible for issues generating discontent. In fact this 'rational' model of how protest is directed is not entirely valid. Protests against local government about unemployment in the UK have taken place despite it not being responsible for national economic policy and only able to make a limited impact through local economic development policy. Hence the fact that Dunaújváros town council is only responsible for a few aspects of the environment does not preclude it from being the target of environmental protest. All one can say is that the fragmentation of environmental responsibilities has a partial shielding effect.

Perhaps the most significant fact is that Dunaújváros is not the site of an active environmental movement. The only relevant citizen organization is the City Improvement Association. This has two representatives on the council environmental committee and receives financial support and free premises from the council. It is regarded by a Public Health Department official as representing the public and by a council ofice-holder as 'very positive'. With this sponsorship it is unlikely to act as a vehicle for public feelings about the environment. There are also a few very small environmental groups in particular parts of the town. For example one formed in Kadar Valley in 1997. But their main concern is with self-help efforts to bring about environmental improvements.

Turning to less organized forms of expression of public opinion, at neither the 1990 nor the 1994 elections were environmental issues significant. They were largely fought on national issues. According to one official:

> Dunaújváros, because it was a newly built town, and because of the politics of the past 20 years, is a very automated town. Therefore not only the environment but many other political problems are not articulated, don't come to the surface, are not discussed and represented. The local residents don't have civil contacts. Everybody is trying to live their own lives in their two room flats. Or if they have a garden [or allotment] they try to escape there. (E 7)

He also suggested that although residents are aware that environmental problems, such as dust, smells and air pollution, exist, they don't express their views in political forums, because they feel the problem is too big to deal with.

A similar view was expressed by a Dunaferr manager, who said that:

> The population here is very understanding of the environmental situation. They know that this is an industrial city. They are mostly workers, so they tolerate the problems more than in an agricultural place. (E 2)

Likewise a colleague said that:

as far as the workers are concerned there is no pressure from there whatsoever. The workers are only interested in their pay packet. Their view is 'to survive somehow'. Workers are still preoccupied with raising their living standards short term, rather than improving their quality of life long-term. (E 11)

An exception to this picture of a quiescent public is the ban on heavy lorries in the centre of the town. This went against Dunaferr's interests since it meant that the firm's lorries had to take much longer routes. This is a counter-example to the general picture of council weakness vis à vis Dunaferr. The measure was only passed after what were described by one official as 'serious fights' – presumably verbal not physical. This is an interesting case and as suggested earlier implies that public opinion on environmental issues, even if it is not expressed in active environmental groups, can have some influence on policy. Perhaps the fact that the measure was not explicitly against Dunaferr but could be presented as a measure in the 'general interest' helped it to be passed. This may be a sign of future trends and if the workforce of Dunaferr declines in size[6] the firm's influence over policy is likely to be weakened.

However it seems likely that as the dominance of Dunaferr wanes in the local economy, and as initiatives such as the ban on heavy lorries in the town centre are seen to work environmental demands will increase.

We now examine Dunaferr itself.

Dunaferr and its environmental practices

Dunaferr is a small firm by international steel industry standards. It is the thirtieth largest steelworks in the world producing 1.4 million tons per year compared with 10–12 million in the largest firms. It is inefficient in its energy consumption. It produces raw iron, steel, cold sheet metal and products such as radiators, spiral tubes and steel frames, and over time has switched to making more steel products.

The 'external' owners of Dunaferr are the State Property Agency (65%), Ministry of Finance (20–25%), and Dunaújváros council (10–15%). However a concept of 'internal' ownership has also been introduced. The company has been broken up into 40 or so units which are owned by each other, as well as the three external owners. The biggest of these is the steelworks which employs 3000. The firm has not been privatized. As Stark (1997) argues, this type of reorganization is essentially defensive and is a means of preserving the management's power of decision. The company has strong links to central ministries and these are crucial in the running of the company. In many ways this represents a continuity with the state socialist period when state enterprises were not subject to any financial discipline due to their leverage with state ministries: they were simply too important to the state for it to jeopardise their functioning. Dunaferr is also one of the 'Dirty 13' companies which the state has

---

6   As it has in fact done since 1998.

continued to support financially. Smaller steelworks within Hungary have not been supported and are struggling to survive.

Dunaferr has an impact on the environment in many ways. The company's main reference group is central ministries. As a non-privatized company it is still part of the old culture in which state subsidies could be obtained through maintaining ties with the right cliques at ministerial level. It is perhaps interesting that this has continued even after 1990. This reflects the somewhat cautious initial progress on privatization in Hungary, the fear of losing control of key industrial plants to foreign interests, and the privileged position of the 'Dirty 13' state enterprises. The company plays a leading part in the national federation of steelworks, a representative and lobbying body. Senior managers also make contact with politicians directly.

Dunaferr's environmental practices can be assessed by examining the hierarchical position of the main environmental manager, the opinions of managers, the level of investment in less polluting equipment and the level of environmental fines. In order to preserve interviewee anonymity while giving some idea of the interviewee's hierarchical position we will use the terms M1 to M4 to refer to the levels of management involved (M1 being at the top, M4 at the bottom).[7]

It was an M4 manager at the Dunaferr steelworks, the largest of the divisions of the restructured firm, who suggested that the priority the company gave to environmental issues was indicated by the low hierarchical position of the Environmental Manager in the central management structure. Without comparative knowledge of similar sized steel works it is hard to judge this comment.

As far as managers' opinions are concerned, there was a sharp contrast between the more optimistic views of the M3 manager interviewed and the more pessimistic views of the M4 manager.

The environmental role of the M3 manager is to find external financial resources (for example, from PHARE, and the Environmental Fund!), to be aware of legal requirements, to keep abreast of international practice, and to keep in touch with the REI. But his role extends well beyond environmental matters since it covers the technical side of all new investment.

According to the M3 manager the firm takes a long term view in its investment decisions:

> We make very careful calculations about how much the environmental damage and investment and all aspects cost. We are fully aware and clear about these. But we think long term. The regulations are becoming stricter, the tolerance level of the local population will decrease and we want to change our technology to the better. (E 2)

---

[7] The company is not primarily accountable to the council as far as its environmental impact is concerned but to the REI. The council would like Dunaferr to inform it about pollution levels but it lacks the power to require this. The M4 manager at Dunaferr in fact has minimal contact with the council, though out of courtesy he sends a copy of their plans for pollution reduction.

The firm has already switched from coal to gas and oil for heating which reduced the amount of dust released by 20,000 tons per year. Its priorities are reducing water and air pollution and it has plans for four major investments in the metal melting works, in the cokery, in insulation and in oil filtering of effluent. These will cost 4 billion ft. This is all in the future and a loan is being sought from a Danish partner. The company monitors its employees' health but interviewees said the results were kept secret.

According to the M3 manager the REI was 'very harsh with us'. The REI was said to make unannounced visits to do measurements of air, soil, and water pollution, and noise levels and to leave part of the samples for the Company to analyse. If it finds an infringement it asks for immediate action, failing which, it imposes a fine. The company also does its own measurements. This manager says that twice daily measurements are made, but that none are made at night or at weekends, which is 'a problem'. These measurements cost the company 30 million ft per year (£120,000), very significantly above the figures for Chinoin and Rába mentioned earlier. Measurements are analysed by Dunaferr and also sent to the Ministry of the Environment, the REI and the Chamber of the Steel Industry (which sends them to the Ministry of Industry.) The latter is interesting since it shows how a large firm is able to make use of contacts with government in its interest. The role of the REI in relation to Dunaferr is discussed further below.

The M3 manager said there were 40 staff 'in charge of the environment' at Dunaferr and two or more in each unit. Responsibility for some activities is centralized (for example, the planning of investment projects, and responsibility for water pollution throughout the site) and for others decentralized (for example, each unit is responsible for measurements, and the prevention of accidents). He acknowledged the existence of some weaknesses in accountability: all employees are responsible, but middle managers are not accountable for actions by their subordinates.

Turning to the opinion of the M4 manager, a less optimistic picture of the company's environmental practices emerges. His view regarding Dunaferr's environmental practices is that: 'they do whatever they must, but that is all.' (E 11) At best they consider environmental aspects of new investments; at worst they do the minimum because environmental investment is seen as unproductive. In his view:

> the company is worried about its image! So they keep using PR activities for creating an environmentally concerned picture of the firm. They keep talking abut how much less in fines we have to pay now, how much less air pollution we cause, how many beautiful plans we have got for improving the environment, but actually doing anything is a bit slower. (E 11)

Some new investments were said to have led to even more pollution than before. On the other hand one favourable factor is that the company is shifting from steel production to making processed products which are less polluting. Future possible investments such as replacing the cokery, main melting and metal shrinking works with a single works would reduce pollution but would need 600 workers in place of 2400.

In relation to regulatory authorities, the M4 manager states that:

> on the whole we do observe the law and regulations, but some of them we do ignore, because the authorities do not force us to observe them. They do not know what we do or do not do. They do not often come to check things. In the last three years we have not even had any serious written assessment of the situation within the company. Usually there is a very cosy relationship between us and those from the authorities who are supposed to come and check up on us, so things are pretty relaxed here. (E 11)

The REI is located in Székesfehérvár and 'does not bother us very often' according to this manager.

> We turn to them because we want to solve certain problems. So they see that we take the initiative and try very hard and that seems to satisfy them. It is not in the Inspectorate's interest to fine us all the time, as they would not get any money directly from these fines. And they are fully aware that Dunaferr is well equipped with good lawyers! So they do not seek conflicts with us! At the same time it is in the interest of the REI to make sure that no articles appear in the paper about left-over waste or polluted water which causes a deterioration compared with our present situation. So they keep things under control but do not like stirring things up too radically. (E 11)

Calculative reasoning characterises the company's approach. This view is supported by evidence about the company's record in terms of pollution which is far from good. It has been fined for various types of pollution. The cokery produces 1300 tons of particles per year. There is excessive CO_2 emission. Iron and oil contaminate the water. On the other hand new equipment introduced in the metal shrinking works in 1994 led to a reduction of metal particle pollution in the air from 15,000 tons per year to 4,000, which is below the permitted level, but is 'still bad'. There is also a problem of asbestos waste which they would like to burn because they consider that at 2150°C (the cokery temperature) it will be well above the level at which it ceases to be dangerous (900°C). The REI and local public health service, however, disagree.

In 1992 Dunaferr was fined 80 million ft (£300,000) but got this reduced by splitting the measurements into separate items. In 1995 they paid 6.2 million ft (£25,000) and in 1996 12 million ft. (£50,000) for air pollution and in 1995 2 million ft for water pollution (£8,000). By comparison their profit in 1996 was 4 billion ft (£16 million). The M3 manager pointed out that whereas the new investment will cost 4 billion ft the fines are below 100,000 ft, but nevertheless it was planning to go ahead with these investments, presumably because of their other advantages.

There is clearly a sharp difference of opinion between the M3 and M4 managers, with one stressing the progress made and the toughness of the regulatory process, while the other stresses the lack of progress and the weakness of the regulatory process. Clearly the shift to steel products, and away from coal burning have had favourable effects on the environment. Equally clearly there is extensive pollution which the planned investment will only partially deal with (if it indeed goes ahead – which, as the Chinoin example in Chapter 4 shows, cannot be assumed). The real issue is the viability of the firm in the world market. It seems to be a small player in its industry which is unlikely to be profitable enough to pay for the major investments which are needed to keep up with the latest pollution reducing technology. It may abandon some of its products and concentrate in specialised products.

We now consider further the question of the impact of REI regulation on Dunaferr.

The REI and its relations with Dunaferr

Dunaújváros is covered by the Central Trans-Danubian Environmental Inspectorate which is also responsible for Székesfehérvár. The towns are 45km away from one another. Our interview with an official in this organization was rather mixed in quality.[8] To start with the official offered a rather formal description of the REI's responsibilities and gave an account of how the REI should work. Only later did some interesting comments emerge concerned the resourcing of the REI and its operations.[9] All the quotations which follow were from this official (E 27).

We were told that the division of labour between the REI and the council was satisfactory ('The responsibilities are divided. No change is necessary. I think this is fine.') The official said that the REI has no influence on the environmental committee of the council and that it had not had any conflicts with it or with the Ministry to which the REI reports.

As far as its relations with Dunaferr are concerned, 'We have a lot of contact with Dunaferr. There are no disputes. In fact they [relations] are very harmonious. This hasn't changed. Our relationship is just as harmonious now as before.' The flow of information regarding environmental matters is 'excellent, regular and formalised. For example Dunaferr works in a self-control [that is, self-reporting] system and works very well'. In answer to the question 'does Dunaferr have any influence on the environmental policy of the Inspectorate?' the answer was 'they don't have any influence or right to interfere, although Dunaferr is a very important company in the country as well'. Likewise the interviewee denied that Dunaferr had ever opposed the environmental policy of the REI. ('Such a thing has never happened. We have a very good relationship.')

---

8 The REI interviewees referred to in Chapter 3 and in the present chapter are therefore employees of the same organization. I have kept separate the two data sources for the time being. However, comparisons between them will be made in Chapter 7.
9 Our interviewer commented that the interview was shorter than planned, that the interviewee was doing other things at the same time. The interviewer commented that when she 'emphasized the international importance of the research, unfortunately it did not work. According to [the interviewee] this work is similar to spying, and reduces Hungary's chances of joining the EU.'

The same responses were made concerning other local companies. In answer to the question whether company ownership (Hungarian or mixed) or size made a difference to the amount of pollution the answer was that 'We can't distinguish between them. Like Dunaferr, the other companies also keep to the rules, there are no problems.'

The more informative responses by this official concerned the practical operation of the REI.

The official pointed out that the new (1995) law did not introduce any new sanctions: the old ones still apply. ('There should have been a few sanctions added, in areas where the environment is particularly suffering, but this wasn't made possible by the law. But of course this is not the aim of the law.')

Regarding the question of how the Hungarian environmental law compared with those in western Europe and other Eastern European countries the official said that:

> I think that Hungary used to have regulations – not environmental ... for example, regulations on water, and others, with which we can stand comparison. The problem in Hungary is not with the law but with the fact that we don't obey the law, and we don't enforce it.

Interestingly the official said that the REI had little time for activities such as 'prevention, education, media'.

Regarding its activities, the official said that once a year they inspect sewage effluent and calculate fines, but in the case of air pollution the data on which they work is self-reported, and they calculate any fines on the basis of such data. The official did not state directly that the REI did not inspect air pollution at Dunaferr but this is the most likely interpretation. If it did not, it means that the fines for air pollution levied on Dunaferr referred to earlier are based on self-reporting. This picture of infrequent inspections is consistent with the view reported by the Dunaferr M4 manager quoted in the previous section. It is also in line with the comment by Morris et al. (1997) that in general REIs carry out relatively few inspections due to the other pressures on them. However, it conflicts with their suggestion that REIs restrict inspections to the most likely potential polluters, since one would expect Dunaferr to fall into the latter category.

In answer to a question about the aims of fines and whether they were educational or punitive, the official's response was 'It's nothing like that, because the fines are very low. We are not for fines, but if one of us discovers something during inspection which requires fines, then we impose them'.

This led to the question of resourcing. The Central Trans-Danubian Environmental Inspectorate covers 13.6% of Hungary by area and has 108 employees of all kinds. 'This means that there are only about 36 people dealing with the problems.' We take this to mean that only 36 have professional qualifications.

In answer to the question 'How effective do you think your organization is?' the response was:

It could be more effective if there were more of us. It is our number which prevents us from being more effective, and ... the fact that the salaries in public administration are extremely low. As such it's not an attractive field.

The official added that the REI has to earn 'one twelfth of its budget' which it does by taking samples for companies. He also pointed out that it does not benefit from any of the fines it imposes since they go to the Central Environmental Fund.

The official said the main problems as perceived by the public in Dunauvaros were air pollution and sewage treatment.

We can combine this evidence with that in the previous section from Dunaferr managers who, as we saw, gave a varying emphasis to the severity of REI regulation. It appears that the regulatory process largely relies on self-monitoring which Dunaferr does which leads to environmental fines by the REI and that the REI lacks the resources to conduct more than occasional inspections of sewage effluent.

The obvious interpretation of this pattern is that it is attributable to the resourcing position of the REI, and the fact that any fines the REI imposes accrue to the Central Environmental Fund not to itself. However the evidence we presented in Chapter 3 based on interviews with other officials from the same REI carried out as part of the Székesfehérvár study gave a much more active picture of the inspection process and did not emphasize the shortage of resources. This is a striking difference and means we cannot accept the shortage of resources as the whole explanation for the pattern of REI activity observed in Dunaújváros. The question of whether the fact that the Central Trans-Danubian Environmental Inspectorate is located in Székesfehérvár, and that Dunaferr has a special status as one of the state-owned 'Dirty 13' have any relevance to the behaviour of the REI will be considered in Chapter 7.

Conclusion

Dunaújváros is in the unusual position of being a town dominated by a single enterprise but where that enterprise remains state-owned and retains a privileged position as one of the 'Dirty 13'. The dominance of Dunaferr has been shown in several ways: as local employer, as contributor of local taxes and services, and as participant in the planning of and as part owner of the 'Inno Park' industrial estate. It was involved in the work of the local council in numerous ways – both formal (for example its employees acting as elected members of the council) and informal (through direct dealings between top managers and mayor). This influence had not taken the form of resistance to any council policy to attract new industry which might rival Dunaferr as employer. Rather the firm had accepted the idea that a diversified economy was a good thing even if its close involvement meant that it remained very much a 'hands-on' participant.

Unlike the other three localities Dunaújváros lacked any environmental group. This meant that policy-making could be a more 'closed' affair with less conflict. It also meant that if environmental issues were raised at all it was by individuals. Hence the probability that environmental concerns would be given priority in council policy or in the practice of the REI was low. It was significant that whereas the council had an active local economic policy its efforts in the environmental field were almost non-existent. The town centre lorry ban was the sole example. The REI claimed only to make visits to inspect sewage and for other types of pollution relied on self-reported pollution by Dunaferr. The distance of the REI office from Dunaújváros (45km) was pointed out by one Dunaferr employee. Dunaferr paid the largest fines of any firms covered in this study yet even so the fines were too low to give it an incentive to introduce pollution-reducing investment. None of the stimuli mentioned by other firms as pressures to introduce more environmentally friendly equipment operated here, for example customer pressure (Rába), own management (Gardenia), or corporate policy (Alcoa). It seems that remaining state-owned and having undergone a defensive restructuring in which each unit is owned by others (but where the state is the main ultimate owner) minimises the likelihood of undertaking pollution-reducing investment.

Thus Dunaújváros can be seen as an example of the continuing legacy effects of having a dominant and state-owned employer. In many ways the relations between Dunaferr and council are unchanged (even if they experienced a hiccough in the early 1990s while Dunaferr reorganized itself). Dunaferr retains its 'natural' authority vis à vis the local council, and is highly involved in its workings. It tries to use its connections with the Ministry to counteract the fines imposed by the REI (even if it ends up paying relatively high fines). The cultural attitude among local people that the environmental situation cannot really be changed can also be traced back to the old regime. The lorry ban is a rare sign of changing expectations between residents and council.

7 A Comparative Analysis of Environmental Regulation in the Four Localities

The starting point of this book was the idea that there was a local dimension in environmental regulation. In other words we argued that what happened at local level could not be read off from national legislation but needed to be studied directly. While acknowledging that government had a large impact on the local level we chose to concentrate on four types of sub-national actor with potential direct effects at the local level: regional environmental inspectorates, local governments, firms, and the public (either via environmental groups or not).

In this chapter we make a comparative analysis of the data presented on the four localities in the previous chapters. We examine in turn: what is meant by comparative analysis, what measures we give the four localities on our dependent and explanatory variables, and the utility of the explanatory model set out in Chapter 2 in making sense of the observed patterns. In this way we shall seek to explain the variations in the levels of local environmental regulation in the four localities set out in Chapters 3 to 6.

Comparative analysis

We start by examining what is meant by comparative analysis and identify some of its strengths and weaknesses. It is often thought that comparative analysis is a straightforward concept. We hope to demonstrate that this is not so.

Comparative analysis needs to be distinguished from the juxtaposition of descriptions of a series of cases. While sequential presentations of descriptive data are undoubtedly informative about the cases concerned they are only comparative in the weak sense of making the reader aware of differences and similarities. They whet the appetite to know more. Comparative analysis also needs to be separated from the sense in which all analysis is comparative: all attempts to find causes involve comparing what happened with a mental image of what is likely to have happened in the absence of certain features (Smelser, 1976, pp. 160–2).

Two features define comparative analysis as understood here:

1. an interest in the explanatory question of why the observed similarities and differences between cases exist, and
2. reliance on the collection of data on two or more cases, ideally according to a common framework.[1]

It should be noted that comparative analysis is applicable to units of any scale from micro to macro. Here the locality focus leads to cross-locality comparison. It is only by convention that comparative analysis is often treated as synonymous with cross-national comparative analysis.

We explore the above two features in turn. The primary reason for comparative analysis is the explanatory interest of gaining a better understanding of the causal processes involved in the production of an event, feature or relationship. Typically it achieves this by introducing (or increasing) variation in the explanatory variable or variables. For example in Chapter 2 it was shown that environmental regulation took the form of negotiation between the regulatory agency and firms in the UK, but also in the US and China. In other words by studying environmental regulation[2] under varying socio-economic systems we were able to suggest that these systems were irrelevant to the nature of the regulatory process, that is, the latter was context-invariant. If only the UK had been studied we might have concluded that negotiation in regulatory relationships was a feature linked to some specific feature of the UK socio-economic system. In this case comparative analysis allows the elimination of a number of explanatory variables. In other cases comparative analysis may lead to the introduction of additional explanatory variables.

Comparative analysis may focus on the explanation of differences or the explanation of similarities or both. Tilly (1984) uses the terms 'variation-seeking' and 'universalizing' to refer to these objectives. This sounds like a straightforward contrast but is not. The reason is that what counts as a similarity or a difference depends not only on the observed values but also on the analyst and should therefore be regarded as a social construct rather than as an objective reality. For example if a study includes three cases which have values 15, 18, 21 on some variable, then one might be inclined to classify them as low, medium and high. If a subsequent study discovered two further cases with values 50 and 80, then one might be tempted to reclassify the 15, 18 and 21 as all 'low'. The decision about whether one has observed differences or similarities therefore depends on the scale of measurement used, and what assumptions are made about the actual distribution of values on the scale. Put

---

[1] Some writers have adopted more restrictive definitions but I see no reason to follow them. For example Prezworski and Teune (1970) argue that comparative analysis is only present when it is shown that a societal level feature has explanatory power. This makes the outcome of the analysis rather than the intention behind it the criterion of whether an analysis is comparative or not.
[2] We use the term in an approximate way. Clearly the regulatory agencies studied were not carefully matched. A more thorough study would need to pay attention to this. (NB this is a post-hoc comparison and should not be regarded as a serious comparative analysis.)

another way one can either emphasise the sameness of 15, 18 and 21 or their differentness. This is a matter of the analyst's perception. Research which starts from similarities on the other hand is always faced with differences of some type but involves a decision that the differences are insignificant and can be ignored. In some cases similarities may be 'created' by excluding data which do not fit and to attributing them to exceptional conditions. In both the last cases the analyst's decisions are guided by theoretical judgements which may or may not be justified. Thus the idea that comparative analysis deals either with similarities or differences is more complex than it seems, and any decision made is always open to future revision.

The second issue in comparative analysis is what units should be included. Przeworski and Teune (1970) distinguish two strategies for choosing the cases to be compared: the 'most different systems' and 'most similar systems' designs. In the first the logic is that a relationship which is invariant across highly diverse (for example societal) conditions is thereby shown to be valid irrespective of these conditions (as in the UK–US–China comparison just mentioned). The second design is based on the idea that it is preferable to compare similar societies (which are assumed to be more familiar to the researcher) to reduce the risk of uncontrolled variables 'intruding' into the relationship of interest.

It is at this point that the relevance of the earlier argument about similarity and difference is relevant. If one's aim is to explain a similarity in values of the dependent variable the mainstream procedure is to search for similarities in values of the explanatory variables. For example if two societies have similar environmental standards it must be because they have similarities in some other respect, for example membership of the EU, a similar level of national wealth. Conversely, if one's aim is to explain differences in dependent variables the procedure is to search for differences in explanatory variables. For example cross-national differences in environmental standards could be explained by differences in national income, on the assumption that the more wealthy a country the more likely environmental quality was to be given a high priority.

This procedure is the 'normal' one. However, as I have argued elsewhere it is not the only one and leads to the neglect of a number of significant alternatives. This is due to its denial of plural causation, the idea that on different occasions the 'same' phenomenon can be produced in different ways (Pickvance, C.G., 1986; 2001). This is a separate idea from that of multiple causation which refers to the number of explanatory variables.

The strength of comparative analysis as a research design is its ability to introduce additional explanatory variables, and to show that relations are more or less general than had been initially thought. Its weaknesses are that it requires the commensurabilty of concepts across cases (for example, terms like 'environmental regulation' must have consistent meanings so we are not comparing apples and oranges), that the introduction of new variables brings with it the introduction of unknown variation too, and that like all non-experimental research it has to rely on 'naturally occurring variation' which rules out many combinations of values of interest to the researcher.

What are the implications of the above arguments for the present study? First we are interested in explaining both similarities and differences in environmental regulation between the four localities. We are interested in sub-national not cross-national variation. Second the way we have measured our concepts is rather rough so we will only use nominal (yes–no) and ordinal (more–less) levels of measurement. Third our conclusions are relative to the cases studied only. It is for subsequent studies using a wider set of localities, or different measures, to decide whether this is a valid approach or not. Last but not least plural causation is excluded.

Local environmental regulation and local economic policy: attributing values to the four localities on the dependent variables

We now discuss in turn local environmental regulation and local economic policy in the four localities. Our central concept and dependent variable is local environmental regulation and we start by explaining how we have measured this concept and how we have attributed values to each locality on each measure.

Local environmental regulation has been measured in two ways. We were interested in:

1. the strength of local government environmental policies; and
2. the strength of the role of the regional environmental inspectorate.

Strength is a loose concept. In the first case it refers to the extent to which the local government has developed policies which either act directly to improve the environment or which have indirect effects on the environment, for example, by changing the costs and benefits of decisions made by individuals and firms. In the second case strength refers to the extent to which the REI took measures which had the potential or actual capacity to change the behaviour of firms in an environmentally beneficial way. Most of this chapter will be concerned with these two measures.

We will also refer to a second concept, the strength of local government economic policy. This is not directly related to local environmental regulation but we included it because changing the local economic structure can often have a direct effect on the local environmental situation. This will be of secondary interest.

Our main interests were in:

1. why some local governments had stronger local environmental policies than others;
2. why in some localities the role of the regional environmental inspectorate was stronger than in others; and
3. why some local governments had stronger local economic policies than others.

In this section we shall present our measures of the three dependent variables for the four localities. The values we give will be based on the evidence presented in

Chapters 3 to 6. We shall refer to this data in summary form but will not repeat it in detail. Since the research on the four localities was not quantitative the variables are measured in ordinal terms. This means that we shall place the localities on the various variables in terms of scales such as 'High–Medium–Low' or 'Strong–Weak' rather than using numerical indicators.

Local environmental policy

Our earlier discussion of local environmental policy in the four towns can be summarized as follows.

Székesfehérvár this had the strongest local environmental policy since some potential investors had been rejected on environmental grounds, land had been reclassified to provide greater environmental protection, and various pro-environmental decisions had been taken by the local council. Although these measures were accompanied by a well-developed environmental rhetoric on the part of the local council we felt this was more a measure of the council's intentions than of its actual achievement and it is not therefore used as a measure of local environmental policy.

Győr local environmental policy here was weaker than in Székesfehérvár. Environmental rhetoric was accompanied by a number of pro-environmental council decisions, and a centrally located foundry had been relocated, but there was no evidence of the rejection of new potential investment on environmental grounds.

Nagytétény local environmental policy here was probably weaker than in Győr as measured by pro-environmental council decisions. However a 'medium' value is justified by the council's continuing lawsuit against the government to obtain compensation for a polluted site. This involved a considerable mobilization of resources by the council; a council which gave the environment less priority would simply have abandoned the struggle in the face of the lack of success.

Dunaújváros the only example of an environmental policy in the town was the lorry ban in the town centre.

We therefore classify the four localities as follows in respect of environmental policy:

    Székesfehérvár: Strong
    Győr: Medium
    Nagytétény: Medium
    Dunaújváros: Weak

Regional environmental inspectorate policy

Our discussion of REI policy covered a range of activities. The ones where there seemed to be most variation were the undertaking of unannounced visits, discussions with firms in anticipation of investments, and responsiveness to members of the public. The evidence presented in Chapters 3 to 6 can be summarized as follows.

Székesfehérvár this was the only town where the REI had a regular programme of unannounced visits, the toughest form of regulation.

Győr the REI seemed to undertake virtually no unannounced visits. However it had an active educational role through meetings with local firms, though these were concentrated in Győr where the REI is located at the expense of the rest of the area covered. It was also active in response to complaints by members of the public.

Nagytétény the REI here also seemed to undertake only rare unannounced visits. It complained strongly of resource constraints.

Dunaújváros the REI here, which though the same as the one at Székesfehérvár, was less active.

We therefore classify the four localities as follows in terms of REI policy:
Székesfehérvár: Strong
Győr: Medium
Nagytétény: Weak
Dunaújváros: Weak

Local economic policy

Our evidence on local economic policy was as follows.

Székesfehérvár this was the locality with the strongest economic policy. It had taken the lead in building industrial estates in the 1980s and continued after 1990, the economic incentives offered to business were the largest of all, and there was an active international effort to put the town on the map.

Győr this town had also built an industrial estate and offered economic incentives to firms coming to the town, but on a lesser scale than in Székesfehérvár.

Nagytétény this locality had not built an industrial estate and had the weakest economic policy of all.

Dunaújváros this town had built an industrial estate and offered economic incentives.

We therefore classify the four localities as follows in terms of local economic policy:
Székesfehérvár: Strong
Győr: Medium
Nagytétény: Weak
Dunaújváros: Medium

The values of the four localities on the three dependent variables are shown in the first three rows of Table 7.1.

It must be pointed out in line with what we said earlier about differences and similarities that our measures from 'strong' to 'weak' reflect differences among the localities we included in the study. It cannot be ruled out that if we had chosen a larger set of localities, which included the four chosen here, the range of differences would have been greater and the levels of each locality of the three dependent variables would have been different. This is what is meant by the contextuality of the notion of difference.

A Comparative Analysis of Regulation in the Four Localities 117

Table 7.1 Positions of the four localities on the dependent variables and explanatory variables hypothesized to be of relevance

	Székesfehérvár	Győr	Nagytétény	Dunaújváros
Dependent variables				
Local environmental policy	Strong	Medium	Medium	Weak
Local REI role	Strong	Medium	Weak	Weak
Local economic policy	Strong	Medium	Weak	Medium
Explanatory variables				
1. Dominant employer	No	No	No	Yes
2. Reputation for power of firm studied	No	No	No	Yes
3. Major contributor of local taxes	No	No	No	Yes
4. Interest from outside investors	Strong	Medium	Fair	Weak
5. Strong networks to local government	Medium	Medium	Weak	Strong
6. Strength of environmentalist public opinion	Medium	Medium	Medium (focused on one conflict)	Weak
Additional variables applicable to REI role				
7. REI resources	Weak	Moderate	Weak	Weak
8. Spatial effects	Favourable	Favourable	Favourable	Unfavourable

Attributing values to the four localities on the explanatory variables

Any attempt to explain the variation in the dependent variables just described requires some sort of framework to channel efforts to discover causes since potentially there is an unlimited number of potential causes. In our case the theoretical framework set out in Chapter 2 does this. It identifies a selected number of potential explanations of observed differences in local environmental regulation.

We now turn to the hypotheses set out in Chapter 2 and explain the values we have given to each locality on the explanatory variables. By explanatory we mean that they have the power to change the dependent variables. We also include two additional variables which did not appear in Chapter 2. The variable numbers refer to Table 7.1.

Variables 1–6

1–3 *Dominant employer, reputation for power of firm studied, major contributor of local taxes* (Features of the enterprise) We consider these three concepts together since in each case the contrast was between Dunaújváros and the other three localities. In Dunaújváros, Dunaferr was the dominant employer, had a reputation for power which we showed was backed up by various indicators, and contributed a very large share of local taxes. In the other localities there was a mix of firms of large, medium and small sizes, none of which had the overwhelming position of Dunaferr. We therefore classified Székesfehérvár, Győr and Nagytétény as lacking these three features, and Dunaújváros as possessing them. Hence the pattern: No–No–No–Yes in Table 7.1 for each of variables 1–3.

4. *Interest from outside investors* In this respect we regard Székesfehérvár as the leader, followed by Győr, then Nagytétény, then Dunaújváros. Hence the pattern: Székesfehérvár: Strong, Győr: Medium, Nagytétény: Fair, Dunaújváros: Weak.

5. *Strong networks to local government* From our evidence networks linking firms and local government were strongest in Dunaújváros. In Székesfehérvár and Győr there were fairly close links over specific issues such as local taxes and planning needs. In Nagytétény links seemed to be particularly distant. We therefore classify the localities as follows: Székesfehérvár: Medium, Győr: Medium, Nagytétény: Weak, Dunaújváros: Strong.

6. *Environmentalist opinion* This was absent from Dunaújváros but fairly well developed in the other three localities, each of which had an environmental group: Gaia in Székesfehérvár, Reflex in Győr, and Green Future in Nagytétény, though in each case our interviews with group leaders or members revealed that these groups had passed their peak of activity which had coincided with the period of regime change 1989–91. We therefore classify the towns as follows: Székesfehérvár: Medium; Győr: Medium; Nagytétény: Medium; Dunaújváros: Weak.[3]

---

[3] Four explanatory variables which were included in Chapter 2 are absent from Table 7.1. The reasons for their exclusion are as follows:
  1. *Strength of pro-environment management.* We encountered two firms in the research where there was some evidence of environmentalist management. Alcoa in Székesfehérvár was introducing corporation-wide standards in the fields of asbestos and underground storage which it claimed went beyond the requirements of Hungarian legislation. Management at Gardenia in Győr also showed a determination to appear to be a good environmental citizen. However in both cases 'pro-environmentalism' was a matter of degree. At Alcoa there was an unsolved effluent problem, and Gardenia's expansion plan involved environmental detriment. Since these characteristics relate to firms rather than localities this variable is omitted from the Table 7.1. It would only be possible to characterize a town's firms on this variable if a large sample of firms was drawn.
  2. *Policy as responsive to or isolated from local interests as expressed by business and the public.* This variable is also difficult to measure given the limited information we have on business views. Data on it are therefore omitted from Table 7.1.

Variables 7–8

These variables arise from new hypotheses about REI behaviour set out below. In Chapter 2 we suggested that REI behaviour would reflect the adequacy of its funding by central government and the priority given to environmental issues over economic issues. We did not raise the possibility that REI behaviour might differ from one area to another and therefore did not suggest any hypotheses about this. However on the basis of the evidence about REI behaviour in Chapters 3 to 6 we would like to add two further hypotheses regarding REI behaviour to help explain the observed differences. These are that REI policy depends on: the level of resourcing of individual REIs, and the geographical location of the localities in question vis à vis the REI office.

7. *REI resourcing* In three of the four locations REI interviewees emphasized the constraints they experienced due to a shortage of resources. These interviewees backed up their statements with evidence about the size of their staff, the workload that they had to cope with and the increasing demands of new legislation. There is no reason to doubt their claims. We therefore classify the REI resourcing situations in the four localities as: Székesfehérvár: Weak, Győr: Moderate, Nagytétény: Weak, and Dunaújváros: Weak.

8. *Spatial effects* Evidence from interviewees at the North Trans-Danubian Environmental Inspectorate in Győr made clear that it concentrates on firms and public complaints in the Győr area. This leads us to put forward a general hypothesis that the regulatory activity of REIs is not evenly spread across the territories for which they are responsible, but that they concentrate on the areas close to their office at the expense of the peripheral parts. This of course is linked to resource constraints, but it is also an effect of having a single office to cover a large area. The elongated shape (see Figure 9.1) of the North Trans-Danubian area which falls under the responsibility of the Győr office may have made this uneven coverage particularly marked. This hypothesis also relates to the comparison between REI behaviour in Székesfehérvár and Dunaújváros which both fall under the Central Trans-Danubian Regional Inspectorate. Since the REI office is located in Székesfehérvár we would hypothesise that the weaker REI policy in Dunaújváros is in part related to the distance between Dunaújváros and the REI's

---

3. *Financial position of local government.* This depends on the local government's share of central grants (and whether these meet the locality's needs) as well as its ability to raise taxes locally (mainly from firms). In the latter respect we suspect that Székesfehérvár was in the best position due to its success in attracting foreign investment. However Dunaújváros is also likely to have been in a good position due to the position of Dunaferr. However in the absence of the necessary data on central grants our data on this concept were weak and we therefore omit this feature from Table 7.1.

4. *Local residents also employees.* The reasoning here was that when employees are residents too this generates an additional pressure on councils and the REI to be tough in environmental standards. Unfortunately we were not able to collect good data on this concept. We therefore omit it from Table 7.1.

office in Székesfehérvár. Hence on the basis that in Székesfehérvár and Győr the REI office is located in the town, and that in Nagytétény it is located nearby in Budapest, whereas the REI responsible for Dunaújváros is located in Székesfehérvár, we classify the four localities in terms of the spatial effects variable as: Székesfehérvár: favourable, Győr: favourable, Nagytétény: favourable, Dunaújváros: unfavourable.

It should be noted that we are suggesting that REI behaviour can be explained by a similar explanatory model to council behaviour; in other words, that local social forces (understood here as pressure from the public and from firms) have a bearing on REI regulatory behaviour. The role of firms is in line with our hypothesis in Chapter 2 that, whatever legislation said, regulatory bodies had discretion in their application of environmental standards, and that the position of firms and the likely impact of a measure on them was taken into account by regulatory bodies in deciding how toughly to apply these standards. This was backed up by international evidence on regulatory processes. The model put forward here suggests that public opinion can also influence the way an REI operates.

In our view these two hypotheses help to make sense of the data we collected on REI behaviour. In Chapters 3 and 6 we showed that the contrast between the operation of the Central Danubian Environmental Inspectorate in Dunaújváros and Székesfehérvár was particularly revealing. As we noted, the same REI operated in both towns. The contrast was that in Székesfehérvár we classified its operation as 'Strong' while in Dunaújváros it was 'Weak'. To make sense of this we can refer to our argument above about spatial effects. The REI was based in Székesfehérvár and therefore if spatial effects operate in the way hypothesized the effect will be to increase the strength of regulation in Székesfehérvár and decrease it in the 'peripheral' location of Dunaújváros (45km away).

We do not consider that the 'spatial effect' argument is sufficient to make sense of the differences in strength of REI regulation. Spatial effects do not operate in isolation from social effects and to emphasize them exclusively would be to fail to do justice to the huge differences between Székesfehérvár and Dunaújváros as places. In Székesfehérvár the council has pursued a dynamic economic policy, its environmental policy has been the strongest of the four localities studied here, and the public is quite mobilized over environmental issues. In contrast in Dunaújváros the council and dominant firm are bound together in a tight nexus and neither the town council nor the public is active on environmental issues. The result is that the combination of social forces in Székesfehérvár creates an incentive for the REI to be more active there while the social forces present in Dunaújváros discourage the REI from action.

In sum it is the contrasting patterns of local social forces as well as resourcing and spatial effects which, we hypothesize, are relevant in making sense of why the REI is drawn into a more active role in Székesfehérvár than in Dunaújváros.

Analysing the pattern of values of dependent and explanatory variables: the four localities compared

How should Table 7.1 be read? The aim of this study is to make sense of local variation in environmental regulation measured by two main variables: local council environmental policy and REI policy. The first two rows of Table 7.1 present our summary measures for the four localities on these variables. The third row refers to local economic policy. The remainder of the table lists the measures of the four localities on the eight variables which we have designated as explanatory. The explanatory variables which appear in Table 7.1 were chosen because there were theoretical reasons for believing that they had a causal relation with the dependent variables of interest here. These reasons were set out in Chapter 2, or, in the case of variables 7 and 8, immediately above.

We now proceed to the empirical part of the evaluation of the explanatory power of our hypotheses. In order to establish whether the hypothesized relations between explanatory and dependent variables are supported or not we need to examine the co-variation (or correlation) between them, since this is a necessary condition for the presence of a causal relation. It is not a sufficient condition since causal relations require co-variation of the predicted kind, the correct temporal order and a theoretical rationale. The latter has already been set out. However as Galtung's 'principle of variety of theories' (1967, p. 455) makes clear, there are numerous potential theoretical explanations for any given correlation so even if the co-variation between two variables is as we expect it does not confirm the theroetical rationale that led us to make the prediction. On the other hand an absence of co-variation means that our hypotheses are not supported.[4]

To say that causal influence exists is the first step in a complex discussion of what causal models might make sense of the co-variation observed. A wide variety of possibilities exists ranging from two variable models (for example, A causes B), to multivariate models, with or without reciprocal causation, and with or without plural causation. Some of these were set out in Chapter 2 when the hypotheses were elaborated. However in interpreting the data in the discussion below we shall develop further models.

To establish the presence of co-variation we will search for monotonic trends or 'gradients' in the patterns of values for each pair of dependent and explanatory variables. But before we do this we need to adopt some ground rules. If co-variation is positive we would expect to find for example that the gradient Strong–Medium–Medium–Weak in row 1 was also found for an explanatory variable. Alternatively if

---

4 In fact the link between co-variation and causation depends on the nature of the underlying causal model. Our conclusions about the rejection of hypotheses apply only to bivariate models. If we consider more complex causal models, for example multivariate, these conclusions do not follow. For example an absence of covariation between two variables could conceal the influence of a third variable. This would show up as two non-zero (for example, equal and opposed) partial correlations.

co-variation is negative, we would expect the gradient Strong–Medium–Medium–Weak to be matched by the opposite gradient Weak–Medium–Medium–Strong. The defect of this approach is that the larger the number of localities one chooses and the larger the number of values for each variable the more difficult it becomes to demonstrate the necessary co-variation rule, and so the more likely the hypothesis is to be rejected.

We shall therefore adopt a looser requirement: namely, that for the two variables being compared, as long is there is not a 'reversal' (or non-monotonic trend) in the pattern then we regard co-variation as present. For example, Strong–Medium–Medium–Weak and Strong–Medium–Weak–Weak would be considered to contain gradients and therefore co-variation, while Strong–Medium–Medium–Weak and Strong–Medium–Weak–Medium would be considered not to show co-variation because Strong–Medium–Weak–Medium contains a reversal. The justification for this procedure is that the ordinal level of measurement (Strong–Weak) is not precise and that too much weight should not be placed on the values of the variables used.

Local council environmental policy

Let us first consider the co-variation between local council environmental policy and the six variables shown as relevant to it in Table 7.1, variables 1–6.

Using the ground rules just explained it can be seen that the three explanatory variables (variables 1–3) related to the presence of large influential firms which contribute to the council's coffers all co-vary with strength of local environmental policy in the way expected (Strong–Medium–Medium–Weak v. No–No–No–Yes in each case).[5] Local environmental policy was stronger in areas lacking dominant firms and weakest in the area where a dominant firm was present (Dunaújváros).

The fourth explanatory variable, interest from outside investors, varied in the predicted way (Strong–Medium–Medium–Weak v. Strong–Medium–Fair–Weak). Localities which were more attractive to outside investors were more likely to have stronger environmental policies. This correlation raises the question of the direction of causality. Does the presence of demand from outside investors stimulate the council into a more active environmental policy or does the presence of a more environmentalist policy stimulate outside investment? The data in Table 7.1 are compatible with either interpretation. However there could also be a more complex causal model. For example both processes might operate simultaneously creating a 'virtuous circle' in which the greater the outside investor interest, the more environmentalist the policy, which again stimulated more investor interest. Alternatively a model with additional variables might be present. For example a western location in Hungary might be partly responsible for a town's attractiveness to investment and for the council adopting a stronger environmental policy.

The fifth variable, local environmentalist opinion, also shows the expected co-variation with council environmental policy (Strong–Medium–Medium–Weak v.

---

5 In each comparison we show the pattern of values for the dependent variable first.

Medium–Medium–Medium–Weak), that is, localities with stronger local environmental policy also had stronger local environmental opinion. There are two interpretations here. The first is that the council is responding to local environmentalist public opinion in developing its policy. The second is that local policy has an educational effect on the public, for example that the more environmentalist the council the more environmentalist the public. All the evidence we have cited would support the former interpretation. The councils in the localities we studied have been reluctant converts to environmentalism and have usually acted under pressure from environmental groups or public opinion in a less organized sense.

The sixth explanatory variable, the strength of networks between firms and local government, fails to co-vary with local environmental policy (Strong–Medium–Medium–Weak v. Medium–Medium–Weak–Strong). Why should this be? We showed earlier that there was co-variation between the three firm-related variables and the strength of local environmental policy in a way that suggested large influential firms could influence policy towards a 'Weak' position. The rationale for including the strength of the network as an explanatory variable was that this might facilitate such influence, but this does not seem to be the case. Our findings suggest that the network pattern is of little significance compared with the power of the firm.

REI role

The second dependent variable was the REI's role, which we measured as ranging from strong to weak. It should be noted that the conventional picture of state agencies is that they act in a standardized way to ensure similar standards throughout a national territory. The analysis below, which suggests the contrary, thus represents an interesting departure from this picture.

The patterns of covariation show that the three firm-related explanatory variables (1–3) vary inversely with the strength of the REI's role (Strong–Medium–Weak–Weak v. No–No–No–Yes). In other words the more a single firm was dominant the more likely the REI was to operate in a weak way. This is exactly what one would expect from the argument that powerful firms are able to 'throw their weight around' in dealings with regulatory agencies. However we should not be too confident that this is the only process present. It could equally well be argued that if firms in an area were very weak economically that the REI would be likely to be weak in its implementation of standards. If so, this would suggest a curvilinear relation, with REI policy being weak when firms were weak, strong when firms were economically strong enough to bear the economic effects of the policy (and where they lacked the collective power to resist it), and weak when firms were very strong. (The possibility of such patterns shows the limitations of linear causal models.) However we found no evidence of such a curvilinear relation.

The pattern of co-variation between the REI's role and the fourth explanatory variable, the degree of interest from outside investors, was also positive: the greater the investor interest the stricter the REI's operation (Strong–Medium–Weak–Weak v.

High–Medium–Fair–Low). Again one can ask what the causal order is here. If the REI's tough policy precedes the investor interest, this would show that the REI becomes an active force in the creation of the conditions which make localities attractive for investment. On the other hand if investor interest precedes an active REI role, this could be because firms with pro-environmental managements seek to promote the environmental standards of the area. Both processes are possible and may operate together. Alternatively a more complex model may be considered in which for example the state of the local economy is the key variable. If the local economy is weak this may explain why there is little investor interest and why the REI feels unable to operate strictly: in case firms went bankrupt.

The co-variation between the sixth explanatory variable, environmentalist public opinion, and the REI's role is also positive:[6] areas where public opinion is more environmentalist are more likely to have stronger REI policy (Srong–Medium–Weak–Weak v. Medium–Medium–Medium–Low). This is an interesting relationship since REIs are governmental agencies responsible to a ministry and do not have an elected element. This makes it strange to find that the way they operate does vary between areas (rather than obeying a centralised requirement to operate in a standardized way), and that it appears to vary according to the state of public opinion in the area. This should not be too much of a surprise since all agencies of central government have to make adjustments to the local environments in which they operate. In different literatures this is described as 'going native' or having 'permeable boundaries'. Adapting to local conditions may indeed be regarded as a positive and desirable aim and failure to adapt could be portrayed as applying central targets in a mechanical way. This permeability is a condition of the effect both of environmentalist public opinion and of local firms.

Finally in discussing REI policy we will emphasize again the relevance of the two variables which were introduced as a result of our analysis of the data (but which were not among our initial hypotheses): REI resources and spatial effects. Since these explanatory factors were introduced after we had observed the results we do not claim that they were hypotheses which preceded the investigation.[7] We will simply emphasize that they are both theoretically meaningful and compatible with the patterns of REI policy strength observed across the four localities.

---

6 The fifth explanatory variable is omitted as it refers specifically to local government rather than the REI.
7 This raises the well-known question of whether the order in which research is written up (theory–hypothesis–data collection–data analysis–return to hypotheses) replicates the order in which it is carried out, or is an idealization required by academic publishing norms. In the present case I chose not to rewrite my hypotheses to anticipate the results concerning REI policy. The slightly awkward presentation of the last section is the price paid for presenting the analysis in the order in which it was carried out!

Local council economic policy

Local council economic policy, our third dependent variable, was strongest in Székesfehérvár, followed by Győr and Dunaújváros, and weakest in Nagytétény.

A first question is whether the localities which had the strongest local economic policy also had the strongest local environmental policy. It can be seen from Table 7.1 that Székesfehérvár is strongest in both respects followed by Győr but that Dunaújváros had a stronger economic policy than Nagytétény whereas for local environmental policy the reverse was the case. This merits some discussion.

We have seen that Dunaújváros had a weak council environmental policy. On the face of it, it is surprising to find that its local economic policy was not equally weak. For example a council which lacked expertise and policy-making policy might be expected to have weakly-developed policy in many fields. But the weak environmental policy in Dunaújváros is not due to this. Rather it is due to the continuing influence of Dunaferr. If we conceptualize Dunaújváros town council as working within limits set by Dunaferr then it becomes apparent why it has a weak environmental policy but a 'medium' developed local economic policy. The fact is that Dunaferr was very much an active partner in local economic policy (and co-owner of the industrial estate) rather than a passive onlooker. This meant it could influence the shape of local economic policy. In other words the fact that local economic policy in Dunaújváros is not formed as independently of local firms as in the other localities helps explain why Dunaújváros's position in terms of the local economic policy gradient across the four towns is a 'deviant' one.

Turning to the patterns of covariation between council economic policy and the independent variables, it can be seen from Table 7.1 that none of the independent variables vary in a way which matches the pattern of variation in the dependent variable: Strong–Medium–Weak–Medium. This means that none of the hypotheses which we thought would explain the strength of local economic policy in fact does so. This could be because most of the independent variables we have included refer to the context in which councils operate rather than to features of councils themselves. No variable relating to councils' staffing resources, expertise, connectedness to national networks, and dynamism in policy formation in all spheres was included. The example of Székesfehérvár, the town with the most active local economic policy, where Mr Balsay was Mayor then MP and whose political leadership there started before 1990 suggests that links to local and national political elites may be relevant. However it is possible that unmeasured contextual variables are also relevant. Lastly as suggested above we are assuming that local economic policy is a unidimensional variable, and that the difference between local economic policy in Dunaújváros and the other three towns is simply one of degree rather than kind.

Conclusion

In this chapter we have reached two main conclusions.

First, it has been shown that there is variation across the four localities in the two main dependent variables, local environmental policy and the role of the REI. The existence of this inter-locality variation indicates the limits of national level studies which by definition can only speculate about what happens at local level. We also showed that there was variation in local economic policy but it did not correspond to that in local environmental regulation.

Second, it has been shown that the explanatory variables included in Table 7.1 were largely successful in explaining the variation in local environmental policy and the role of the REI. In particular the presence of powerful dominant firms, the level of interest from outside investors, the strength of local environmentalist opinion, REI resourcing, and spatial effects due to the location of the REI office, were all shown to have played a role. However for the reasons explained earlier we cannot rule out the possibility that excluded variables are also of relevance. (By contrast the explanatory model was unsuccessful in examining variation in local economic policy and some possible reasons for this have been suggested.)

In Székesfehérvár the combination of a lack of dominant firms, strong interest from outside investors, strong local environmentalist opinion, a dynamic local council and an active REI led to the relatively favourable outcome on our measures of local environmental regulation. This was accompanied by a strong environmentalist rhetoric. Győr and Nagytétény ranked second and third in strength of local environmental regulation and Dunaújváros came last. The former two localities showed some evidence of environmentalist activity among the public and in other respects generally showed weaker levels of the variables on which Székesfehérvár was strongest. Dunaújváros was a very different type of locality with its dominant firm in continued state ownership (though it had undergone an internal reorganization for definitive purposes), lack of environmentalist opinion, and lowest level of investor interest. The council was heavily under the influence of Dunaferr. This led to its inability to develop a local environmental policy, but also to the fact that it had developed a local economic development policy in which Dunaferr played an active role.

What is interesting is that these findings do not seem distinctive in relation to studies carried out elsewhere in more advanced capitalist countries or in China as described in Chapter 2. We will return to this question in Chapter 10.

How much reliance can we place on our conclusions? The fact that the study is based on only four localities is a reason for caution. The argument for conducting studies on a small number of cases is that one gains more knowledge of them and is therefore more likely to reach valid conclusions. This has been put in a strong form by Mitchell (1983). Against this is the argument of Lieberson, that we find more persuasive, that inference based on small samples is very risky. A key issue is the range of variation in the independent variables. We have classified the four localities from strong to weak in respect of the different variables. However these measures are relative. Within our sample of four we feel these measures are justified. What remains unknown is whether if we had taken a sample of 20 localities including the four localities we would have placed them in the same categories on this variable, or whether in the extreme case they would all have been classified in the same category. In brief our conclusions about the effects of the independent variables are dependent on the range of variation actually present in the independent variables.

A further reason for caution concerns the difference between relative and absolute measures of local environmental regulation. Our focus in this chapter has been on local council environmental policy and REI activity and their relative strength and weakness across the four localities. If we are concerned about the local environmental situation we have to acknowledge that it depends not only on the relative strength of local environmental regulation but also on its absolute strength, and on other factors such as the incentives which firms have to improve their environmental impacts as well as on other factors. This was made very obvious by the fact that Székesfehérvár, which had the strongest level of local environmental regulation, had the second worst environmental situation among the four study localities as measured by the presence of certain air pollutants (see Table 2.5). This suggests that at its strongest the impact of local environmental regulation is rather moderate.

To explain this we can point to the evidence of Chapters 3 to 6 which showed that the level of environmental penalties was very low and that they failed to act as incentives to invest in new and cleaner equipment. A Rába interviewee even claimed that environmental investment had to pay for itself within two years, which indicates the low priority given to such improvement. (It would be interesting to know how widespread such a view is.) Chapters 3 to 6 also revealed the delayed investment in waste water treatment plants in a number of firms. The REI rule by which firms which had 'plans' for investment in such improvements were exempt from penalties acted as a significant factor delaying the reduction of levels of water pollution. Both examples suggest the weakness of environmental regulation in absolute terms in Hungary. These chapters also drew attention to the incentives internal to firms to reduce pollution apart from environmental fines. For example we found evidence of multinational corporate policy (Alcoa), managerial policy (Gardenia) and consumer pressure (Rába) all contributing to a reduction of pollution. Last but not least the industrial structure of the locality is important, especially because many established firms have been allowed to continue operations although they would not meet current requirements imposed on new investment. Thus our focus on the relative strength of local environmental regulation in the four localities does not enable us to measure the absolute level of local environmental regulation, which has a more direct influence, together with other factors, on levels of actual environmental pollution.

8 Settlement Type and Local Government Environmental Policy in Hungary: the Role of Local Economic Structure and Local Government Resources*

In the previous five chapters we have reported and analysed the results of our case studies of four localities. In this chapter and the next we present the result of another part of our research.

Case studies are useful in gaining a detailed understanding of particular cases and when used comparatively as in Chapter 7 enable one to examine some hypotheses about the reasons for the variation between the cases. However, I share with Hammersley (1992) the view that this intensity does not guarantees privileged access to truth (see Mitchell 1983; Pickvance, 1995). The very intensity of information gathered does not provide unmediated access to causal relationships. The drawback of case studies is that unless one has immense resources the number of cases chosen will be small and the validity of conclusions drawn from them more generally is therefore unknown (Gomm et al., 2000).

In order to complement the four case studies we undertook a large scale interview survey of local governments. This survey involved a nationwide sample of 600 out of the total of 3149 local governments. It was a stratified sample covering all city governments (including all Budapest districts) and a random sample of town and village governments. (In the very few cases of refusals or non-response, replacement local governments were used to achieve the target of 600.) The sample included all 46 cities (Budapest city council, the 23 Budapest district councils and the 22 provincial cities), 179 towns (all but two), and a sample of 31 large villages and 344 small villages. All of the analyses below retain the settlement type classification since there were large differences on most variables of interest between settlements of different types. The person who was interviewed in the survey varied with the settlement type. In villages the respondent was generally the mayor or notary, while in towns and cities

---

* An earlier version of this chapter was published as 'Settlement type and local government environmental policy in Hungary: the role of local economic structure and local government resources' in *European Environment*, 12, 2002, 90–104. Copyright John Wiley & Sons Ltd. Reproduced with permission.

it was an official (usually with environmental responsibilities). A standardized interview schedule was used. Most of the findings of the survey are presented by settlement type since as explained local governments of different types had a greater or lesser number of responsibilities. The survey was conducted in December 1998.

It should be noted that while surveys have some advantages over case studies they are not without their weaknesses. They offer wider coverage and representativeness but at the expense of intensity of information. In particular attitudinal data is usually given in abstraction from particular cases and cannot be used to gauge action. In a case study the multiple sources of data mean that cross-checking is more likely to be possible and normative statements can be checked against what a person actually did.

In the remainder of this chapter, the findings of the survey are presented in the following order: a) commitment to environmental policy at local government level, b) local economic policy measures, c) local environmental problems, d) local government environmental measures, and e) the perceived effectiveness of environmental measures.

Commitment to environmental policy at local government level

If local environmental policy is a significant local government activity one would expect adequate resources to be committed to it and an explicit policy to exist. However since resource levels vary greatly between settlement types we would expect a correlation between measures of commitment to environmental policy and settlement type. We used two measures of commitment: the existence of a local government official with specific environmental responsibilities, and the existence of a written local environmental policy. We expected a strong correlation between settlement type and the first measure since we expected the larger and better-resourced local governments to be much more likely to have a specific environmental official due to the costs involved. We expected a weaker correlation between the second measure and settlement type since a written environmental policy is less costly and might not be beyond the means of even a village.

Having a person with specific environmental responsibilities proved to be very strongly correlated with settlement type (Cramer's V=0.61).[1] The proportion of local governments with no specific person in charge ranged from 100% in big villages and 98.3% in small villages to 76.4% in towns and 24.4% in cities. Commitment to environmental policy measured in this way therefore reflected the different level of resourcing of local governments of different sizes. However, the 'cities' category splits into provincial cities where only 4.5% had no-one with specific responsibility

---

[1] Cramer's V, a chi-squared based measure of association, is used throughout since it has the desirable properties of varying between 0 and 1 and being uninfluenced by the number of rows and columns in the table to which it refers (Blalock, 1960).

for environmental matters, and Budapest and its districts,[2] where this figure was surprisingly high at 43.4%. There is little difference in the typical size of the two categories (about 100,000). The likely explanation for this is the socio-economic differentiation of Budapest which means that some districts are very poor and have other priorities.

The second measure of the priority given to the environment was whether the local government has a written environmental policy. This figure ranges from 20.9% in small villages and 35.5% in large villages to 54.7% in towns and 82.6% in cities, showing a moderate correlation with settlement type (V=0.30). In view of the small size of the villages it is interesting that even a minority had written policies. The fact that less than 100% of towns and cities had written environmental policies means that the formal requirement to have such a policy was not being met. Breaking down the cities figure, provincial cities proved once again to be more likely to have environmental policies than Budapest councils (95.5% v. 70.8%.) This supports the evidence based on staffing just presented. On closer examination there was a substantial overlap between the Budapest councils which did not have a person responsible for the environment and those which had no written environmental policy: of the 13 councils which had a written environmental policy, ten had a specific person responsible for the environment while of the seven councils without a written policy only two had a specific person in charge.

Overall, the pattern of environmental commitment measured in these ways follows the expected pattern with commitment increasing with settlement size, in line with increasing resources. The two unexpected results are the extent of commitment in some small villages, and the fact that provincial cities give more importance to environmental issues than some district councils in Budapest.

Local economic policy measures

To be committed to environmental issues is one thing; to turn this into action is another. We therefore consider now the more practical question of what measures local governments are planning or using. We start by considering local economic policy measures. Although such measures may not be conceived first and foremost as environmental measures they have a clear impact on the environment since the economic structure of a locality is the main factor shaping the local environment. This is so both in a historical sense (the relics of past economic activity shape the character and image of the local environment) and in a future sense (existing environmental features can be deployed in local economic policy as assets with attractive power). The question of how far local economic policy measures used or had regard to the local environment will be examined below. We consider whether local governments

---

[2] Throughout this paper figures referring to Budapest refer to the 23 district councils and the city council. Where a different meaning is intended, this is stated.

had plans to change their local economic structure, what methods they were using, and with what hopes of success.

It is difficult to set out clear-cut hypotheses on this topic. There are two factors favouring action by local governments.

- The ideology that local governments should be 'responsible' for their localities in economic terms rather than being dependent on central government as in the past is quite well developed.
- The difficult post-1989 economic experience of Hungary (see the figures quoted earlier) which has led to growing income inequality and particularly severe economic impacts in rural areas.

On the other hand there is one obvious constraining factor.

- The limited likely impact of local government compared with that of national economic policy given their relative levels of resources. This makes it likely that whatever measures are used by local governments they will not be expensive. For example whereas publicity for a locality's attractive features is within the means of a wide range of local governments, major investment projects such as the building of factories and industrial estates, or the provision of large grants and loans, will be limited to large settlements.

This suggests that action will be widespread and on a scale proportionate to the resources available.

In fact the survey revealed that almost all local governments had plans to change the economic structure of their settlement (100% of cities, 97.2% of towns, 93.5% of large villages and 86.3% of small villages). These are surprisingly high figures and are in line with our hypothesis. However to make sense of these responses we need to explore what types of action were planned and with what expectation of success.

When interviewees were asked what were the three most important methods of achieving economic change that they planned, the most common first choices were: supporting local entrepreneurs, followed at some distance by attracting clean hi-tech industry, tourism, and attracting any industry (see Table 8.1). These responses were only weakly correlated with settlement type overall (V=0.22), but this conceals one clear trend: a systematic decline in the preference for hi-tech industry with settlement size.

Helping local entrepreneurs was by far the most common response in all types of settlement. This is interesting because one might conceptualize entrepreneurship as something that relies on the initiative of the individual without state support. The fact that it is the first choice for support by local governments results from several factors: an ideological commitment to private enterprise as the way forward for the country, a belief (derived from state socialism) that the state should offer support for the people, and a conception of local politics in which the new, more autonomous, local

Table 8.1 Distribution (%) of first choices of planned measure by local governments to change the local economic structure, by settlement type

	Budapest	Provincial cities	Towns	Large villages	Small villages
Local entrepreneurs	47.8	63.6	60.9	58.1	52.0
Hi tech industry	30.4	27.3	18.4	9.7	6.7
Tourism	13.0	0	5.0	9.7	13.4
Any industry	0	9.1	11.2	6.5	5.2

government gains political support by providing direct benefits to local people. (Interestingly in Budapest support for local entrepreneurs was less popular than in provincial cities. This may be because Budapest has more public sector employment or because political parties are more strongly rooted there and local politics relies less on offering personal benefits to voters.) Typically, the value of support for local entrepreneurs would be on a very small scale and was thus feasible even for small local governments. In small settlements it could include support for individuals making use of assets left after the collapse of many co-operatives.

Attracting hi-tech industry came second as a priority in Budapest and provincial cities and showed a strong correlation with settlement type, being little mentioned in villages. In contrast attracting industry other than hi-tech comes last as a first choice measure. In bigger settlements the relative preference for hi-tech industry was much stronger. Since they were the location for existing industry they would be more aware of the polluting effects of traditional industry. They would also feel that their industrial tradition and infrastructure made them more attractive to hi-tech industry. Small settlements on the other hand would be in a weaker position to choose and would be pleased to attract even traditional industry.

Tourism is the third most common first choice measure, though it was not mentioned in any provincial cities. This does not mean that these cities do not consider themselves attractive to tourism (see Table 8.2), but only that supporting local entrepreneurs and hi-tech industry are preferred options.

When second choice options are considered (Table 8.2), both tourism and hi-tech industry come out strongly in all types of settlement. The fact that tourism comes second to hi-tech industry in Budapest, which is a popular tourist destination, is on the face of it surprising. This is probably because tourist-related activity is concentrated in the central area of Budapest and the majority of district councils do not see it as being of direct benefit to them. Attracting industry other than hi-tech comes only third as a second choice measure, reflecting its unattractiveness as an economic option. The gap between the pattern of choices for the two types of industry is very striking. Like Table 8.1, Table 8.2 shows that hi-tech industry is more often chosen than 'any industry', especially in bigger settlements.

Table 8.2 Distribution (%) of second choices of planned measure by local governments to change the local economic structure, by settlement type

	Budapest	Provincial cities	Towns	Large villages	Small villages
Local entrepreneurs	0	0	3.0	0	1.2
Hi tech industry	38.1	50.0	31.5	33.3	12.4
Tourism	19.0	40.9	31.5	31.5	38.0
Any industry	0	4.5	19.4	19.4	8.1

Totalling the figures in these tables reveals that hi-tech industry and tourism, which are, rightly or wrongly, often perceived as environmentally-friendly economic activities, are well represented among the first two choices of planned economic change. Hi-tech industry is first or second choice in 68.5% of Budapest local governments, 77.3% of provincial cities and 49.9% of towns, while combined figures for tourism range from 51% in small villages to 32% in Budapest.[3] Certainly one can argue that cities have comparative advantage as locations for hi-tech industry due to their more skilled labour forces and better infrastructure and that small settlements have advantages for certain sorts of tourism. But it is likely that the favourable environmental images of these activities is also a factor in their popularity with local government officials.

Turning to the question of how quickly these efforts at economic diversification could be brought about, there was an interesting division of opinion: although a minority of local governments felt they were happening already, the majority felt they would take three years or more (Table 8.3). This polarized pattern appears across the board (which explains the very low V of 0.14) and suggests a spatial differentiation between localities expecting improvement soon and those expecting it in the longer term. The fact that this polarization was most marked in Budapest (which had the

Table 8.3 Distribution (%) of local government responses to the question 'In what period can these changes [in the economic structure] be achieved?', by settlement type

Period	Budapest	Provincial cities	Towns	Large villages	Small villages
Ongoing	47.8	27.3	21.8	25.8	20.6
1–2 years	4.3	4.5	6.9	3.2	10.5
3–5 years	8.7	40.9	40.8	32.3	30.8
Over 5 years	39.1	27.3	27.0	25.8	24.6

---

3 Needless to say there is not enough hi-tech industry to allow these aspirations to be realized.

largest proportions of local governments expecting change in the very near future, and in over five years) may reflect the spatial inequalities produced by land market and housing processes, with some areas having favourable prospects and attracting investment, while others see little hope. Interestingly, the five districts of Budapest identified earlier which had neither a responsible person for the environment nor an environmental policy all gave responses in the 'over five-year' category. This suggests a syndrome in which those districts which give environmental issues the lowest priority are also likely to be most pessimistic about the speed of economic change.

What is striking about local economic policy is therefore that it is so widespread, and that the hi-tech industry and tourism policy options which have the image of being environmentally friendly are very popular compared with 'any industry'. The most popular option however, 'supporting local entrepreneurs', is not related to the environmental dimension. It is more connected to a conception of local politics in which small amounts of financial support are used to spread benefits and secure political support.

Local environmental problems

Before turning to the content of the explicitly environmental policy that local governments planned it is useful to outline the environmental problems which local governments said they faced. The process by which certain activities or objects come to be defined as environmental problems is partly, but not entirely, a matter of social construction (Hannigan, 1995). It reflects both the state of knowledge prevailing about cause-effect relations impacting on the environment and the activities of different actors ('issue entrepreneurs') who wish to promote certain problems at the expense of others. The problems reported by local governments and discussed here are therefore 'perceived' problems which may not be in accord with an external (for example, national government) assessment. This does not mean however that they have no 'objective' content at all.

To discover the perceived environmental problems in an area one can either a) ask respondents for a list of the problems in a locality, b) ask what the most important problems are, or c) ask people to place a list of problems in rank order. Each method has pros and cons. The first allows the respondent to choose the problems but does not indicate their relative importance; the second forces a discrimination between most important and other problems but cannot distinguish between localities that have more or less other problems; and the last also requires discrimination among problems but may force respondents to rank order even unimportant problems.

In the present study the second method was used: interviewees could choose up to three options from a card showing eight options. Almost all interviewees (96%) chose one problem; 79% chose two and 54% three. However there was a strong correlation with settlement type. Whereas 96% of Budapest and 95% of provincial city interviewees mentioned three problems this figure fell to 73% for towns, 48% for big villages, and 44% for villages.

There was some correlation between the most commonly mentioned environmental problems and settlement type (V=0.23). Table 8.4 reveals the contrast between cities where a wide spread of 'first choice' environmental problems was mentioned and where traffic and various forms of pollution are most often cited, and towns and villages where a narrower range of problems was mentioned (and in small villages where waste predominated).

Table 8.4 Distribution (%) of first choice environmental problems as seen by local government officials, by settlement type

	Budapest	Provincial cities	Towns	Large villages	Small villages
Waste	12.5	13.6	31.6	25.8	39.3
Traffic	20.8	18.2	11.9	16.1	2.2
Air pollution	20.8	18.2	9.6	9.7	3.7
Industrial pollution	12.5	4.5	9.6	6.5	2.5
River/lake pollution	8.3	9.1	4.0	3.2	4.3

The other environmental problems mentioned on the card were: polluting agricultural activity, insufficient green space, and noise. First choice responses on these were: 1.6%, 1.4% and 1.0%. Agricultural pollution is a good example of an issue which is not so easily constructed as a problem.

In interpreting these results we need to allow for the effect of the method.[4] As shown above the average number of environmental problems cited declined with settlement size, but Tables 8.4 and 8.5 show the ordering of environmental problems as a proportion of those who cited environmental problems. The method allows respondents in settlements with multiple problems to quote only one of them as 'most important' whereas they may feel that their second most important problem is also serious. In contrast, in a locality with only one major problem the next most important problem may not be very significant, but the method cannot reveal this. This effect of the method can be seen, for example, in Table 8.4 where in large villages traffic seems to be nearly as important a problem as in Budapest. But since in larger settlements there were many more problems the low figure for traffic is deceptive. The full extent of traffic problems in Budapest is revealed only when second choices are taken into account in Table 8.5.

Turning to second choice environmental problems (Table 8.5), there is a moderate correlation with settlement type (V=0.28). Again, waste looms largest for villages and

---

4 I acknowledge helpful comments from Chris Rootes about the effects of number of problems on interviewee responses.

Table 8.5 Distribution (%) of second choice environmental problems as seen by local government officials, by settlement type

	Budapest	Provincial cities	Towns	Large villages	Small villages
Waste	20.8	9.1	33.3	44.4	36.4
Traffic	29.2	13.6	11.9	11.1	3.8
Air pollution	25.0	22.7	6.9	3.7	2.1
Industrial pollution	4.2	9.1	5.7	0	1.7
River/lake pollution	0	18.2	6.3	3.7	7.5
Lack of green space	4.2	4.5	3.8	3.7	7.1

various forms of pollution are mentioned most in cities. There are some differences: Budapest's waste problems show up more strongly, as do provincial city river and lake pollution and big village waste problems, and lack of green space creeps into the table.

The most striking result is that the pattern of second choice environmental problems is relatively similar to that of first choice environmental problems. This is particularly clear in the concentration of responses mentioning waste in virtually all types of settlement, and in the concentration of responses mentioning traffic and air pollution in Budapest and provincial cities. This 'convergent' pattern (which means that local governments include the same two problems (but in different order) in their first and second choices) is most likely to occur when the aggregate distribution of environmental problems for local governments is highly skewed, that is, when most local governments experience a small number of generally shared problems. (The opposite pattern will be shown when we consider responses to environmental problems.)

It is impossible without a very different type of data to know how far the perceived environmental problems described here have an 'objective' base or how far they are entirely socially constructed. But this is irrelevant in so far as it is perceived environmental problems which are the focus of policy debate.

Local government environmental policies

Turning to local government environmental policies, it would be misleading to expect them to show a high correlation with local environmental problems as perceived by our interviewees, since, as was shown earlier, responsibility for environmental problems is distributed across levels of government, and local government is only one of the levels involved. Thus only some of the problems reported in Tables 8.4 and 8.5 are matters for local government action. Issues requiring high capital investment such as sewage treatment, are funded by national government working through counties and through cities with county status.

We now examine what kinds of *environmental policy measure* local governments planned to undertake in response to 'these environmental problems' (those mentioned in Tables 8.4 and 8.5). The survey allowed the interviewees three choices; 96% made three choices, 75% made two and 42% made one. Table 8.6 shows the first choices of policy (V=0.20). The question in fact contained an ambiguity since only some of the problems it referred to were within the remit of local government. This mainly affects the 'investment' response in which the role of supra-local governments was crucial. The other responses were largely within the power of local governments.

Table 8.6 First choice responses (%) to the question 'How does the local government plan to solve these environmental problems?', by settlement type

	Budapest	Provincial cities	Towns	Large villages	Small villages
Investment	20.8	45.5	38.1	33.3	39.6
Fines	25.0	0	22.7	33.3	32.1
Agreements	16.7	31.8	19.9	16.5	7.5
Reduce traffic	29.2	22.7	11.9	6.4	3.1
More green space	0	0	3.4	3.3	11.5

Considering the five responses in turn, investment was the most frequent response in all types of settlement except Budapest. The fact that this response was frequent in villages which lacked investment resources makes clear that respondents were referring to investment by higher levels of government. The lower investment response in Budapest is probably due primarily to the traditionally better infrastructure provision in the capital compared with smaller settlements,[5] and the latter's greater need for waste, sewage treatment and water related investment.[6]

Fines, the second most cited response, are a new option for local governments and have the advantage that they appear to be a cost-free type of policy. In fact this is not always the case; local governments may have to pay an expert to measure pollution due to their lack of equipment. More important, fines bear on firms which are the main source of local taxation. Hence the uses of fines can antagonise major local interests. Not surprisingly the actual level of fines levied was very low. According to our survey, among the 30% of local governments which knew how much they had

---

[5] This originates in the state socialist policy of economising on infrastructure costs (Ofer, 1977; Pickvance, C.G., 2002).

[6] The effect of the method of asking questions does not seem to have been significant here since 'investment' is not a significant second choice response in Budapest – see Table 8.7.

received in fines in the previous year the median amount was 200,000 ft (£800).[7] The others either did not know or levied no fines. This policy is not likely, therefore, to give rise to significant income. There is a sharp difference between the fines figure for Budapest (25.0%) and provincial cities (0%). This may be because the environmental problems in Budapest were more linked to pollution by companies and less related to waste (where investment, not fines, is a more likely response).

Reaching agreements with firms as a response was more common in provincial cities as a first response (31.8%) than in Budapest (16.7%). This may be because firms had closer relations with local governments outside the capital and agreement was thought feasible.

Reducing traffic was a more common response in Budapest and declined progressively with settlement size. This is in line with the acute traffic problem there.

Turning to second choice responses (Table 8.7), the most striking result is that 'more green space' moves from bottom first choice (Table 8.6) to top second choice in three settlement types. Third choice patterns (not tabulated) show a further rise to prominence of 'more green space': it is mentioned by 53.8%, 55.0%, 53.1%, 41.7% and 49.5% of the five settlement types respectively, and was by far the most frequent third choice response. Adding these figures to those in Tables 8.6 and 8.7, one can see that providing more green space is felt to be one of the three most important ways of solving environmental problems in 68.6% of provincial cities, 81.6% of towns and over 90% of villages, big villages and Budapest local governments. This indicates the presence of significant environmentalist feeling.

Table 8.7 Second choice responses (%) to the question 'How does the local government plan to solve these environmental problems?', by settlement type

	Budapest	Provincial cities	Towns	Large villages	Small villages
Investment	4.5	4.5	18.6	30.8	22.8
Fines	0	0	0	0	0.5
Agreements	0	0	3.1	3.8	5.9
Reduce traffic	27.3	68.2	28.6	7.7	4.6
More green space	40.9	13.6	26.1	46.2	46.6
Divert traffic	22.7	13.6	14.9	0	0.9

Turning to the other second choice solutions to environmental problems, investment is mentioned as a second choice by villages again but less by towns and least by the cities. Fines disappear as a second choice across the board whereas they

---

[7] The £800 figure is compatible with the figures for fines reported by individual firms in our four case studies.

were the second most often cited first choice policy. Likewise, agreements with firms almost disappear for all settlement types whereas previously they were cited by a minority of cities, towns and big villages. Reducing traffic increases its frequency strongly among provincial cities and towns, while diverting traffic as a city and town policy choice emerges as an infrequent second choice.

Comparing Table 8.7 with Table 8.6, it can be seen that there are big differences in the distribution of responses by settlement type. In other words, local governments are highly 'divergent' in their choices of policy response in the sense that their first and second choices of policy are likely to be different. This difference reflects a lack of skew in the aggregate distribution of responses, or in other words a relatively uniform distribution of responses. This contrasts with the pattern shown in Tables 8.4 and 8.5 concerning perceived environmental problems.

Comparing the pairs of Tables (8.4 and 8.5, and 8.6 and 8.7), the reason why the first and second choices of environmental problem were largely convergent, while the first and second choices of environmental measure are largely divergent, is probably that while there is relative agreement (at least within settlement types) as to what the environmental problems are, there is considerable disagreement about what policy responses are possible or feasible to these problems. There are two reasons for this: a perception among local governments that a diversity of ways of responding to environmental problems exists, each of which may make some contribution, and a lack of experience in using many of these measures and hence ignorance or uncertainty about whether they are workable or which is best.

Perceived effectiveness of environmental policy measures

Finally we turn to local government officials' perceptions of the effectiveness of environmental policy measures. Theoretically one can hypothesize that perceived effectiveness will be influenced by a) the number and intractability of the problems in question, b) past experience of effective policy and c) the resources likely to be available.

We defined environmental policy measures in two ways: broad and narrow. Table 8.8 uses a broad definition. It includes all the measures mentioned in response to the question 'How does local government plan to solve these environmental problems?' and presented in Tables 8.6 and 8.7.[8]

The overall correlation between perceived likely effectiveness of environmental measures and settlement type in Table 8.8 is very weak (V=0.11). However, inspection of the table reveals that larger settlements are likely to be less satisfied than small

---

8   In an ideal world it would have been desirable to separate out individual policy responses and ask about their effectiveness in dealing with individual environmental problems. Apart from the fact that this would have required a highly complex interview schedule, it would still have failed to cope with inter-locality variability in the severity of environmental problems (and hence in the probability that policy measures would be judged effective).

Table 8.8 Local government officials' perceptions of the likely effectiveness of the environmental policy measures mentioned in Tables 8.6 and 8.7 (%)*

	Budapest	Provincial cities	Towns	Large villages	Small villages
Satisfactory	16.7	27.3	37.6	53.3	47.5
Quite satisfactory	62.5	72.7	48.3	36.7	38.6
Not satisfactory	12.5	0	11.8	10.0	10.1
Insignificant	8.3	0	1.7	0	2.5

Note: * Question: 'In your opinion how effective would these measures be?'

ones. This is probably because, as we have seen, smaller settlements have fewer and less severe problems and hence the chance of dealing with them is greater. In particular, waste, the biggest problem in small settlements, was the object of national government action, and not dependent on local resources.

Interpretations of questions which measure satisfaction are always open to subjective interpretation depending on the observer's expectations: the glass may be half full or half empty. But it is fair to say that Table 8.8 reveals at least a moderate overall level of confidence in the effectiveness of environmental measures broadly defined. In general some caution should be exercised in interpreting the results in Table 8.8 since the interviewees are local government officials who are referring to their own activities. A survey of the public may not have shown so much confidence.

We then asked interviewees about the effectiveness of 'local government environmental activities'. This differs in two ways from the previous question. It refers more narrowly to the activities of local government, and it has a greater 'present-orientation' than the question in Tables 8.6 and 8.7 where the 'measures' had previously been defined as 'planned'. The responses are set out in Table 8.9. Again

Table 8.9 Local government officials' perceptions of the effectiveness of local government environmental activities (%)*

	Budapest	Provincial cities	Towns	Large villages	Small villages
Very effective	4.2	4.5	5.6	3.2	6.8
Quite effective	58.3	72.7	58.1	64.5	56.3
Not very effective	29.2	22.7	31.3	22.6	30.4
Not at all effective	4.2	0	4.5	9.7	4.1

Note: * Question: 'To what extent do you consider local government environmental activities effective?'

there is a very weak correlation with settlement type (V=0.08) and no trends are discernable.[9]

Compared with Table 8.8, the responses again show a moderate level of perceived effectiveness, but the level is lower across the board than in Table 8.8. This is probably because when local government officials reflect on their present activities they are more realistic than when they think about the potential effectiveness of environmental measures.

Conclusion

The decentralization of local government in Hungary was a deliberate attempt to escape from the centralism of the former system and was an essential aspect of the democratization process. The resulting structure is both highly fragmented and highly diverse. As Bennett (1988) foresaw, this has led to large differences in resourcing, with villages having insignificant resources and becoming dependent on county governments.

The emphasis here has been on the significance of settlement type. This has two aspects. The resourcing differences associated with settlement type have a strong relationship with environmental commitment as indicated by the presence of specialized environmental officials (which were only to be found in larger settlements and even in these were not universally present) and with having a written environmental policy (nearly half of all towns and even some cities lacked one). Other differences associated with settlement type were connected with local economic structure: larger settlements were shown to be linked to particular types of environmental problem (traffic, air pollution), planned environmental policy (making agreements with companies, reducing traffic) and planned local economic policy (hi-tech industry).

In other cases no difference or only slight differences were found with settlement type. This was true in the case of waste as a widely perceived environmental problem, the use of investment, fines and more green space as planned local environmental policies, the moderate level of perceived effectiveness of local government environmental policies, and the popularity of tourism as a planned local economic policy. We would interpret this as due to a) certain common problems which are independent of settlement type (waste), b) certain supra-local means of addressing environmental problems (central government investment), and c) local government policy measures which are compatible with limited resources (fines, increased green space – a planning measure, support for tourism – which can be cheap). Note that the latter measures do not imply that village local governments can escape from their limited resources. The moderate confidence in local government environmental policies is probably a reflection of the overall policy capacity of local government by

---

9 Table 8.9 shows no tendency for the perceived effectiveness of environmental activities to rise in smaller settlements as was the case in Table 8.8. This is because the narrower question excludes the impact of supra-local levels of government on local environmental problems.

people working in it and is proportionate to the level of resources available to local government. Finally there was a polarization between local governments expecting quick and slow change which was found within all settlement types, suggesting that differences within settlement types (for example between relatively poorer and richer localities) were significant.

In conclusion, whereas at national level the Hungarian government is developing the necessary legislative framework, institutional capacity, and infrastructure investment required in the environmental field by its 'accession strategy', when one examines local government the picture is perhaps less optimistic. The complex decentralized governmental structure and the limited resourcing available have held back local government environmental policy. Since the conclusions in this chapter are based on a survey of local government officials, who could be expected to be more optimistic about their achievements than the public at large, the picture presented here is more likely to be too optimistic than too pessimistic.

9 Local Economic Situation, Local Environmental Mobilization and Local Government Environmental Policy in Hungary*

Much writing on environmental policy starts from an administrative or legal standpoint and focuses on the powers and scope of legislation and how this evolves over time. The present chapter has a different starting point. It is concerned with what influences the making of environmental policy at local level and assumes that this can only be discovered by research on the agents involved. The approach is therefore sociological rather than administrative or legal and gives importance to informal processes of influence rather than formal legal powers.

Our point of departure is the well-known argument that the main reasons for the unequal territorial distribution of unattractive facilities, such as polluting factories or waste incinerators, in a country, are not differences in legal powers but differences in area economic prosperity and in the extent of local public mobilization around environmental values. In a nutshell the proposition is that regions and towns with poorer economic situations will be keen to attract workplaces and facilities which have negative externalities. These negative externalities may be physical, such as air pollution, or social, such as stigmatising reactions provoked by 'marginal' social groups. As a corollary, firms and other organizations wishing to set up these facilities will target areas of economic and social deprivation which they expect to be unlikely to resist. Conversely regions and towns in the best economic situations will seek to avoid workplaces and facilities with negative externalities.

This model underlies, for example, Blowers and Leroy's (1994) theory of why some areas attract Locally Unwanted Land Uses (or LULUs) while others avoid them. It is also the foundation of the 'environmental justice' movement in the US, which seeks to defend minority groups from hazardous waste and other activities with negative externalities (Cole and Foster, 2001). A parallel argument can be made on

---

* An earlier version of this chapter was published as 'Local economic situation, local environmental mobilization and local government policy in Hungary', *Journal of Environmental Policy and Planning*, 4, 2002, 87–99. Copyright John Wiley & Sons Ltd. Reproduced with permission.

the international level to explain why some less developed countries become recipients of environmental bads, such as household waste.

One reason for the unequal territorial distributions of such facilities and activities within countries is that in most countries some types of areas have institutionalized protection of some kind.[1] For example green belts and national parks bring with them special protective statuses which impose higher standards on the activities permitted within them. It is to be expected that some degree of territorial environmental differentiation will exist due to the efficacity of these institutionalized statuses, even if studies of planning decisions in protected areas show that the protection they ensure is far from total. (See for example Munton's (1983) study of the London green belt.)

However, over the vast majority of most national territories there are no special protective statuses. Typically, local environmental policy is in the hands of subnational governments applying common legislation which gives them strong formal powers over the location of activities, for example the power to refuse permission for them.[2] This poses the question of why common legislation does not lead to an equal territorial distribution of unattractive facilities.

There are two obvious answers. The first is that legislation is never totally prescriptive, but allows choice or discretion in local policy-making. The scope for this arises in two ways. In the case of permissive legislation (which allows but does not require an authority to do or prevent something) the scope for choice is self-evident. But even in the case of mandatory legislation (which specifies that a certain activity must be carried out or prevented) there will be some discretion as to how and when this is to be done since concepts can never be defined to meet all situations, and local circumstances will vary. It is the scope for variation made possible by formally identical legislation which allows the unequal territorial distribution of unattractive activities to occur, in areas where there are no special protective statuses. The existence of such choice or discretion goes against the model of 'central control' which is often unthinkingly applied and by which local government gives the impression that its hands are totally tied by higher levels of government. In my experience this is rarely the case and is best seen as an ideology by which local governments transfer responsibility for decisions over which they retain considerable influence. (On the question of centralization see Pickvance and Preteceille (1991).)

The second reason for the unequal territorial distribution of economic activities is that the existence of choice or discretion allows the exercise of informal influence. A study of legislation would make it appear that local governments have enormous powers. For example local government powers to grant planning permission could be used to refuse all industrial development. In the real world however these formal powers come into conflict with the various interest groups which stand to gain or lose

---

1 This protection may result from past public environmentalist mobilization or top-down imposition and is not always welcomed by residents because of the restrictions they entail.
2 The term environmental policy is used here to refer to planning and pollution related policies implemented by local government. It excludes policies affecting local areas applied by national bodies and their field offices.

through policy. The real, or 'effective', power of local government depends on the balance of power between it and external actors.

A simple model of how local governments' decisions influence the location of activities is influenced could start from five factors:

1. the economic situation of the area and its need for facilities and employment;
2. the real and perceived influence of external actors such as businesses and environmental groups;
3. the values of the local politicians and officials implementing the legislation;
4. the perceived characteristics of the local population; and
5. the settlement type.

Thus local politicians would be hypothesised to pay attention to the economic situation of the area and the interests of firms but also be open to the influence of residents and environmental groups. Their opportunities for policy making would vary according to the settlement type due to the differing powers given to local governments in different settlement types. This is the approach taken by many classic sociological studies of environmental policy implementation as well as by studies of other types of local government policy: Blowers (1984), Crenson (1971), and Saunders (1979).

The aim of the present chapter is to explore two of these processes, the influence of local economic conditions and of environmental groups on local government environmental policy implementation in Hungary. We shall not pursue the questions of politicians' or staff values, or perceptions of the local population's characteristics.

The chapter is divided into three parts: concepts, hypotheses and operationalization; a presentation of the findings; and a conclusion.

Concepts, hypotheses, and operationalization

From the above arguments we derive two hypotheses:
For any given settlement type

A. *the more affluent the locality, the greater the extent of environmental mobilization,*
B. *the more affluent the locality, the greater the effect of environmental groups on local government environmental policy.*

Figure 9.1 expresses these two propositions.
These propositions make two assumptions.

1. An assumption about mobilization: namely, that when economic deprivation in an area is less, people are *more* likely to form environmental groups and the groups are *more* likely to influence environmental policy. The underlying theoretical rationale is that environmental groups are a) not formed by the deprived but by the

Figure 9.1 Hypothesized model relating economic situation, environmental mobilization and environmental policy for any settlement type

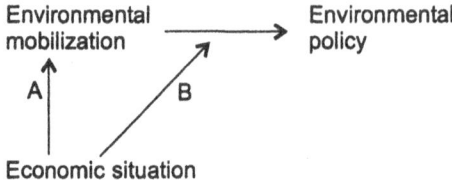

more educated or affluent, and b) because of this are better organized and more likely to be successful, perhaps even relying on links with local officials and politicians. This idea is common to the new social movement and resource mobilization approaches within social movement theory (Rucht, 1991). Hence we should expect that the priority given by the public to environmental issues over economic issues would increase the greater the economic prosperity of the area.

2. An assumption about the relation between local prosperity and local population composition. This involves two elements: population selectivity effects and human capital effects. The proportion of higher educated people (who are known to be more likely to espouse environmentalist values – see Parry et al., 1992) is a) higher in richer areas than in poorer areas (due to differences in occupational structure, migration flows and the unequal distribution of higher education institutions) and b) also contributes directly to the wealth of the area.

We shall measure the concepts of interest in the following way:

1. *Settlement type:* this is measured directly. The local governments studied were classified into the following categories: Budapest, provincial city, town, big village, small village. The sample used was described in Chapter 8.
2. *Environmental mobilization:* this is measured by the presence of environmental groups in the area as judged by local government officials.
3. *Local government environmental policy:* this variable is not measured directly. Instead we measure the influence of environmental mobilization on local environmental policy as judged by local government officials.
4. *Economic situation of settlement:* the measurement of this concept requires a lengthy discussion.

Ideally it would have been desirable to have measures for the economic situation of all the settlements, but no such data was available. Instead it was decided to group localities into macro-regions of similar economic situation and use these as the unit of analysis. The choice of macro-regions was made in the light of two conflicting requirements. We wanted to ensure a) that each macro-region represented a distinct average economic situation (which suggested having more of them), and b) that the cell frequencies in the cross-tabulations were not too small so that analyses by settlement type could be made (which suggested having fewer).

Any delineation of macro-regions is open to debate since decisions on their number and boundaries are a matter of choice. Ideally they should be internally homogeneous and sufficient in number for internal differences to be insignificant. In practice neither criterion is often met. Macro-regions always have some degree of internal economic differentiation. The fewer the number chosen the greater this will be and the more serious its effect, with the consequence that it will be more difficult to demonstrate inter-regional variations.

In Hungary a threefold division is often made between the West, Budapest and the East. This has a certain appeal. However it has the major disadvantage from our point of view that Budapest is entirely made up of urban district councils, whereas the counties that make up West and East have a mix of city, town and village governments. This means that one of our aims – to examine the effect of both economic situation and settlement type on local environmental policy – could be pursued in only two out of three macro-regions.

A second possible choice is to use the seven NUTS2 regions, each of which is made up of two or three counties. (NUTS2 regions are the middle of the three-level EC territorial classification; they are the level at which national and EC regional polices are usually applied.) This has the advantages that Hungarian government data is available in this format and that regional economic differences are more likely to be visible than if fewer regions are chosen. The disadvantage is that seven is too many for our purposes, since with seven regions and five settlement types in each the cell frequencies in a cross-tabulation of 600 local governments would be too small to separate out economic and settlement type effects.

A compromise was therefore decided on, in which the seven NUTS2 regions were grouped into three macro-regions, which we have labelled Northwest, South, and Northeast. This grouping was made using measures of GDP per capita, hourly earnings, and unemployment. As can be seen from Table 9.1, although the three measures do not show sharp breaks between the economic situation of the three macro-regions, the Northwest is overall the most affluent and the Northeast overall the poorest, with the South in an intermediate position. The Northwest is considerably wealthier than the other two macro-regions. Hence we shall expect differences between the Northwest and South to be greater than those between the South and Northeast. Local governments were therefore classified into these three types as measures of economic level. Figure 9.2 shows the location of these regions and their component counties.

The drawback of using only three macro-regions is that intra-regional economic differences are greater and inter-regional differences are smaller than if more were used. The importance of intra-regional differences is made clear in Enyedi's (1994) analysis of the economic prospects for 'regions' in Hungary in which the eight regions he uses frequently cross county boundaries or involve splitting counties. Nevertheless Enyedi's analysis also provides some backing for the choice of the three macro-regions used here. His categories 'regions with industrial depression' and 'external

Figure 9.2 Counties and 'macro-regions'

From a map © Kóvári József, Márton Mátyás, Zentai László at http://lazarus.elte.hu/

Table 9.1 Characteristics of the Hungarian NUTS2 regions, and how they were grouped into three 'macro-regions'

Names of macro-regions used here	Names of official NUTS2 regions and their component county governments	GDP/capita, 1998 (100 = national average)	Net earnings of full-time employees/ month, 1999	Unemployment rate, 1999
Northwest	Central Hungary: Budapest, Pest County	148	60	5.2
	Central Transdanubia: Fejér, Komárom-Esztergom, Veszprém	98	47	6.0
	Western Transdanubia: Győr–Moson–Sopron, Vas, Zala	110	46	4.4
South	Southern Transdanubia: Baranya, Somogy, Tolna	77	43	8.2
	Southern Great Plain: Bács–Kiskun, Békés, Csongrád	76	44	5.7
Northeast	Northern Hungary: Borsod–Abaúj–Zemplén, Heves, Nógrád	68	43	11.5
	Northern Great Plain: Hajdú–Bihar, Jász–Nagykun–Szolnok, Szabolcs–Szatmár–Bereg	68	42	10.1

Source: Hungarian Central Statistical Office website: www.ksh.hu/eng

periphery' are mainly in the Northeast macro-region. Of the 'dynamic poles and axes', three are in the Northwest, one in the Northeast and two in the South. 'Upgraded western Hungary' is entirely in the Northwest. The South has a mixture of types of area. In other words the combination of types of area help to make sense of the differences in economic performance in the table and suggests that the three-fold macro-regional division used here is an effective way of measuring the economic situation of settlements.

In the rest of the chapter the term region will be used in place of macro-region for brevity.

In sum, local economic situation is measured by allocating each locality to a region: Northwest – most affluent, South – less affluent, Northeast – least affluent.

Following from the use of the region as a substitute for economic situation, our initial hypotheses that local environmental policy is affected by local economic situation and local environmental mobilization, and that this varies by settlement type, can be translated into the propositions that for any locality:

- *the more affluent the region, the greater the perceived extent of environmental mobilization,*
- *the more affluent the region, the greater the perceived effect of environmental groups on local government environmental policy.*

In interpreting our results three points should be noted:

1. If the expected relationships exist our results should show a regional gradient from Northwest (the most affluent region) through the South to the Northeast (the poorest region), with the largest difference being between the Northwest and other two regions for the reasons mentioned earlier. However as explained earlier the decision to choose only three regions makes it less likely that inter-regional differences in economic situation will be revealed as having an effect on mobilization. Conversely if we find striking inter-regional differences these will be indicative of even stronger underlying effects.
2. Since we also expect settlement type to make a difference, comparisons of inter-regional differences will only be carried out within the same settlement type. In this way the separate effects of settlement types and regions will be distinguished.
3. Lastly, in order to avoid giving excessive weight to possibly insignificant differences, no reference will be made in the interpretation of the tables below to differences of 2% or less, or to percentages calculated on a base of less than ten.

The data were collected through the national survey of 600 individual local governments mentioned in the last Chapter. Since the economic situation and settlement type of areas are hypothesized to have effects on local environmental policy, a satisfactory research design needs to build in variation in these variables in order to study their effects (King et al., 1994). The national sample did this. It covered all regions of Hungary and hence settlements of all economic levels, and by including Budapest city council and its 23 district councils, all 22 provincial cities, and a sample of 179 towns, 31 large villages and 344 villages, it ensured that the full range of settlement types was represented in the sample. In all the tables which follow the settlement type classification is used so that comparisons can be made within local governments belonging to the same settlement type.

Presentation of findings

This section considers in turn: measures of local government environmental commitment, and the presence of environmental groups and their perceived influence on environmental policy.

Measures of local government environmental commitment

We suggested earlier that even when common legislation applied to a category of local governments this did not ensure similar behaviour. Before examining the hypotheses set out earlier it is therefore useful to examine the variation between settlement types in environmental commitment and also to see whether there is any regional variation within settlement types in this respect.

This can be done by looking at the proportion of local governments of a given settlement type a) with a written environmental policy and b) with an official with environmental responsibilities. From what has been said both measures should show a decline as one moves from large to small settlements, in line with their decreasing competences and resources. However, we do not hypothesize that there will be any regional differences since our assumption is that these these measures of environmental commitment measure formal aspects of policy rather than the informal processes of influence.

We examine first the 'All regions' data in Tables 9.2 and 9.3 which was discussed in the last chapter, and then turn to the regional differences.

The 'All regions' row in Table 9.2 shows the expected decline in commitment with settlement size. However it also shows an unexpected result, that provincial cities are more likely to have a written environmental programme than Budapest council. This is despite the fact that the average population size of provincial cities and Budapest districts is similar (about 100,000). The probable reason for this is that as a city Budapest is socially and economically differentiated and the district councils have very different social and economic bases which are reflected in their practices (see below).

A second measure of environmental commitment is whether a local government has a specific official with environmental responsibilities.

The 'All regions' row of Table 9.3 shows the same decline with settlement size as Table 9.2, with the difference that no large villages and almost no small villages had an environmental official whereas significant minorities had written environmental

Table 9.2 **Percentages of local governments in a given settlement type and region with a written environmental programme**

	Budapest[a]	Provincial cities	Towns	Large villages	Small villages
Northwest	70.8	100.0[b]	54.9	45.5	24.1
South		100.0[b]	54.4	20.0	19.2
Northeast		83.3[b]	54.9	40.0	18.5
All regions	70.8	95.5	54.7	35.5	20.9
N[c]	24	22	179	31	344

Notes
a In the tables and text Budapest refers to the city council and 23 district councils unless otherwise indicated.
b Percentages calculated on a base of less than ten.
c Number of local governments in that settlement type category from which data available.

Table 9.3 **Percentages of local governments in a given settlement type and region with a specific official with environmental responsibilities**

	Budapest	Provincial cities	Towns	Large villages	Small villages
Northwest	56.5	100.0*	32.0	0	1.5
South		100.0*	28.1	0	2.0
Northeast		83.3*	14.1	0	1.9
All regions	56.5	95.5	23.6	0	1.7
N	23	22	178	31	343

Note: * Percentages calculated on a base of less than ten.

policies. This no doubt reflects the relative resource cost of each. Once again the district councils of Budapest are shown to be less committed to environmental policy than the provincial cities. An analysis of Budapest councils showed that there was a substantial overlap between those which did not have a person responsible for environmental matters and those which had no written environmental policy: of the 13 councils which had a written environmental policy, ten had a specific person responsible for the environment while of the seven councils without a written policy only two had a specific environmental official. There is also evidence of a link with socio-economic differentiation. If Budapest districts are ranked in terms of dwelling values into high, medium and low[3] then there is a strong relation with the proportion having a specific environmental official, which rose from 4/10 (low value districts), to

---
3 Based on 1991 housing value data in Kovacs (1994).

4/7 (medium value) and 2/2 (high value). The corresponding proportions for districts having a written environmental policy are: 6/10, 5/7 and 3/4, a weaker relationship that is to be expected because of the ease of writing a policy compared with employing a staff member.

Tables 9.2 and 9.3 also show some regional differences. Table 9.2 shows regional differences only within the two village categories. Both show the most affluent region, the Northwest, as most likely to come first, but the other two regions do not take up their expected relative positions. Table 9.3 shows the full hypothesized regional gradient in the case of towns, with the Northwest most likely to have environmental officials. Although we did not hypothesize that these formal measures of environmental commitment would reveal any regional differences, it is interesting that what evidence there is mostly supports the idea of a regional gradient from Northwest to Northeast, suggesting that in certain settlement types economic situation leads to differences in the application of formal measures of policy.

The presence of environmental groups and their influence on environmental policy

We now turn to our main foci of interest, and start with the link A in Figure 9.1 and first proposition: that the level of environmental mobilization within each settlement type shows the expected regional/economic gradient. To examine this we consider the local government officials' perceptions of the prevalence of environmental groups in their area. The question asked was whether there were any environmental groups in the area. It was therefore a measure of their perceptions rather than a measure based on conducting a census of groups. The question did not ask how many groups there were. It therefore did not measure the 'breadth' or the 'intensity' of such mobilization, but only whether it existed at all.[4]

The results are shown in Table 9.4. This shows two things. Firstly, as is evident in the 'All regions' row, which reveals an interesting gradient by settlement type (with provincial cities leading the way as in Tables 9.2 and 9.3), there is a strong bivariate correlation between settlement type and reported presence of environmental groups.[5] Only large villages deviate from the pattern in Tables 9.2 and 9.3. The levels of the figures, if perceptions correspond to reality, show the extent of environmental group activity throughout Hungary: environmental groups are present in most districts of Budapest and nearly all provincial cities and are rare only in the small village

---

[4] In addition, we cannot claim that officials' perceptions are proportional to the number of groups since a threshold effect may operate by which officials are totally unaware of low level group activity, and become aware of it only when it exceeds some level, for example when it is reported in local media.

[5] The value of Cramer's V, the correlation coefficient for the whole table which treats settlement type and region as nominal variables, is 0.51, a high figure. When the data for each region is considered separately the corresponding figures are also high: 0.57, 0.51 and 0.44.

Table 9.4 Percentages of local government officials in a given settlement type and region reporting the presence of environmental groups in the area

	Budapest	Provincial cities	Towns	Large villages	Small villages
Northwest	70.8	88.9*	60.0	72.7	13.1
South		85.7*	49.1	30.0	8.4
Northeast		100.0*	40.6	30.0	11.2
All regions	70.8	90.9	48.9	50.0	11.2
N	24	22	174	31	339

Note: * Percentages calculated on a base of less than ten.

category. This is an important finding since it makes clear that environmental groups do not only exist in the places which are most notorious for their pollution such as Ajka (power station), Dorog (waste incinerator), Nagytétény (galvanizing plant) and Ofalu (radioactive waste) (Juhasz et al., 1993, Szirmai, 1993).[6] It also ties in with analyses of the political opportunity structure in post-socialist Hungary which suggest that the media are favourable to environmental groups, that local and central government is responsive to citizen activity, and that environmental activism prior to 1989 was a channel through which local politicians gained prominence and office (Pickvance, K., 1998; Pickvance, C.G., 1996; Szirmai, 1997).

Secondly, Table 9.4 shows some regional differences in the towns and two villages categories. In each case the Northwest takes the leading position as our regional gradient hypothesis suggests. But the South comes unexpectedly third in the small village category, though the differences are in any case very small, and in large villages does less well than expected. Therefore the evidence on the effect of local economic situation (as measured by region) on environmental group presence as perceived by local government officials generally supports our hypothesis in the case of the position of the Northwest, but fails to explain the relative positions of localities in the South and Northeast. Since as we showed in Table 9.1 the economic differences between the Northwest and the other two regions are greater than those between the South and Northeast this finding is not too unexpected.

We now turn to link B in Figure 9.1 and our second proposition: that the influence of environmental groups on environmental policy is greater in affluent regions, for any given settlement type. We were able to measure the impact of environmental groups on policy directly by interviewees' responses to the question 'What are the most influential forces on environmental decision-making?', to which one response

---

6 In such areas environmental groups are more likely to be directed at changing local environmental policy. The question throws the net more widely to include all environmental groups many of which are engaged in educational and practical activities.

was allowed. The response frequencies across the whole sample were: the public (46.3%), elected representatives (40.6%), environmental bureaucrats (5.5%), environmental groups (3.2 %), firms (2.5%) and the media (0.8%). (It should be noted that these totals are arithmetic means and therefore reflect the large proportion of villages (62.5%) in the sample.)

Since the interviewees were local government officials one would perhaps expect them to conform to the conventional picture of representative democracy and give the answers 'the public' and 'local politicians'. It is therefore likely that the impact of environmental groups (and firms – another unconventional answer) were underestimated and the fact that they were mentioned even by small minorities is all the more interesting. It should be noted that the form of the question is likely to isolate 'extreme' cases since one would expect far fewer interviewees to say environmental groups had 'most' influence than if we had asked whether they had 'any' influence. Clearly the settlements where they had the most influence are quite unusual.

The All regions row of Table 9.5 shows that the 'environmental group' response was most often given in provincial cities (13.6%) and Budapest (12.5%) and least often in large villages (nil). These are quite striking figures and again bear witness to the relatively favourable situation for environmental (and other citizen) groups in Hungary. Comparing Tables 9.4 and 9.5 it can be seen that there is a proportionality between the order of the figures for Budapest, provincial cities and towns in terms of both presence of environmental groups and their having 'most influence' on policy. The leading position of provincial cities in both tables conforms to the pattern in the previous tables.[7]

Table 9.5 **Percentages of local government officials in a given settlement type and region who said that environmental groups had the most influence on environmental decision-making in the area**

	Budapest	Provincial cities	Towns	Large villages	Small villages
Northwest	12.5	22.2*	12.0	0	1.5
South		14.3*	0	0	0
Northeast		0	4.2	0	1.9
All regions	12.5	13.6	5.1	0	1.2
N	24	22	177	31	342

Note: * Percentages calculated on a base of less than ten.

As far as the regional pattern in this table is concerned, only the figures for the towns can be examined, given our rules about interpreting data. As can be seen they

---

[7] In this case the V values refer to all responses to this question. The V values for the three regions are less than in Table 9.4: 0.23, 0.29, 0.24 but they were much higher than for the unregionalized bivariate crosstabulation, V = 0.17.

show the expected dominance of the Northwest (12%, or six towns, listed below), but the Northeast (4.2%, or three towns) does better than the South (nil) which is contrary to the hypothesis. This result thus offers only partial support for our hypothesis about the importance of economic situation and environmental group mobilization in understanding local government environmental policy.

So far we have adopted an aggregate analysis of survey responses on the question of perceived influence of environmental groups on local environmental policy. Since the number of localities where environmental groups were judged to be the most significant influence on local environmental policy are so exceptional (3.2% of the total) and few in number we now consider the individual cases involved. The assumption here is that the analysis of exceptional or 'deviant' cases can be revealing. We therefore now provide some more information on these highly unusual localities.

Budapest
- Budapest city council (NW): the city-wide council is led by the mayor, a former social worker and dissident; keen to promote Budapest on the European and world stage.
- Budapest I (NW): the castle area, with high house prices.
- Budapest XVIII (NW): an outer low-price 'petit bourgeois' area of houses and gardens.

The provincial cities
- Kecskemét (S): a county town and agricultural centre with higher education institutions and a strong civic culture.
- Sopron (NW): a tourist and commercial centre, and university town, near the Austrian border with a strong civic culture.
- Szombathely (NW): a rail centre and county town of 21,000 also near the Austrian border. Mixed industry and fruit farming.

The towns
- Balassagyarmat (NE): a historic town of 18,000 with a mixed and declining economic base seeking to promote itself as a tourist centre.
- Balatonfüred (NW): a pre-war spa, tourist resort and conference centre of 13,500 on Lake Balaton.
- Encs (NE): an industrial town in a wooded hilly area 200km from Budapest, with at least one environmental group.
- Nagykáta (NW): a town of 13,000 to the east of the capital, in the Great Plain, where there was a Canadian government programme to develop municipal decision-making with an emphasis on participatory planning.
- Ráckeve (NW): a town on the Danube south of Budapest in an area popular for dachas and angling. Situated in the middle of an ecologically sensitive region, like Nagykáta it received Canadian support for participatory environmental management.

- Szentendre (NW): an artists' town on the Danube north of Budapest popular for day trips and for residence among the nouveaux riches. Not coincidentally it is also the location of the Regional Environmental Centre (for central and eastern Europe).
- Szigetszentmiklós (NW): an industrial town of 20,000 on the Danube in the southern periphery of Budapest.
- Tiszafüred (NE): a resort on Lake Tisza near Hortobágy National Park, promoting green tourism.
- Vác (NW): a mixed industrial town of 36,000 on the Danube north of Budapest, with a number of environmental groups mobilized around the cement works there.

There is no single feature which is common to all these localities. However a large number of them fall into two categories:

a) places with higher education institutions and a strong civic culture; and
b) towns located in attractive environments (especially on the Danube or on lakes) which are trying to exploit this asset as part of an economic development strategy.

Both of these provide fertile ground for environmental groups. The two cases where the Canadian municipal programme was introduced also show the influence of external ideas. (However the 'external' factor should not be stressed exclusively. The Canadian instigators may have chosen localities which they considered propitious for their participatory experiment.)

Finally we can draw on Tables 9.4 and 9.5 to measure the extent to which the presence of environmental groups was converted into perceived influence on policy. This 'conversion ratio' could be treated as a measure of particularly successful group activity, and/or of a local government which was particularly receptive to citizen pressure. (It would be difficult to separate these two processes. Indeed the receptiveness of local government at one point in time may be a response to earlier environmental group action, so there is a spiral of reciprocal relations.)

In practice this raises an issue of definition. Some environmental groups try to influence policy while others are engaged in education or practical activities so it could be argued that only the former type should be included in any measure of environmental groups influence. Against this it could be argued that there is an indirect effect of the activities of the latter group, and that whatever their intentions they have the effect of making environmental issues more prominent on the political agenda.

The data available from the survey concerns the presence rather than the number (or character) of environmental groups so it falls short of what is desirable.[8] However

---

[8] Other data suggest the predominance of environmental groups with a practical orientation. See for example the list of Hungarian environmental groups on www.rec.hu, or of those receiving small grants on www.okotars.hu.

it is useful to compare it with the evidence on perceived influence of environmental groups.

The bottom row of Table 9.6 shows that the highest conversion ratio was found in Budapest and the provincial cities. It was much lower in the towns except in the Northwest and small villages except in the Northeast. As suggested above this is likely to be due both to differences in numbers of environmental groups (and their involvement in political activity) and differences in receptiveness to them by local government. Finally Table 9.6 shows a mixture of supportive and contradictory evidence for the idea of a regional/economic gradient. This suggests that the 'conversion process' between environmental group activity and influence on policy takes place more within the political realm and is less influenced by economic forces than some of the other processes discussed earlier. In turn this implies that patterns of political influence are not determined by the economic situation of a locality but have some autonomy.

Table 9.6 A measure of the 'conversion ratio' between the presence of environmental groups and the perception that they have 'most influence' on environmental policy, for local governments of a given settlement type and region

	Budapest	Provincial cities	Towns	Large villages	Small villages
Northwest	0.18	n.a.	0.20	0	0.11
South		n.a.	0	0	0
Northeast		n.a.	0.10	0	0.17
All regions	0.18	0.15	0.10	0	0.11

Note: Each figure is calculated by dividing the entries in Table 9.5 by those in Table 9.4. Provincial city data by region were based on too small a base to be included.

Conclusion

The starting point of this chapter was the proposition that variations in local environmental policy could be explained in part by the economic situation of the locality and the extent of environmental group mobilization. The underlying rationale was that localities with more highly educated people are likely to be more affluent, that affluent localities (and more educated people within them) are more likely to mobilize and to mobilize effectively around environmental issues, and that local governments were responsive to this mobilization. This proposition derives from studies in advanced capitalist societies and one reason for examining it in Hungary was to see how far it had validity in a lower income 'transition' society.

The first finding was that settlement type was an important influence on environmental group presence and environmental group influence on policy. The provincial cities and Budapest led the way in both respects. However the unexpected finding was that the provincial cities were the settlement type in which environmental groups were most prevalent and where their influence was greatest. The socio-economic differentiation within Budapest meant that some areas had no environmental groups and therefore no influence on environmental policy.

The second finding concerned economic situation (measured at the regional level). Unfortunately the numbers of cases were not sufficient to test this hypothesis satisfactorily across the whole range of settlement types. In particular although all 22 provincial cities were included in the survey the numbers were too small for inter-regional comparisons to be made with any confidence. The clearest result was that local governments in the most favourable economic environments (the Northwest region) were most likely to have environmental groups and these groups were most likely to be the single most influential force on environmental policy. On the other hand, the differences in the last two respects between the poorest and intermediate areas (Northeast and South regions) were less consistent. This conformed with our expectations given that the Northwest is considerably more affluent than the other two regions and should show more marked effects.

The third result concerned the perceived extent of environmental groups. This varied greatly with settlement size and showed a strong relation with economic situation among towns. (In other words in towns environmental groups were more likely to be found in the most favoured areas economically than in the poorest areas.) Large villages in the richest areas were also very likely to have environmental groups.

Fourth, regarding the perceived influence of environmental groups on environmental policy, the survey question was an 'extreme' one since it asked who had the most influence and not surprisingly the proportions giving the response 'environmental groups' were low. Nevertheless, in addition to the clear positive relation between perceived influence of environmental groups and settlement size, this influence was more likely to be mentioned by interviewees in towns in the wealthiest region than by those in the middle and poorer regions. Analysis of the individual localities where environmental groups were considered most influential on environmental policy showed that many fell into two categories: a) those with higher education institutions and a tradition of citizen activism, and b) those that were basing their economic development partly on environmental assets such as rivers, lakes and national parks.

Overall (and particularly for the richest region), economic situation as measured by regional category worked well in demonstrating the consistent advantage of localities in the richest areas both in environmental group presence and influence on environmental policy. The corollary of this, that localities in the poorest regions should be most disadvantaged in these respects, failed to appear consistently across settlement types. Whether this is due to a 'real' lack of gradient or to the inadequacies of our regional measure is for future research to explore. One possibility is that the advantages of localities in the Northwest are overwhelming. This could be related to the proximity of the Northwest to Austria and Germany and its consequent attractiveness for foreign investment, the relation between affluence and higher education, and the probable greater degree of contact between environmentalists in Northwest Hungary and those in western Europe.

In sum the balance of the evidence provided here supports the idea that in Hungary in localities which are relatively wealthy, environmental groups are more likely to organize and more likely to influence environmental policy. In other words the model shown in Figure 9.1 is probably not restricted to advanced capitalist societies. This conclusion is subject to two qualifications. First, the measure used could be improved. It relies on a measure of local economic wealth which is at the regional level. Although relationships which emerge despite such an aggregate measure hint at stronger underlying relationships, ideally a more localised measure of local prosperity should be used. Likewise, levels of education should also be measured for each locality given the importance of education in the mobilization process. Second, it should be acknowledged that survey research is only one way of getting at the relationships explored here. Its advantage is that it is comprehensive and systematic but its weakness is that statements about the perceived influence of environmental groups on policy may be normative and not be borne out in actual cases. Conversely, case studies of a small number of localities may show the actual influence of environmental groups but leave open the question of whether the influence observed is peculiar to those localities or to the issues involved.

10 Conclusion

The aims in writing this book were threefold: to describe some aspects of local environmental regulation in Hungary, to explain the patterns observed, and to relate the Hungarian experience of local environmental regulation to the wider academic literature on environmental policy and post-socialism.

In this chapter we pull together our main findings and relate them to the initial theoretical debates. We will not repeat the comparative analysis of the four localities in Chapter 7 or the detailed analysis of the survey data in Chapters 8 and 9. We consider in turn our findings and how useful our explanatory model is in making sense of them, how these findings relate to research on environmental regulation internationally, and what role should be given to the legacies from state socialism. We shall emphasise the cross-national parallels in local environmental regulation but will argue that, contrary to mainstream comparative methodology, it is not necessary to deny Hungarian specificities such as legacy effects in explaining them.

An overview of the main findings

The main findings are about a) variation between localities, and b) constant patterns across localities.

Patterns of local variation

1. There is considerable variation between the four localities in terms of local environmental regulation as measured by the strength of local government environmental policy. This was reinforced by the survey evidence which showed variation between local governments of different types in their environmental policy.
2. There is also considerable variation between the four localities in terms of local environmental regulation as measured by the strength of regional environmental

inspectorate activity. This was an unexpected conclusion since REIs are government agencies and as such might have been expected to have uniform practices across the four locations.
3. The variation in strength of local government environmental policy in the four localities followed the same pattern as the variations in strength of REI behaviour, namely that localities which were strong in one respect were also strong in the other.
4. The survey data suggested that local government environmental policy was most developed (in the sense of there being a written policy and an official in charge) in larger local governments (except that in provincial cities it was more developed than in the districts of Budapest).
5. The survey data showed that larger settlements were perceived by officials as having more environmental problems than smaller settlements. Waste was the problem most mentioned in all settlements. Traffic and air pollution were next most often mentioned in larger settlements.
6. The survey showed that the most popular types of local government environmental policy measures in the eyes of officials were investment and fines and that this did not vary much with settlement type. Measures concerning traffic were most mentioned in larger settlements but more green space was very popular among officials in all types of council when first, second and third policy choices were aggregated. There was considerable confidence in the effectiveness of environmental policy measures (widely defined) in all settlement types but this was lowest in Budapest. A narrower definition, restricted to policies directly controlled by local government, revealed less confidence in their effectiveness.
7. Turning to local government economic policy, there was also considerable variation both among the four locality case studies and in the survey. However the pattern of variation among the four localities did not match that of the variation in local government environmental policy. The survey data revealed that there was an almost universal commitment to local economic policy among local governments whatever the size. The most popular policy among interviewees was supporting local entrepreneurs, with the promotion of tourism and the attraction of hi-tech industry coming second. There was an interesting polarization in responses concerning the speed of impact of local economic policy with some officials expecting rapid impact and others a much slower impact.

These findings demonstrate the value of a local level study, since a national study could not have revealed such differences.

Constant patterns across localities

So far we have emphasized variations between localities. However it would be misleading to give the impression that variation was the whole story. We also found two common features across all the research sites. Our interviews revealed that the legislation governing the actions of local governments and REIs allowed them considerable flexibility in dealing with firms. As a result local environmental regulation was characterised by negotiation rather than the mechanical imposition of requirements or penalties.[1] There were numerous ways in which the rules allowed an accommodation between the interests of firms and the policies of local governments and REIs.

Our evidence on low fine levels, on exemptions from environmental requirements, and on their negotiability, suggested that the absolute degree of severity of environmental regulation is at most moderate rather than high.

Before considering explanations of these findings it may be useful to spell out some of the ways we encountered in which the scope for negotiation was manifested and in which weak environmental regulation was expressed. The first list refers to the REIs and the second to local government.

REI policy

1. Legislation does not exist concerning the type of pollution concerned.
2. Legislation exists but no standards have yet been set.
3. Standards have been set but they are loose.
4. Standards have been set but allow variation depending on circumstances.
5. Standards are set but exceptions are made.
6. Exemptions are allowed for firms that have plans to reach higher standards in the future.
7. Initial approval of equipment is lenient.
8. Companies may under-report pollution levels.
9. REI-initiated inspections are rare or ineffective, so the chances of any breaches of standards being discovered are low.
10. Residents do not report possible breaches to the council but direct to the firm so REI inspections are not carried out following complaints and the council is unaware of breaches.
11. The resourcing of the REI is inadequate so it cannot carry out its functions and has to divert efforts into earning money, for example, by doing consultancy work.
12. Alleged breaches of standards are contested by the companies.
13. The greater resources of companies enable them to spend more on expert opinion than can the REI or local government.
14. When fines are set, companies lodge appeals. Again the size of the resources of the respective parties are crucial.
15. Fines are typically set at levels which are so low that they remove the economic incentive to reduce pollution.

---

1 Since our research method was not intended to allow us to observe any negotiations between REIs and firms we could only rely on reports about negotiations.

Local government

1. In preparing plans environmental considerations are given low priority.
2. In giving permission for environmentally unfriendly activities little consideration is given to environmental considerations.
3. In classifying land by category of protected status too much land is placed in the least protected category.
4. In acting as a channel for complaints the council is ineffective.
5. Fines are set at low levels in areas where the council has this responsibility.
6. The enforcement of planning decisions and fines has low priority.

These lists indicate the points at which negotiation may occur and allow firms to exert influence, leading to weak local environmental regulation.

Explaining inter-locality variation in environmental regulation

Turning to the explanatory question of how to make sense of the findings on local variation in environmental regulation, we return to the hypotheses presented in Chapter 2 and the further lines of enquiry developed in Chapters 8 and 9.

Local government environmental policy

As far as local government environmental policy is concerned we showed that it varied among the four localities in a systematic way. It was stronger in localities where no employer was dominant in employment, power or fiscal terms, where there was more interest from foreign investors and where there was environmentalist opinion among the public. It was weaker in localities where there was a dominant employer, where there was less interest from foreign investors and where there was least development of environmentalist opinion among the public. Unfortunately the co-variation between the explanatory variables meant that localities with certain combinations of features were absent, for example, those with high foreign investor interest and low environmentalism. Hence we are unable to separate out the influences of these factors. The strength of social network links proved not to be significant in explaining variation; this we suggested was because other factors dominated it.

The findings regarding dominant employers or their absence, and regarding the role of environmentalist opinion are in line with the research in North America and Western Europe referred to in Chapter 2. The finding about foreign investment is not one which I have encountered before. The general idea that in times of unemployment and shortage of investment local governments are likely to undertake measures to attract investment is a very familiar one, and the possibility that these measures might include lowering environmental standards is very plausible. The argument here is a variant on this. The finding that it was the localities which were most attractive to foreign investment which had the highest environmental standards could be explained as due to a deliberate policy of upgrading the environment as a means of attracting investors. This implies a selective policy in favour of firms who can meet higher environmental standards and against those that want low standards. The existence of such policies of course reinforces the polarization of a national territory into areas with the least polluting investment and those with the most polluting investment. Since all our four case study localities were in the west of Hungary, which is relatively more affluent and which has attracted the lion's share of foreign investment, the implication is that in Eastern Hungary environmental standards may be yet lower. This hypothesis would require a new study to explore it.

The survey data suggested some causal interpretations of the variation in local government environmental policy. There was significant co-variation between having a written policy and having a specific official responsible on the one hand and settlement type on the other but there was no systematic trend for local environmental policy to be more developed in more prosperous parts of the country for any given settlement type. This suggests that the formal responsibilities placed on local governments of different types translate fairly directly into policy strength. This could be taken as a measure of institutional maturity, or in other words that policy capacity follows the hierarchical position of a local government given by its settlement type. It should be noted that this finding refers to having an environmental policy rather than to its content. As suggested above we would expect that the more prosperous the settlement the more likely its environmental policy to be strong.

Our other finding was that, while it was rare for environmental groups to be perceived as having most impact on local government environmental policy, where this happened it was in more prosperous settlements. This is in line with the proposition based on research in western Europe and North America that in settlements where the population is more educated and affluent, public opinion is more likely to be environmentalist, and people are more likely to form environmental groups and to have an influence on local environmental policy. Our analysis of the exceptional localities where environmental groups had most influence on local environmental policy lent support to this argument given that the localities were often university towns, or towns with a well-developed civic culture.

REI policy

The strength of REI policy in the four localities co-varied with the same variables as local government environmental policy. It was strongest in the localities where there was no dominant firm, where there was more foreign investor interest and where environmentalist opinion was stronger. In addition we showed that the level of resourcing of the local REI was a key factor in the strength of its policy as was the proximity of the REI office to the locality in question. It is quite striking to find that local social forces (as indicated by environmentalist public opinion and economic actors) co-vary with the strength of REI policy, since as the REI is a state agency there is no obvious reason why this should be. By contrast it is much more understandable that the resourcing and proximity to a locality of an REI have an influence on its behaviour. There is a however a plausible explanation. This is that the REI is less closed to local pressures than the label 'state agency' suggests, and that state agencies are typically much more open to their local operating environment than one might think. This is a finding of a French study for example (Grémion, 1976). One reason for this is of course the practice of negotiation, which as we have shown was as common a feature of the regulatory process in Hungary as it was in the other countries referred to in Chapter 2. The effect of this is that local REIs are part of the local socio-economic structure rather than detached from it. This makes it quite understandable that the same forces that affect local government environmental policy should also affect REI policy in an area.

The co-variation which we found between the strength of local government environmental policy and of REI policy in an area can thus be attributed to the fact that both are responsive to the socio-economic structure of the locality. In addition it is likely that there is an interactive process by which a strong local government environmental policy encourages the REI to take a stronger line in its own policy, while weak local government environmental policy encourages the REI to take a weaker line in its own practices.

This explanation of the strength of local government environmental policy and REI policy appeals to factors external to these institutions. A fuller model would build in features of the institutions themselves such as their leadership, the quality of the staff they recruit, and local traditions of activism.

Local government economic policy

The strength of local government economic policy in the four localities did not vary with any of the explanatory variables we considered. This may also be because we did not include in our explanatory model features of local government itself.

We consider the two findings which showed constancy across localities (the presence of negotiation between local governments, REIs and firms, and the level of severity – at most, moderate – of environmental regulation) in the next section.

Explaining cross-national similarities in environmental regulation

In this section we stand back and adopt a cross-national perspective. So far we have emphasised the parallels between our findings concerning variation between localities in environmental regulation in Hungary and those in previous studies. We now turn to our findings regarding negotiation as a feature of environmental regulation, and the lack of overall severity of environmental regulation.

The important point about these findings is that they are exactly in line with the findings of the research referred to in Chapter 2. Negotiation appears to be the norm internationally in environmental regulation, and the conclusion that environmental regulation is not severe is also very widely reported. This leads to two questions: why

Conclusion   169

is there a tendency for patterns of local environmental regulation in different countries to converge, and whether this means that Hungary's state socialist past is irrelevant to its form of local environmental regulation.

Convergent patterns of environmental regulation

In saying that Hungary shows these similarities in environmental regulation with other countries, we are making a bold statement. As we argued in Chapter 7, any identification of a similarity is a matter of 'construction'. In any comparison one can focus on either similarities or differences. To assert a similarity in our case means abstracting from numerous international differences, for example, in the nature of the regulatory agencies (national, regional, local), in their level of technical expertise, and in whether they have the power to impose fines, and if so whether they retain the income from fines. Such differences are of course perfectly valid foci of interest themselves. However we believe that the broad level similarities in local environmental regulation identified here are no less important and are valid objects of explanation[2]. Since our research was a single country study, rather than being part of a systematic cross-national comparison using a common theoretical framework, our interest in raising the broad question of international convergence goes well beyond our own data. Hence our conclusions are put forward with caution.

We now ask what explanations might exist for these similarities in patterns of local environmental regulation. Most obvious is the materialist and structuralist theoretical argument which can be seen in two examples. Marxist writers argue that in capitalist societies since capital accumulation is the driving economic force there are structural forces which protect capital accumulation against anything which threatens it. On this view environmentalist opinion is a potential threat which has to be accommodated at the least possible cost. The existence and strength of local environmental regulation is thus the result of a 'truce' in the battle between firms and public over the environmental impacts of production processes, with the state acting as a weather-vane reflecting the balance of these two forces in its policies. Under most conditions environmentalist forces are relatively weak and this is reflected in local environmental regulation. Conversely local environmental regulation will be at its strongest when environmentalist forces are at their strongest. This argument certainly fits the experience of environmental regulation in capitalist countries. However that does not mean it is the only possible explanation.

The finding that patterns of environmental regulation in China are similar in the respects identified here to those in Hungary and North America suggests that an explanation that appeals to the logic of capitalism is insufficient, given the unique combination of state socialist and capitalist elements in China. However the materialist argument can be extended beyond capitalist societies to argue that whatever the

---

2   Strictly speaking similarity does not imply convergence. The former refers to a single point in time while the latter refers to a process. It is possible for countries to show a short-lived similarity while moving in opposite directions.

economic system or prevailing political ideology of a society, any force which interferes with the way the society provides for its own subsistence, in other words, how it provides goods and services to its population, must be constrained in order to give priority to the continuity of the production process. The advantage of this explanation is that it is compatible with the marxist argument on capitalist societies and includes it as a special (if extremely frequent) case.

If we accept negotiation within well-defined limits as a feature shared by local environmental regulation in different countries, what role does this leave for legacies of state socialism?

We have encountered a number of these in the book. They can be grouped into three categories:

Institutional and stratification continuity

1. State enterprises with great leverage over local government and environmental agencies.
2. Networks forged under state socialism between party officials and other influentials.
3. A distribution of income and assets among social groups that favoured those with party connections.
4. Political continuity in the case of the mayor of Székesfehérvár, who kept his position after the 1990 elections.
5. The majority of REI staff had worked in the agency since before 1990.
6. Stratification patterns.

Continuity in attitudinal patterns

1. The popular belief that the state has a duty to support the population rather act as a hands off 'enabler' and regulator.
2. A lack of enterprise or initiative due to reliance on the state and the limited scope for private sector economic activity.
3. (In contradiction to the last) the argument that the 'second' (i.e. non-state) economy allowed people to develop new sources of income and encouraged entrepreneurship.
4. The continuing effects of the conflict over pollution in Nagytétény, which started before 1989.

Against these arguments there are a number of claims about change:

1. That extensive privatization means that firms no longer have such leverage over local governments and environmental regulators.
2. That the reform of local government has given it real autonomy vis à vis firms.

3. That the state is no longer as powerful as before in terms of economic and social welfare.
4. That old networks are irrelevant because party connections no longer provide access to significant resources.

The role we give to legacies in our understanding of local environmental regulation depends on which of two approaches to the logic of comparative analysis we take, the orthodox or the heterodox. According to the former, if the same feature occurs in two different societies then we must seek to explain it by one or more aspects of the two societies which they share and which have a theoretical connection to the similarity concerned. The key implication of the orthodox approach to explaining similarities is that differences in the societies concerned are ruled out of court as explanations by fiat. This means that any distinctive features of a society, such as possible legacy effects of state socialism in Hungary, in a Hungary–UK or Hungary–US comparison, are excluded from consideration as explanations of common features. This seems a very strong conclusion to reach on purely logical grounds.

Fortunately an alternative approach is available. The heterodox approach to explaining similarities between countries is based on the concept of plural causation. This refers not to plural in the sense of more than one cause (in other words, multiple causation), but to plural in the sense of the non-uniformity of causal patterns over time and place. It suggests, following Mill (1886), that in the social sciences, in contrast to the natural sciences, we should expect it to be the norm rather than the exception for similar phenomena to be produced in a diversity of ways in different times and places (see Pickvance, C.G., 1986; 2002). To take an example, consider the success of environmental protest groups which most writers would attribute to a series of factors: the type of issue they raise (for example, how radical, how moderate, with what breadth of public appeal), the contextual conditions in which they operate (for example, regime type, support from the media, attitude of political parties), the social composition of the groups involved, the campaigning methods chosen, and the strategy of the opposing authority or agency. By listing a number of factors like this, each of which consists of one or more variable which can take various values, two conclusions could be drawn. The first is that a given level of success can only be attained in one way, that is to say when each of the variables listed takes a particular value. The second is that a given level of success can be attained in a variety of ways, in other words when the different variables take different sets of values. The first suggests that there is a unique combination of values of variables which accounts for a particular level of success; the second suggests that there is a plurality of ways in which this can happen. These represent different combinations of circumstances which lead to the same conclusion. My argument is that 'logical' considerations should not be allowed to rule out the second possibility. Indeed, as Mill argued, this possibility seems far more in keeping with the complex and interactive character of the social world.

The heterodox approach has important consequences for cross-national studies. Contrary to the orthodox (and intuitive) idea that to explain similarities one must look only for similar causes, the heterodox approach allows differences between societies to contribute to explanations of similarities. In the case of a Hungary–US or Hungary–UK comparison it allows legacy effects of state socialism to be considered as potential explanations.

How can the potential legacy effects mentioned above contribute to the explanation of cross-national similarities in environmental regulation according to the heterodox approach to environmental regulation? We can group them as follows:[3]

Largely unchanging features There are several examples of continuities with state socialism which although not showing no change represent only limited change. Firstly, the idea of state enterprises having overwhelming power vis à vis local governments and state regulatory agencies is a feature of the state socialist past. This is directly relevant to understanding the situation in Dunaújváros where as we saw Dunaferr was still in state ownership (even if it had made internal cross-ownership as a defensive ploy) and where the company's relation with the local government still showed overwhelming power. Second, the REI is a continuation of its state socialist predecessor and the staff we interviewed had the long record of public sector employment and commitment to professional ideals that this implied. There was no parallel with environmental regulatory agencies in advanced capitalist societies where personnel may have a private sector background as often as a public sector one and may not have fully taken on a public sector ethos. A third example is the continuity of political leadership in Székesfehérvár.

The past as a model In this case a model of relations from the past may act as a guide in the present. Thus even when many state enterprises are privatized the model of influence in which they are able to exert pressure on local government and the REI may continue. As we found in Székesfehérvár, where the local government had the toughest environmental policy of any of the four localities, an office holder we interviewed made clear the limits to the power that the council could exercise over firms. A second example of the past as model is where people still expect the state to act as it did in the past and do not adapt quickly to it taking in a new role. In the Hungarian case this is reinforced by the state's own caution in introducing changes in the economic sphere, as illustrated by its slow privatization. This was interpreted as due to its fear of laying off workers (Elster et al, 1998). This illustrates Elster et al.'s example of legacies in the form of continuing cultural traditions.

Two points can be made about these legacies. The first is that paradoxically they may facilitate patterns of relations which are congruent with those in capitalist societies. The example of firms exerting leverage over local governments is a familiar

---

[3] Compare Elster et al. (1998, p. 60) who distinguish three types of legacy effect: the effect of socialization and cultural tradition, direct institutional constraints on present policy, and the use of the past in arguments about reform (for example, the pre-communist period may be taken as a model to justify a new proposal).

one in advanced capitalist societies as well as being a legacy of state socialism, whether as a continuing feature or a model. Usually local governments define their role in a way compatible with the interests of major firms. The second is that the fact that a feature originates in a legacy of state socialism does not exclude the possibility that it may form a very viable part of a new system. In other words legacies are not by definition contradictory with a new system. Rather we have suggested that there may be some rather unexpected continuities. In these cases the presence of legacy effects in Hungary is not incompatible with the explanation of cross-national similarities. Rather legacies from state socialism provide one path to some of the similar outcomes we are interested in explaining. Thus the heterodox approach to comparative analysis proves able to explain the cross-national similarities in local environmental regulation without jettisoning the role of some state socialist legacies. To put it another way, while there is a Hungarian way towards the combination of negotiated and moderate local environmental regulation this does not mean that it is the only way. Each society can have a particular way of reaching a common state.

Conclusion

In this study we have drawn on prevailing theories about local environmental regulation based on research in advanced capitalist societies. These have proved surprisingly useful in interpreting our findings. The balance of power between firms, councils, inspectorates and the public, and the resourcing of inspectorates have been shown to have the same role in Hungary as in other studies. (The main additional factors we drew attention were the attractiveness of a locality to foreign investment, and the distance of the office of the inspectorate from the firm being regulated, which is an aspect of resourcing.) However this does not mean that legacies from Hungary's experience of state socialism are irrelevant. We have shown, using the idea of plural causation (the idea that a variety of causal chains can lead to similar outcomes), that legacies can be integrated into the explanatory model since they represent one particular causal chain leading to a pattern of local environmental regulation which shares many similarities with those observed elsewhere.

All research designs and methods of data collection have strengths and weaknesses. Every study makes a choice of both in the light of the aims of the study. It is hoped that the combination of locality case studies using topic guides for the interviews, and surveys using structured interviews helps to overcome some of the individual limitations of the two methods.[4] Nevertheless this study leaves many questions open for future study. The fact that all four localities were in western Hungary raises the question of whether the situation in eastern Hungary follows the model set out here. A greater focus on a few concrete cases of pollution would lead to a different type of study from the one we carried out. Likewise a greater knowledge of

---

4 One weakness was that we did not anticipate the role of the water authorities and did not carry out interviews with officials.

firms or councils could have been gained if either category had been subjected to an intensive study. Lastly, a research team which had legal, administrative, economic and technical expertise would have allowed a closer examination of statements about what pollution control methods were feasible.

Finally, what does the study tell us about environmental pollution in Hungary now and in the future? Actual pollution depends on existing industrial and other processes, the extent of local environmental regulation and the extent of internal pressures on firms and other actors to adopt less polluting methods. The data on air pollution levels in the four localities shown in Table 2.5 were at odds with the claims about the success of local environmental regulation by interested parties. This suggested that local political actors in the pursuit of foreign investment emphasized their wish to achieve a cleaner environment rather than focus on the existing situation which included a heritage of older polluting firms. Our evidence about local environmental regulation was that it was at most moderate in its impact, and that it varied considerably by locality so that firms varied in the degree of control imposed on them. We saw that environmental fines were paid by all the firms studied. However they varied from the minute fines paid by Gardenia (for whom the symbolic value of the fine seemed more important than its monetary value), through the low fines paid by Alcoa, Rába and Chinoin (under £4000 per year) to the considerable fines paid by Dunaferr (£58,000 per year). We did not collect systematic data on how firms chose their production processes or the materials they used. But we found evidence of three sorts of internal pressure: the application of international firm-wide practices (in Alcoa), pressures from (industrial) consumers (in Raba), and an environmentally-committed management (in Gardenia). We also came across the suggestion that environmental investments had to pay for themselves within two years, a very short time scale. These ideas deserve a separate study.

As far as the future is concerned, we have questioned the picture of Hungary as a country which will adopt uniform EC standards once it joins the EU since this misunderstands the bargaining involved in the accession process and the diversity of standards within the EU. A great deal of investment is taking place in the water and sewerage field, but from this study it was striking to find how recurrent an issue pollution from waste water was. The reluctance of firms to invest in waste water treatment plants and the willingness of inspectorates to give firms exemptions from fines on the understanding that plans for improvement had been made are major obstacles.

There is every reason to expect Hungary to continue to experience local variation in environmental regulation as in other countries. The reason is that environmental regulation everywhere is essentially a negotiated activity which is responsive to the individual situation of firms. The argument of this book has been that local environmental regulation results from the interaction between firms, councils, inspectorates and the public. It follows that any long term improvement of environmental pollution depends on a change in this balance due to a greater national political priority for environmental issues, increased resourcing for inspectorates, a strengthening of environmental pressures internal to firms, and greater environmental awareness among the public and councils. These in turn depend on a strengthening of the national economy and of the economic situation of individual firms. All these forces are mutually reinforcing. It is to be hoped they lead to an upward spiral of environmental improvement rather than a downward spiral of environmental deterioration.

Bibliography

Alcamo, J. (1992) 'Emergency care for the East European environment', in J. Alcamo (ed.), *Coping with Crisis in Eastern Europe's Environment*, Parthenon, London.
Anderson, G.D. and Fiedor, B. (1997) 'Environmental charges in Poland', in R. Bluffstone and B.A. Larson (eds) *Controlling Pollution in Transition Economies*, Edward Elgar, Cheltenham.
Andrle, V. (1976) *Managerial Power in the Soviet Union*, Saxon House, Farnborough.
Angel, D.P., Brown, H.S., Broskiewicz, R. and Wronski, S. (2000) 'The environmental regulation of privatized industry in Poland', *Government and Policy*, 18, 575–592.
Atkinson, A.B. and Micklewright, J. (1992) *Economic Transformation on Eastern Europe and the Distribution of Income*, Cambridge University Press, Cambridge.
Baylis, R., Connell, L. and Flynn. A. (1998) 'Sector variation and ecological modernization: toward an analysis at the level of the firm', *Business Strategy and the Environment*, 7, 150–161.
Bennett, R.J. (1998) 'Local government in post-socialist cities', in Gy. Enyedi (ed.) *Social Change and Urban Restructuring in Central Europe*, Akademiai Kiado, Budapest.
Blalock, H.M. (1960) *Social Statistics*, McGraw-Hill, London.
Blowers, A. (1984) *Something in the Air*, Harper and Row, London.
Blowers, A. and Leroy P. (1994) 'Power politics and environmental inequality – a theoretical analysis of the process of peripheralization', *Environmental Politics*, 3, 97–228.
Bluffstone, R. and Larson, B.A. (eds) (1997) *Controlling Pollution in Transition Economies*, Elgar, Cheltenham.
Brieskorn, R., Krikke, B. and Petersen, F. (1996) 'Municipal environmental policy planning in Poland: a self-regulative approach to solving environmental problems', *European Environment*, 6, 5, 150–5.
Brovkin, V. (1990) 'Revolution from below: informal political associations in Russia 1988–9', *Soviet Studies*, 42, 233–257.
Caddy, J. (1997) 'Hollow harmonization: closing the implementation gap in Central European environmental policy', *European Environment*, 7, 3, 73–80.
Carlin, W., Van Reenen, J. and Wolfe, T. (1994) *Enterprise Restructuring in the Transition: An Analytical Survey of the Case Study Evidence From Central and Eastern Europe*, European Bank for Reconstruction and Development, London.
Carter, F.W. and Turnock, D. (eds) (1993) *Environmental Problems in Eastern Europe*, Routledge, London.

Cole, L.W. and Foster, S.R. (2001) *From the Ground up: Environmental Racism and the Rise of the Environmental Justice Movement*, New York University Press, New York.

Crenson, M. (1971) *The Un-politics of Air Pollution*, Johns Hopkins University Press, Baltimore.

Devons, E. and Gluckman, M. (1964) Modes and consequences of limiting a field of study, in M. Gluckman (ed.) *Closed Systems and Open Minds*, Oliver and Boyd, Edinburgh.

EBRD (1997) *Transition Report 1997*, European Bank for Reconstruction and Development, London.

EBRD (1998) *Transition Report 1998*, European Bank for Reconstruction and Development, London.

EBRD (2000) *Transition Report 2000*, London: European Bank for Reconstruction and Development.

Edelman, M. (1964) *The Symbolic Uses of Politics*, University of Illinois Press, Urbana.

Ellingstadt, M. (1997) 'The maquiladora syndrome: Central European prospects', *Europe-Asia Studies*, 49, 7–21.

Ellman, M. (1989) *Socialist Planning*, Cambridge University Press, Cambridge.

Elster, J., Offe, C. and Preuss, U.K. (1998) *Institutional Design in Post-communist Societies: Rebuilding the Ship at Sea*, Cambridge University Press, Cambridge.

Emmott, N. (1997) 'The theory and practice of IPPC: case studies from the UK and Hungary and implications for future EU environmental policy', *European Environment*, 7, 1, 1–6.

Enyedi, Gy. (1994) 'Regional and urban development in Hungary until 2005', in *European Challenges and Hungarian Responses to Regional Policy*, Z. Hajdu and Gy. Horvath (eds) Centre for Regional Studies, Hungarian Academy of Sciences, Pecs.

Eyal, G.M, Szelényi, I. and Townsley, E. (1998) *Making Capitalism without Capitalists: the New Ruling Elites in Eastern Europe*, Verso, London.

Fagin, A. (1994) 'Environment and transition in the Czech republic', *Environmental Politics*, 3, 3, 479–494.

Fineman, S. (2000) 'Enforcing the environment: regulatory realities', *Business Strategy and the Environment*, 9, 62–72.

Fisher, D. (1992) *Paradise Deferred: Environmental Policymaking in Central and Eastern Europe*, Royal Institute of International Affairs, London.

Fleischer, T. (1993) 'Jaws on the Danube: water management, regime change, and the movement against the Middle Danube hydroelectric dam', *International Journal of Urban and Regional Research*, 17, 429–443.

Friedland, R., Piven, F.F. and Alford, R.R. (1977) 'Political conflict, urban structure and the fiscal crisis', *International Journal of Urban and Regional Research*, 1, 447–471.

Galtung, J. (1967) *Theory and Methods of Social Research*, George Allen and Unwin, London.

Gomm, R., Hammersley M. and Foster P. (eds) (2000) *Case Study Method*, London: Sage.

Gouldson, A. and Murphy, J. (1998) *Regulatory Realities*, Earthscan, London.

Grabher, G. and Stark, D. (1998) 'Organising diversity: evolutionary theory, network analysis and post-socialism', in J. Pickles and A. Smith, (eds) *Theorising Transition*, Routledge, London.

Grémion, P. (1976) *Le Pouvoir Périphérique*, Seuil, Paris.

Györ–Moson–Sopron County (no date) Information on Györ–Moson–Sopron.

Hajdu, Z. (1993) 'Local government reform in Hungary', in R.R. Bennett (ed.) *Local Government in the New Europe*, Belhaven, London.

Hajer, M.A. (1995) *The Politics of Environmental Discourse: Ecological Modernization and the Policy Process*, Clarendon Press, Oxford.

Hammersley, M. (1992) *What is Wrong with Ethnography?* Routledge, London.

Hannigan, J. (1995) *Environmental Sociology*, Routledge, London.

Hanson, P. (1986) 'The serendipitous achievement of full employment: labour shortage and labour hoarding in the Soviet economy', in D. Lane (ed.) *Labour and Employment in the USSR*, Wheatsheaf, Brighton.

Harding, A.P. (1988) 'Spatially specific economic development programmes in Britain since 1979', *West European Politics*, 11, 102–115.

Harloe, M., Pickvance, C.G. and Urry, J. (eds) (1990) *Place, Policy and Politics: do Localities Matter?*, Unwin Hyman, London.

Hasko, K. (1998) An elite factory among the 'Dirty 12': the Chinoin Pharmaceuticals and Chemical factory in the 22nd district of Budapest. Unpublished project report.

Hawkins, K. (1984) *Environment and Enforcement: Regulation and the Social Definition of Pollution*, Clarendon Press, Oxford.

Hosking, G.A., Aves, J. and Duncan, P.J.S. (1992) *The Road to Post-Communism: independent political movements in the Soviet Union 1985–1991*, Pinter, London.

Hough, J.F. (1969) *The Soviet Prefects: the Local Party Organs in Industrial Decision-Making*, Harvard University Press, Cambridge, MA.

Jehlicka, P. and Kara, J. (1994) 'Ups and downs in Czech environmental policy: identifying trends and influences', in S. Baker, K. Milton, and S. Yearly (eds) *Protecting the Periphery*, Cass, London.

Judge, D., Stoker, G. and Wolman, H. (eds) (1995) *Theories of Urban Politics*, Sage, London.

Juhasz, J., Vári, A. and Tolgyesi, J. (1993) 'Environmental conflict and political change: public perception on low-level radioactive waste in Hungary', in A.Vári and P. Tamas (eds) *Environment and Democratic Transition*, Kluwer, Dordrecht.

Kerekes, S. and Kiss, K. (1998) 'Hungary's accession to the EU: environmental requirements and strategies', *European Environment*, 8, 61–170.

King, G., Keohane, R.O. and Verba, S. (1994) *Designing Social Inquiry*, Princeton: Princeton University Press, Princeton.

Kornai, J. (1992) *The Socialist System*, Oxford University Press, Oxford.

Kovács, Z. (1994) 'A city at the crossroads: social and economic transformation in Budapest', *Urban Studies*, 31, 1081–1096.

Kramer, J.M. (2001) 'EU enlargement and the environment in Central and Eastern Europe', paper to the Workshop on Environmental challenges of EU enlargement, EUI, Florence, May 2001.

Ladanyi, J. (1992) 'Local government reorganization and housing policy in Budapest: a roundtable discussion', *International Journal of Urban and Regional Research*, 16, 477–488.

Lane, D. (1987) *Soviet Labour and the Ethic of Communism: Full Employment and the Labour Process in the USSR*, Wheatsheaf, Brighton.

Lengyel, I. (1993) 'Development of local government finance in Hungary', in R.R. Bennett (ed.) *Local Government in the New Europe*, Belhaven, London.

Lieberson, S. (1992) 'Small N's and big conclusions: an examination of the reasoning in comparative studies based on small numbers of cases', in C.C. Ragin and H.S. Becker (eds) *What is a Case?*, Cambridge University Press, Cambridge.

Logan, J. and Molotch, H. (1987) *Urban Fortunes: the Political Economy of Place*, University of California Press, Berkeley.

Lowe, P., Clark, J., Seymour, S. and Ward, N. (1997) *Moralizing the Environment: Countryside Change. Farming and Pollution*, University College London Press, London.

Ma, X. and Ortolano, L. (2000) *Environmental Regulation in China*, Rowman and Littlefield, Oxford.

Manser, R. (1993) *The Squandered Dividend: the Free Market and the Environment in Eastern Europe*, Earthscan, London.

Marsh, D. and Locksley, G. (1983) 'Capital: the neglected face of power', in D. Marsh (ed.) *Pressure Politics: Interest Groups in Britain*, Junction, London.

Matláry, J.H. (1994) 'The European Union and the Visegrad countries: the case of energy and environmental policies in Hungary' in S. Baker, K. Milton, and S. Yearly (eds) *Protecting the Periphery*, Cass, London.

Mill, J.S. (1886) *System of Logic*, Longmans Green, London.

Mitchell, J.C. (1983) 'Case and situation analysis', *Sociological Review*, 31, 187–211.

Morris, G.E., Tiderenczl, J. and Kovacs, P. (1997) 'Environmental emission charges and air quality protection in Hungary: recent practice and future prospects', in Bluffstone, R. and Larson, B.A. (eds) *Controlling Pollution in Transition Economies*, Edward Elgar, Cheltenham.

Muller-Rommel, F. (1990) 'New political movements and 'new politics' parties in Western Europe', in Dalton, R.J. and Kuechler, M. (eds) *Challenging the Political Order*, Polity, Oxford.

Munton, R.J.C. (1983) *London's Green Belt: Containment in Practice*, Allen and Unwin, London.

Nee, V. (1989) 'A theory of market transition: from redistribution to markets in state socialism', *American Sociological Review*, 54, 663–681.

Ofer, G. (1977) 'Economizing on urbanization in socialist countries', in A.A. Brown et al. (eds) *Internal Migration*. Academic Press, London.

Offe, C. (1991) 'Capitalism by democratic design? Democratic theory facing the triple transition in East Central Europe', *Social Research*, 58, 865–892.

O'Toole, L.J. (1998) *Institutions, Policies and Outputs for Acidification – the Case of Hungary*, Ashgate, Aldershot.

Parry, G, Moyser, G. and Day, N. (1992) *Political Participation and Democracy in Britain*, Cambridge University Press, Cambridge.

Pavlinek, P. and Pickles, J. (2000) *Environmental Transitions*, Routledge, London.

Persanyi, M. (1990) 'The rural environment in a post-socialist economy: the case of Hungary', in P. Lowe, P. T. Marsden, and S. Watmore (eds) *Technological Change and the Rural Environment*, David Fulton Publishers, London.

Pickvance, C.G. (1986) 'Comparative urban analysis and assumptions about causality', *International Journal of Urban and Regional Research*, 10, 162–184.

Pickvance, C.G. (1995) 'Comparative analysis, causality and case studies in urban studies' in A. Rogers and S.Vertovec (eds) *The Urban Context: Ethnicity, Social Networks and Situational Analysis*, Berg, Oxford.

Pickvance C.G. (1996a) 'Environmental and housing movements in cities after socialism: the cases of Budapest and Moscow', in G.D. Andrusz, M. Harloe and I. Szelenyi (eds) *Cities After Socialism*, Blackwell, Oxford.

Pickvance, C.G. (1996b) 'Urban and regional policy: the political dimension', in W. Lever and A. Bailly (eds) *The Spatial Impact of Economic Changes in Europe*, Avebury, Aldershot.

Pickvance, C.G. (1997) 'Mediating institutions in the transition from state socialism: the role of local government', in G. Grabher and D. Stark (eds) *Restructuring Networks in Post-socialism*, Oxford University Press, Oxford.

Pickvance, C.G. (1999) 'Democratization and the decline of social movements: the effects of regime change on collective action in Eastern Europe, Southern Europe and Latin America', *Sociology*, 33, 353–372.

Pickvance, C.G. (2001) Four varieties of comparative analysis, *Journal of Housing and the Built Environment*, 16, 7–28.

Pickvance, C.G. (2002) 'State socialism, post-socialism and their urban patterns: theorising the central and Eastern European experience', in Eade, J. and Mele, C. (eds) *Understanding the City: Contemporary and Future Perspectives*, Blackwell, Oxford.

Pickvance, C.G. and Preteceille, E. (eds) (1991) *State Restructuring and Local Power: a Comparative Approach*, Pinter, London.

Pickvance, K. (1998) *Democracy and Environmental Movements in Eastern Europe: a Comparative Study of Hungary and Russia*, Westview, Boulder.
Przeworski, A. and Teune, H. (1970) *The Logic of Comparative Social Inquiry*, Wiley, London.
Radosevec, S. and Yoruk, D.E. (2001) *Videoton: the Growth of Enterprise Through Entrepreneurship and Network Alignment*, Working Paper No. 3, Centre for the Study of Economic and Social Change in Europe, University College London.
Rév, I (1987) 'The importance of being atomized: how Hungarian peasants coped with collectivization', *Dissent*, 34, 3, 335–350.
Richardson, G., Ogus, A. and Burrows, P. (1982) *Policing Pollution*, Clarendon Press, Oxford.
Rucht, D. (ed.) (1991) *Research on Social Movements*, Campus, Frankfurt.
Rutland, P. (1985) *The Myth of the Plan: Lessons of Soviet Planning Experience*, Open Court, La Salle, Illinois.
Saunders, P. (1979) *Urban Politics: A Sociological Interpretation*, Hutchinson, London.
Shomina, E.S. (1992) 'Enterprises and the Urban Environment', *International Journal of Urban and Regional Research*, 16, 222–233.
Sik, E. (1994) 'From the multi-coloured to the black and white economy: the Hungarian second economy and its transformation', *International Journal of Urban and Regional Research*, 18, 46–70.
Sleszynski, J. (1996) Economic instruments in environmental policy: a profile of Poland, *European Environment*, 2, 126–134.
Slocock, B. (1996) 'The paradoxes of environmental policy in Eastern Europe: the dynamics of policy-making in the Czech republic', *Environmental Politics*, 5, 3, 501–521.
Slocock, B. and Sowinski, M. (1996) 'Regional management of industrial air pollution in eastern Europe: air pollution in Katowice province, Poland', *European Environment*, 6, 21–7.
Smelser, N.J. (1976) *Comparative Methods in the Social Sciences*, Prentice-Hall, Englewood Cliffs.
Smith, A. and Swain, A. (1998) 'Regulating and institionalising capitalisms: the micro-foundations of transformation in Central and Eastern Europe', in J. Pickles and A. Smith (eds) *Theorising Transition*, Routledge, London.
Soveroski, M. (2001) 'Flexibility, subsidiarity and environmental present and future implications for enlargement', paper to the workshop on environmental challenges of EU enlargement, EUI, Florence, May 2001.
Stark, D. (1992) 'From system identity to organizational diversity – analyzing social change in Eastern Europe', *Contemporary Sociology*, 21, 299–304.
Stark, D. (1997) 'Recombinant property in East European capitalism', in G. Grabher and D. Stark (eds) *Restructuring Networks in Post-socialism*, Oxford University Press, Oxford.
Stepanek, Z. (1997) 'Integration of pollution charges systems with strict performance standards: the experience of the Czech republic', in Bluffstone and Larson (1997).
Stoker, G. (1995) 'Regime theories and urban politics', in D. Judge, G. Stoker, and H. Wolman (eds) *Theories of Urban Politics*, Sage, London.
Swain, A. (1998) 'Governing the workplace: the workplace and regional development implications of automotive foreign direct investment in Hungary', *Regional Studies*, 32, 653–671.
Swain, N. (1992) *Hungary: the Rise and Fall of Feasible Socialism*, Verso, London.
Szirmai, V. (1993) 'The structural mechanisms of the organization of ecological-social movements in Hungary', in A. Vári and P. Tamas (eds) (1993) *Environment and Democratic Transition*, Kluwer, Dordrecht.
Szirmai, V. (1997) 'Protection of the environment and green movements in Hungary', in K. Láng-Pickvance, N. Manning and C.G. Pickvance (eds) *Environmental and Housing Movements: Grassroots Experience in Hungary, Estonia and Russia*, Avebury, Aldershot.
Temesi, I. (2000) 'Local government in Hungary' in T.M. Horvath (ed.) *Decentralization: Experiments and Reforms*, Open Society Institute, Budapest.

Tickle, A. and Welsh. I. (1998) 'Environmental politics, civil society and post-communism', in A. Tickle and I. Welsh (eds) *Environment and Society in Eastern Europe*, Longman, London.

Tilly, C. (1984) *Big Structures, Large Processes, Huge Comparisons*, Russell Sage Foundation, New York.

Vári, A. and Tamas, P. (eds) (1993) *Environment and Democratic Transition*, Kluwer, Dordrecht.

Vogel, D. (1986) *National Styles of Regulation: Environmental Policy in Great Britain and the United States*, Cornell University Press, Ithaca.

Vogel, D and Kun, V. (1987) 'The comparative study of environmental policy: a review of the literature', in M. Dierkes, H.N. Weiler, and A.B. Antal (eds) *Comparative Policy Research: Learning from Experience*, Gower, Aldershot.

Waller, M. and Millard, F. (1992) 'Environmental politics in Eastern Europe', *Environmental Politics*, 1, 159–185.

Weale, A. (1992) *The New Politics of Pollution*, University of Manchester Press, Manchester.

Yeager, P.C. (1991) *The Limits of Law: The Public Regulation of Private Pollution*, Cambridge University Press, Cambridge.

Index

Alcoa 50–56, 93, 110, 118, 127, 174
   environmental practices of 50–53
   and REI, see Regional Environmental Inspectorate and Alcoa
   assets 10

Central Environmental Fund 34, 104
Chinoin 79, 82–93, 174
   and council 82–3
   and fines 87–8, 92
   and public 86
   and REI, see Regional Environmental Inspectorate and Chinoin
   environmental practices of 85–8, 90–92
   history of 85
   comparative analysis 111–14, 121–7
   of local government policy 129–61
   convergence 3, 169–70
   cross–national comparison 3, 168–73

Danube Circle 7
disciplines 3
Dunaferr 95–110, 118, 125, 174
   and environmental practices 103–7
   and local council 98–101, 109–10
   and pollution 103–9
   and REI, see Regional Environmental Inspectorate and Dunaferr
Dunaújváros 39–41, 76–7, 92, 95–110, 115–27
   council 96–101, 109

development 95
environmental problems in 97
local economic policy in 96–7, 100–101, 110
local environmental policy in 97–8, 101–3, 110
public opinion 101–3, 109

ecological modernization 1–2
economic policy, see local economic policy
environmental groups
   influence of 147–8, 151, 154–9
   see also Gaia, Green Future, Reflex
environmentalism 1
   of local government 22–3
environmental mobilization 147–8, 151, 154–61
environmental quality in Hungary 37–8
environmental regulation 1–4, 7, 14–15, 17–20, 112, see also local environmental regulation
   and central government 29–30, 32
   and local government 21–3, 28–9, 32
   and the public 21–3, 31, 32
   comparative analysis of 111–27
   cross–national similarities in 168–73
   defined 3
   fines in 165
   firms and 18–23, 27–9, 32, 37
   in Czech Republic 34
   in Hungary 33–7
      role of county councils 36

role of local government 36
role of ministries 33–5
in Poland 34
in post–socialism 26–30
negotiation in 18–20, 26, 55–6, 165, 168, 174
under state socialism 7–8, 30
European Union enlargement 2, 14–15, 30, 174

Gaia 47–9, 118
Gardenia 69–72, 78, 110, 118, 127, 174
   council and 71–2
   development of 69–70
   environmental practices of 70–71, 78
   fines 78
   pollution by 70–71
   and REI, *see* Regional Environmental Inspectorate and Gardenia
Green Future 79–80, 83, 85–6, 92, 118
Győr 39–41, 59–78, 93, 115–27
   and fines 65–7, 69, 70–77
   council 60–63, 71–2, 77
   council and firms 63
   development of 59
   influence of environmental groups in 62–3
   local economic policy in 60–61
   local environmental policy in 61–2, 77

Hungary 6–7
   and European Union 2, 14–15
   citizen action in Hungary 7
   decentralization reform in 12
   divided into regions 148–51
   economic performance of 14
   economic reform in 13
   enterprises in 13
   political parties in 11–12
   privatization in 13
   transition in 11

legacy effects 9–10, 92, 170–73
local economic policy
   comparison and explanation of 125, 163, 168
   effect of settlement type on 129–43, 145–61
   in the four localities 114, 116–17
   measures of 131–5, 142
local government
   decentralization of 142–3
   finance 12–13
   post 1990 12, 21, 28–9
   under state socialism 5, 8
local environmental policy, *see* Dunaújváros, Győr, Nagytétény, Székesfehérvár, and local environmental regulation
local environmental regulation 1–3, 17–31
   and municipal public health service 37
   comparison and explanation of 116–17, 122–3, 125–7, 163, 166–8, 174
   effect of settlement type on 129–43, 145–61
   in advanced capitalist societies 17–23
   in China 26
   in Czech Republic 24
   in Hungary *passim*
   influence of public on 21–3
   in Poland 24–5
   in the four localities 114–15
   measures of 131–5, 142
   reasons for weak 165–6
   role of fines in 165, 174, *see also* Regional Environmental Inspectorate
local environmental problems
   comparison of 135–7, 142
localities under state socialism 5
LULUs (Locally Unwanted Land Uses) 21, 145

Metallochemia 79–81
Nagytétény 39–41, 63, 76, 79–93, 115–27
   and Chinoin 82–3
   and firms 82
   council 80–81
   development of 79–81
   environmental groups in 79–80
   environmental problems in 84
   local economic policy in 82–3
   local environmental policy in 83–5, 92
   pollution in 79–81, 84–8
'new legalism' 24

path dependence 11

PHARE 14, 47, 64, 104
pollution
  in Hungary 37–8, 174
  in Czech Republic 37–8
  in Poland 37–8
pollution legislation 18, 24–6

Rába 53, 64–9, 77–8, 93, 110, 127, 174
  and council 68–9, 77
  and REI, *see* Regional Environmental Inspectorate and Raba
  environmental practices of 66–9
  history of 64
  pollution 64–6
Reflex 62, 77, 118
Regional Environmental Inspectorate 34–6, 165
  and Alcoa 53–7
  fines 55–7
  inspection visits 54–5, 57
  self-reporting 54
  and Chinoin 89–93
  fines 92
  inspection visits 73–7
  resources 89–90, 93
  and Dunaferr 101, 104–9
  fines 105–10
  inspection visits 105, 110
  resources 109
  self-reporting 108
  and Gardenia 71, 76
  and Győr 73–7
  and public 74–5, 77
  fines 77
  inspection visits 73–5
  resources 76–7

  and Nagytétény 80–81, 83–5, 88
  and Rába 64, 66, 68–9, 176
  comparing policy of 115–17, 123–4, 163
  explaining policy of 119–20, 126–7, 167–8
  functions of 35
  integrated permitting by 35
REI, *see* Regional Environmental Inspectorate
research design 31, 38–41, 129–30, 173–4
settlement type
  effect of on local environmental and economic policy 129–43, 145–61

state socialism
  collapse of 1–2
  in Hungary 6–8
  in practice 6
  legacy effects of, *see* Legacy effects
  mass participation organizations in 5–6
survey of local governments 129–61
symbolic politics 3
Székesfehérvár 38–41, 43–57, 63, 76–7, 85, 92–3, 97, 115–27
  council 44–5
  development of 43–4
  environmental conflicts in 47–8
  environmental problems in 49, 53–5, 57
  local economic policy in 45–7, 56
  local environmental policy in 47, 57
  pollution in 40, 53, 57

transition 8–11
  from state socialism 3
  sociological approaches to 9–11